Man of Letters

The early life and love letters of
Robert Chambers

edited by
C. H. Layman

EDINBURGH UNIVERSITY PRESS

© C. H. Layman 1990

Edinburgh University Press
22 George Square, Edinburgh

Set in Linotronic Garamond
by Koinonia Ltd, Bury, and
printed in Great Britain by
the Alden Press, Oxford

British Library Cataloguing
  in Publicaiton Data
Layman, C. H.
    Man of letters: the early life and
    love letters of Robert Chambers.
    I. Scotland, Publishing, Cham-
    bers,
    Robert, 1802–1871
    I. Title   II. Chambers,
    Robert,   1802–1871
    070.5092

ISBN 0 7486 0164 3
     0 7486 0193 7 pbk

The publisher acknowledges subsidy
from the Scottish Arts Council towards
the publicaiton of this volume

Contents

CONTENTS

Foreword

by

The Rt Hon. Sir David Steel

This book sheds much awaited light on one of the greatest figures of nineteenth century Scotland of whom comparatively little has been written. True, in the firm of W. & R. Chambers, he has his lasting memorial in that publishing empire, and indeed in the famous Chambers Encyclopaedia - what an irony that when hard times befell his father the sale of his Encyclopaedia Britannica was one of the deepest felt tragedies in the family. He has, with his brother, another memorial too in the Chambers Institution, a fine collection of buildings in Peebles High Street where formerly the Town Council met and which currently houses an interesting museum, art gallery and public meeting hall. Over one of the doorways is the motto: 'He who tholes overcomes', which is I suspect untranslatable from the Scots.

Yet this collection of his private papers and letters will surely serve as a yet more glorious record of the man's triumph over adversity. The picture of his Peebles childhood is to me the most vivid and arresting section of the book: deeply moving in places, wildly funny in others and consistently graphic throughout.

The dying Laird Grieve bemoans the fact that his daughters denied him his daily tots of whisky while young Robert recalls his father's observation that: 'whatever harm there may be from whisky generally, the sudden abstraction of it from a system which had come to depend on it could hardly be wise, any more than humane'. He describes his two years as a boarder at the local grammar school where the charge for each youngster was subsidised by the heritors: 'The entire expense must have been only eighteen shillings - a fact sufficient to explain how Scotch people of the middle class appear as so well educated in comparison with their southern compatriots'.

We learn also of the impact on the small burgh of Peebles of the prisoners from the Napoleonic war and of their part in the financial downfall of the Chambers family. Robert's subsequent teenage struggles in Edinburgh to make a meagre living selling books, and his remarkably persistent love-letters to his future wife, form the later part of the narrative, in which Sir Walter Scott plays a typically beneficent role.

It may be a little premature to suggest it before the book has even appeared in print, but I hope that Kit Layman will feel encouraged to go on from this superb work of discovery and editing to produce perhaps a script for a one-man stage presentation. Certainly he has brought Robert Chambers dramatically to life to be enjoyed I hope by a wide audience.

David Steel
January 1990
Ettrick Bridge

Illustrations

1. Robert Chambers as a young man. Portrait by an unknown artist in the possession of Sir Mark Norman.

2. The house, 'modern' (1796) and 'sklatit' (slated), where William and Robert were born, beside the Eddlestone Water in Peebles.

3. Mr Sloane's account for William's and Robert's attendance at the Grammar School, Peebles, 1810 - 1811. His addition is faulty and he robs himself of fourpence. He taught classics and English but not arithmetic.

4. The struggling bookseller. In Robert's salesbook for 1819, the summary on the left shows that his first 14 months in business produced a profit of £61-3-9. But in the daily account on the right it is clear that there were many days (probably rainy days) when he sold nothing at all.

5. Robert's faultless penmanship. This title-page was written out by hand, although you would scarcely know it. It is from the book which Robert presented to Sir Walter Scott, and which marked the turning-point in the fortunes of the Chambers family.

6. Anne Kirkwood, wife of Robert Chambers, and mother of their fourteen children. There is reason to think that this old photograph has been printed the right way round, and therefore that Anne was left-handed. Sadly, her letters replying to Robert's have not been found.

7. An example of Robert's cross-written letters. He used both sides of thin paper, writing twice on each side.

8. The anonymous title-page of *Vestiges*, the book that shocked Britain and America in 1844 and paved the way for Darwin's *Origin of Species* fifteen years later.

9. No 1 Doune Terrace, Edinburgh, the home of Robert Chambers from 1844.

10. Anne Chambers and family about 1844. From left to right they are James (3), Amelia (6), Anne (9), Mary (11) with William (1), Anne Chambers at her harp, Janet and Eliza (8), and Nina (14). Robert, the eldest son, is missing, presumably away at school. Three children had already died in infancy. Phoebe and Alice were yet to be born.

Introduction

The first part of this book is about Peebles at the beginning of the nineteenth century, and the early years of Robert Chambers, who was born there in 1802. It is compiled mainly from Robert's own papers which include several auto-biographical pieces.

His brother William also left some reminiscences and I have used them too, but with caution, sometimes changing an unimportant word for continuity. When William's *Memoir* was published in 1872 he had twice been Lord Provost, and was a pillar of respectability in Edinburgh. The *Memoir* quotes Robert's writings extensively, but a comparison with the original reveals that William was being selective, and had not hesitated to amend them as he thought fit. Sometimes he seems to have had clarity in mind, sometimes dignity, and sometimes he appears to be disagreeing with Robert's version of events. The letter dated 13th April 1829 in the present collection makes an interesting comparison with William's extracts from it in the *Memoir*. Of the two brothers Robert seems, in dozens of instances, to be the more accurate, and I have followed him where there is a conflict.

The second part is set in Edinburgh, where Robert, starting at the age of thirteen, tried to make his way in the world following a series of catastrophes which had left the family bankrupt and almost starving. After some daunting setbacks his prodigious capacity for hard work began to bring him success as a bookseller and writer, and by the time he was twenty-one he was famous.

The third part mainly consists of letters written by Robert to his wife-to-be. Like many love letters they radiate growing affection, humour, despair, hope, annoyance, and confusion. The lovers have rows and reconciliations. Only one half of the correspondence has been found and there are tantalising gaps. Though it is hard to believe, during the six-month period covered by the letters Robert wrote two large books between attending to customers in his bookshop; thus he was very busy and many of the letters had to be written late at night after an excessively long day. They are uncorrected emotional outpourings, but the style is easy and elegant – a product of the age and of Edinburgh.

I have transcribed the letters as accurately as I can, but some of them are very difficult to read. Robert wrote at tremendous speed in a fine scrawl. He also made a habit at this date of extreme economy in the use of paper: having finished a page he would turn the sheet through ninety degrees and write over the top of what he had just written. The result is that the 2,000 words of the letter dated 19th April, for example, cover the same area as a single sheet of A4. In a few cases I have had to guess at an indecipherable word, and I have left blanks where even a guess did not seem justified.

In the Epilogue I have sketched Robert Chambers's subsequent career, and hinted at his place in the Edinburgh Enlightenment, a place widely underestimated because his most important contribution was a work published anonymously.

This book is therefore not a complete portrait of the man, which is perhaps another story for another time, but rather a life-and-letters patchwork of fragments stitched together. It seems to me that these are fragments that deserve to see the light, and can themselves throw light on some aspects of Scottish life in those heady days.

Part 1

PEEBLES FOR PLEESURE

Chapter I

Peebles has often seemed to visitors to be an attractive, secluded, tranquil place where not a great deal is happening, and where nothing much has ever happened.

Situated twenty-five miles from Edinburgh and about the same distance from the English border, it appears to baffle the awareness of some people who know other parts of Scotland well. 'As quiet as the grave or as Peebles' said Henry Cockburn in about 1830, and others have said it since. Today six thousand people live there. There are good roads through the pleasant countryside in all directions, but it is not on one of the great arterial highways through the Borders. Casual visitors are few, and many of them would guess that Cockburn's phrase was still apt.

In 1800 the two thousand inhabitants of Peebles knew of their reputation for quietness, and often discussed it. They would remark that theirs was a 'finished' town, in that the population was stable and new houses were very rare. There were no crowds, no bustle; a cannon could be fired at noon, they would say, along the full length of the High Street, without injuring anyone. While being intensely interested in the world outside, they made a virtue of their seclusion, and were apparently content.

A well-known event in the town's annals was the visit by an old Peebles man to Paris. His return caused considerable excitement, and he was of course asked how he found that city. His answer was often quoted, sometimes humorously, sometimes as an example of rustic philosophy: 'Paris, a' things considered, was a wonderful place – but still – Peebles for pleesure!'

The inhabitants were fond of their town and its simple 'pleesures.' They called it a bonny place, and it is easy to see why. It was surrounded by well-doing farms on the smooth hills of Tweeddale. The River Tweed dominated the town, as it still does, looking ceaselessly beautiful. Anyone who wanted a few trout for dinner could fish for them; many did, and many still do. In the centre of the town, on the site of the old royal castle, was a robust-looking church, built to replace the old parish church which even then resembled a fine Piranesi ruin. Nearby was Neidpath Castle, perhaps the most spectacular of Borders castles; it had been captured by Cromwell after a vigorous defence, but was now held by the Duke of Queensberry, who was far too busy in his pursuit of boxing and debauchery in London to bother anyone in Peebles. There was a good deal of small farming, a little weaving, and some desultory shop-keeping. It seemed that little could disrupt the quiet life of Peebles.

Robert Chambers, a native of the town, was well-known for his remarkable, enamel-clear memory. Looking through his papers I have found many extraordinary examples of it, and it was said of him, 'Whatever he saw or learned he never forgot; everything that could interest the mind was treasured up, ready to be of service when wanted.' His reminiscences allow a glimpse deep into the life of a small burgh in the early years of the nineteenth century, where things were not always as placid as they seemed to be on the surface. The next twelve chapters describe it in his own words.

Chapter II

There was an old and a new town in Peebles, each of them a single street, or little more; and as even the New Town had an antique look, it may be inferred that the Old looked old indeed. It was indeed chiefly composed of thatched cottages, occupied by weavers and labouring people – a primitive simple race, of the most homely aspect, in many instances eking out a scanty subsistence by having a cow on the town common, or cultivating a *rig* of potatoes in the fields close to the town. Rows of porridge *luggies*[1] were to be seen cooling on window soles. A smell of peat smoke invaded the place. The click of the shuttle was everywhere heard during the day, and in the evening the grey old men came out in their Kilmarnock night-caps, and talked of Bonaparte on the stone seats behind their doors. If a cow passed and left some token of her presence behind, an old woman with her skirts twisted above her rump was sure to dart from her door and gather up the deposit, which she forthwith baked with coal culm[2] into a roll, precious as an aid to her fire. A child from the New Town, visiting a house in the Old, would be regaled by the housewife with a piece of thick oaten cake with very white fresh butter, which she had used her thumbs in spreading. The platters used in these humble dwellings were all of wood, and the spoons of horn; knives and forks rather rare articles. The house was generally divided into two apartments by a complex of *box-beds* placed end to end, a bad style of bed prevalent in cottages all over Scotland; they were so close as to almost stifle the inmates. Among these humble people all costumes, customs, and ways of living smacked of old times. You would see a venerable patriarch making his way to church on Sunday, with a long-backed, swing-tailed light blue coat of the style of George II, which was probably his marriage coat and half a century old. His head gear was a broad-brimmed blue bonnet. The old women came out on the same occasions, in red scarfs (called cardinals) and white sharp-prowed *mutches* (caps), bound by a black ribbon, with the grey hair folded back on the forehead underneath. There was a great deal of drugget and huckaback and serge in that old world, and very little cotton. One might almost think he saw the humbler Scotch people of the seventeenth century still living before his eyes.

Apropos of the box beds, there was a carrier named Davie Loch, who was reputed to be rather light of wits, but at the same time not without a sense of his worldly interests. His mother, finding her end approaching, addressed her son in the presence of a number of neighbours: 'The house will be Davie's of course, and the furniture too –' 'Eh, hear her!' quoth Davie, 'sensible to the last, sensible to the last.' 'The lying siller –' 'Eh, yes, hoo clear she is about everything.' 'The lying siller is to be divided between my two daughters –' 'Steek³ the bed-doors, steek the bed-doors,' interposed Davie; 'she's raving noo!' And the old woman was shut up accordingly.

Davie in the course of his calling was attacked by two Irish labouring men on the highway, and robbed of five and ninepence. I remember going with some other boys, in the latter part of the year 1814, to a spot beyond Morningside, where, on a gibbet erected at the scene of this petty robbery, the two men were hanged, after joining very decorously in singing the 103rd psalm, Scotch version –

> Oh, thou, my soul, bless God the Lord,
>   And all that in me is
> Be stirred up, his holy name
>   To magnify and bless

which I was near enough to hear distinctly, and never since have read without thinking of those two examples of over-rigid justice.

In this Old Town population there survived one or two aged men who professed an adherence to the Covenant and Covenanted work of Reformation. Of one called Judden (i.e. Gideon) Veitch I remember but little; but the other, designated Laird Baird, remains clearly daguerreotyped on my memory, a tall bony grim old man, with blue *rig-and-fur* stockings rolled half way up his thighs, and a very umbrageous blue bonnet. His secular business consisted in thatching houses; his inner life was a constant brooding over the sins of a perjured and sinful nation, and the various turns of public affairs in which he traced the punishments inflicted upon us by an outraged deity for our laying aside the Solemn League and Covenant. He came up to my mother one summer evening, as she was standing at her door with her first-born in her arms. 'Ye're mickle pleased wi' that bairn, woman,' said the laird gruffly. 'If the French come, what will ye do wi' him? I trow ye'll be fleeing wi' him to the tap o' the Pentland Hills. But ye should rather pray that they *may* come. Ye should pray for joodgements, woman – joodgements on a sinfu' land – pray that the Lord may pour out the vials of his wrath upon us – it wad be for our guid, for our guid!' And then he went on his way, leaving the pretty young mother heart-chilled by his terrible words, and clasping the

infant to her breast with the feeling that there was only too much
reason to fear the French might prove the instruments of divine wrath
in regard to our country. Having known something in my childhood
of these Old Town worthies, there was no novelty or surprise to me
a few years thereafter, when I read of Mause Headrigg and Habakkuk
Mucklewraith in Scott's *Old Mortality*.

I had occasion to know the Old Town well in my earliest years, for
our family then dwelt in it, though in a modern 'sklatit' house which
my father had had built for him by *his* father when about to be married.
Our ancestors had been woollen manufacturers, substantial and respectable people, although living in a very plain style. My father,
growing up at the time when the cotton manufacture was introduced
into Glasgow, had there studied it, and now conducted it on an
extensive scale at Peebles, having sometimes as many as a hundred
hand-looms in his employment. My earliest recollections bring before
me a neat small mansion, fronting to the Eddlestone Water; a tastefully
furnished parlour, containing a concealed bed, one or two other little
rooms, and a kitchen; a ground floor full of looms, and a garret full of
webs and weft. Games at marbles played with my elder brother on the
figures of the parlour carpet, while recovering from the measles, come
back upon me as among the pleasantest things I have experienced in
life. Or, wandering into the workshop below, it was a great entertainment to sit beside one of the weavers and watch the flying shuttle and
the movements of the heddles and treddles, and hear the songs and
gossip of the men. Weavers were topping operatives in those days; for
they could realise two pounds a week, sometimes even more, and
many young men of good connections had joined the trade. My father,
as agent for Mr Henry Monteath, for Mr McIlroy, and others, in
Glasgow, realised a good income, which enabled us to live on an
equality with the best families in the place. There used to be a pleasant
bustle about the house on Saturdays, when the men would come for
new webs or supplies of weft and get payment for their work – good-
humoured worthy men who would take me on their knee, and tell me
'I should be a man before my mother if I only did what I ought to do'
– while I would examine, with the wonder of a young savage, their
silver watches, their curious zig-zag watch-keys, and the cowry shell
or bored sixpence, which usually hung from their fobs.

To a child of course all things are new, and the first occurrence of
any thing to his awakened senses never fails to make a deep impression.
I think I yet remember the first time I observingly saw the swelling
green hills around our little town. The first occasion of a particular
word being used in my hearing I can recall in a great number of

instances. I am sure I could point to within ten yards of the spot where I saw the first gowan and the first buttercup; first heard the hum of the mountain bee; first looked with wonder into a hedge-sparrow's nest with its curious treasure of blue eggs. A radius of half a mile would have described the entire world of my infancy: of that world every minute feature remains deeply stamped within me, and will while life and consciousness endure. There is a great deal of studious observation in a child. Casual, trivial, and thoughtless words spoken by his seniors in his presence go into him, to be afterwards estimated and judged of; so it is a great mistake to speak indecorously before children. Thus it is that I can remember, as a thing of yesterday, these sittings of mine on the knees of weavers, – being regaled with the tick of the man's watch held to my ear or with a peep into the incomprehensible interior, examining his week-old beard and wondering what it was there for, studying the stripes of his waistcoat, marking the style of his speech as being less refined perhaps than that of my parents, and making generally what might be called an analysis of the man, as a (to me) new part of creation.

At the time when I was coming upon the stage of the world, a number of old things were going out of it. The minister of the parish still wore a cocked hat. He died in 1808 and I can just remember seeing him one Sunday, as he walked home from church, with that head-gear crowning his tall and dignified figure. There were still a few men with pig-tails whisking constantly over the collars of their coats. Most people continued to wear breeches which, free from braces, tightened round the haunches, and had ties at the knees, white woollen stockings filling up the space below down to the buckled shoes. There was also one person who exhibited ruffles at the wrists. Rather oddly, he was a poor man, a watchmaker named Law, a relative of the celebrated financial schemer of that name, who nearly ruined France in the time of the Orleans regency. Geordie Law, as he was unrespectingly called, possessed a letter inviting his ancestor to the funeral of the great financier. He was a most miserable creature, with no business, a large family, and an immense stock of personal vanity. The vapouring speculative character of this poor Peebles burgher threw a light on that of his famous relative – all surface and no reality. A woman, whose husband had thriven by extreme diligence, till he was suspected to be worth not less than five hundred pounds, was quoted for a saying – 'There goes Geordie Law, swaggering up the street wi' his ruffles, as if half the toon were his ain; and look at oor Sandy – for a' he has, he's neither proud nor lordly.' There was a legend in our family, extremely tantalising to my brother and myself, of a spare watch which might have been assigned to one of us, but which had lain for years in a dismembered state in a saucer in Geordie Law's dusty shop, – having been entrusted to him to be mended – and which there was no chance of our ever seeing restored to its primitive integrity. The fact was that Geordie used the materials of one such watch to make up what was wanting in another, and consequently a good many horologes which had been entrusted to him lay dismembered and imperfect in their respective saucers. When very much pressed one day for the return of a watch which had been left some months before for repairs, he offered the remains of it in what might be considered as its tomb, – namely its saucer. I have never passed the old fool in the street but I thought with bitterness of the watch of which he had been the means of depriving us.

Another piece of antiquated attire which lingered in my younger days was the spencer, a sort of coat without tails, or what might now be termed a short paletot, which old gentlemen wore in winter days of medium severity. It was believed to be the invention of an Earl Spencer, from whom it obtained its name. All coats were then dress coats – no such thing as a frock or surtout as yet devised – the pockets always opening cross-wise on the exterior, just under the base of the spencer. Spatterdashes (briefly called spats, and sometimes kootikens, i.e. integuments for the *koots* or ankles) were prevalent. It was, however, an era of transition for leg gear. Tight stocking trews tied at the ankle were in favour with men possessing good limbs. Boots, formerly used only in riding and travelling, were also in vogue with men who desired to be smartly dressed. One could either have *top-boots*, that is boots with a moveable cincture of pale leather at top, or *tassel boots*, by which was meant what were afterwards called hessians, terminating in a wavy line under the knee, with a tassel hanging out over the middle in front. A buckish weaver called Willie Paterson had got a pair of tassel boots, on which he could fasten tops, and thus enjoy tops or tassels at his pleasure. People meeting him as he went to church would say, 'Willy, I see this is top day with you.' Top day or tassel day for Willy Paterson's boots was a favourite joke. As an alternative for boots were gaiters, originally tight, but latterly lax, with vertical foldings. 'Lax in their gaiters, laxer in their gait,' is a line in the *Rejected Addresses*[4] which strongly recalls to me the year 1812.

The New Town was a smarter place than the Old; yet it contained many homely old thatched houses and few of any elegance. The shops were for the most part confined and choky places, with what were called half doors, a bell being generally struck or shaken when this door was opened by a customer, so as to summon the worthy trader from an equally stifling back parlour, or quite as likely from some place on the street thirty yards off, where he had been holding conference with a group of neighbours on some gossip of the day. No attempt was made to keep up an appearance of business. The grocer laid no empty sugar cask at his door, for every body would have known that the boys had picked the last particle of the sweet contents out of the chinks of the wood many weeks ago. The draper never thought of busying himself with the packing of imaginary parcels of female fineries, to induce women to come in for their new gowns and shawls. All was quiet and sombre by day; and in the evenings, a dim candle on the counter made the only difference. A favourite position of the shopkeeper was to lean on his arms over the half-door, gazing abroad into the vacant street or chatting with a casual bystander. Custom, where so little of it was going, was felt as a personal matter, and to see any part of it going to a new shop was a thing not easy to be borne. A little girl one day crossed the street with an unhemmed handkerchief in her hand, and accosted a dealer in haberdashery, as he leant over his door, with, 'Mr –, my mother has sent me over for a penny-worth of silk to hem this handkerchief'; to which, without moving from his favourite position, he coolly but tartly responded, 'Go back to your mother, my dear, and tell her to get the thread where she got the handkerchief.'

I do not think there were more than three shop-keepers in the town who had any apprentice or assistant. If the husband was out for a forenoon's fishing in the Tweed, his wife acted as his sufficient lieutenant. No baker had more than one or two journeymen. It seems to me remarkable that, small as their concerns generally were, the family life of these people was of a somewhat refined character. The tone of the females was far from being vulgar. Accomplishments, such as are now so common – music, foreign languages – were unknown; but all had had a sound education in English, and their conversation was not deficient in intelligence. I have since learned that travellers for Manchester and Glasgow warehouses remarked a superiority of taste in the goods ordered for Peebles over that of the goods required in more industrial and wealthy towns not far off. It appears to me in retrospect with regard to the family of a baker, with which I had become familiar through school companionship, that they were very well-bred people. The old mother, in her linen printed gown and white cambric kerchief, as she sat by the fireside working stockings, was a dignified figure. The baker himself, a bailie, was a man of gentlemanly address. I cannot but think with pleasure of intelligence and good manners being thus shown as independent of external circumstances and particularly of a circumstance so vulgar as wealth.

Chapter III

Such worthy burghers as were able to spend their evening quietly at home, generally acquired some little property; but this was not a common case. The absence of excitement in the ordinary life of a small town made it next to impossible for a man of social spirit to avoid convivial evening meetings, and these were very frequent. The favourite *howff* was an old-fashioned inn kept by a certain Miss Ritchie, a clever sprightly woman of irreproachable character, who, so far from the obsequiousness of her profession, required to be treated by her guests with no small an amount of deference, and, in especial, would never allow them to have liquor after a decent hour. When that hour arrived – I think it was the Forbes-Mackenzie hour of eleven – it was vain for them to ask a fresh supply. 'Na na, gang hame to your wives and bairns', was her dictum, and it was impossible for them to sit much longer. Meg Dods in *St Ronan's Well* is what I would call a rough and strong deportraiture of Miss Ritchie – a Miss Ritchie of a lower sphere of life – and, if I may judge from a conversation I once had with Sir Walter Scott regarding the supposed prototype, I think he knew a little about her. The *tout-ensemble* of the actual inn – a laird's town-house of the seventeenth century, with a *grand cour* in front accessible by an arched gate surmounted by a dial – with the little low-ceiled rooms, and Miss Ritchie herself, ruling house, and servants, and guests with her clear head and ready tongue, jocosely sharp with every body, forms a picture in my mind to which I should now vainly seek to find a parallel.

Into one of Miss Ritchie's parlours, or some similar place, would little groups of the burghers converse any evening after the shutting up of their shops, there to talk over the last public news by the Edinburgh Courant, or any petty occurrence that might have taken place nearer home. There was hardly any declared liberalism among them, for the exigencies of the country under the great struggle with Bonaparte had extinguished nearly all differences of opinion. Dear to man is the face of his brother man; pleasant it is every where to hear this brother man's voice, and have an interchange of ideas with him. In that lifeless little town, to have denied the inhabitants these social meetings would have been to practise the greatest cruelty; and on a liberal view, admitting that the means of a more legitimate excitement were not to be had, the jug of whisky toddy at Miss Ritchie's in the evening puts on a defensible aspect. Toddy might there be regarded as the very cement of society – an attraction of cohesion without which a small country town would have been pulverised and dispersed into space. I suppose the same end was served in former times by twopenny ale, a liquor of which only the fame remained in my youthful days; but since the middle of the eighteenth century usquebaugh had been coming into general use, and a hot solution of it with sugar, under a name introduced (strange to say) from the East Indies, namely toddy, was already universal. The decoction was made in stone-ware quart jugs, and poured into the glasses of the company, again and again, in successive rounds, as soon as each person had drained off what was before him, those who lagged in their potations being always duly proscripted and pushed on by their neighbours. They always met under the belief that they were going to have just one jug; but somehow, when that was ended, there was always a painful feeling of surprise, and to have a second seemed only a doing of justice to themselves under an unaccountable wrong continually inflicted upon them by the nature of things. Matters being to far righted, they might have been expected to see the propriety of going home to their beds; but here came in a local circumstance which interested them to an opposite conclusion. The burgh happened to have a most bibulous coat-armorial, consisting of three fishes (by the way, I suspect that fishes drink no more than land animals do, though the contrary is always supposed); and so when the second jug was emptied out, some one was sure to mention 'Peebles Arms', thereby hinting the duty they were under, in loyalty to the town, to have a third jug. Such an argument in such circumstances was irresistible; and thus it came about that the one virtuous jug of the intention always proved to be three in the guilty event.

Two o'clock was the dinner hour of those days, and when there were one or two guests, the toddy jug was always paraded. Men would rise from table, a good deal confused with drink before the afternoon was far advanced, and sometimes had a difficulty in getting home even under favour of day-light. The minister of a neighbouring parish, along with two young gentlemen and a farmer of the same parish, were one day entertained at dinner in Peebles, and were only too hospitably treated. The minister, an odd-looking little thick man with but a limited amount of understanding, and who used to be a good deal laughed at by his brethren, left the town to go home half an hour before his parishioners, who, following him, and passing a place where the road was skirted by whin bushes (gorse), were arrested by faint cries of distress that seemed to proceed from the wayside. Pushing about among the whins, the young men presently found the obese little minister lying on his back, like a gravid ewe, in a hollow from which he was totally unable to raise himself. Just able to recognise one of the young men, he faintly exclaimed, 'Oh, help me up, Maister James – help me up – and take care of my usefulness, take care of my usefulness!' as if this said usefulness had been something of a brittle nature about his person, whereas the term is a cant one applied in the Scotch church to that sustained reputation which gives the clergyman influence over his flock. I do not know if the young men obeyed the poor minister's behest by keeping silence at the time, but I heard one of them relate the story with great humour more than half a century afterwards.

The bailie adverted to a few pages back had one day taken a like early dinner with a friend in Edinburgh, and by four o'clock had got himself elevated into a condition of supreme happiness. According to his previous plan, he set out after dinner to walk to Peebles – twenty-two miles – but when he reached a coach hamlet called Burdiehouse – the place where Dr Hibbert afterwards discovered *holoptychius nobilissimus*[5] in the coal measures – the good drink had taken full effect upon him, and, sad to say, the bailie and his respectable suit of black clothes went sonce into a jawhole. Two or three women, loitering at their doors, observed the occurrence, and came to the bailie's rescue. When they had got him pulled out and reared on his feet, he presented a most dismal spectacle, and one of the women began to rub him down with straw, not using much delicacy in the operation. He felt his dignity outraged, and stammered out, 'I am a bailie of Peebles, woman – I am a bailie of Peebles.' 'And a bonny-like bailie they ha'e o' ye, man!' was the answer. A fellow-townsman, passing, heard this colloquy, and assisted in bringing the begrimed magistrate home.

A neighbour of ours, called Laird Grieve (Laird implied that he was proprietor of his house and perhaps a small bit of land besides) had imbibed more or less of whisky every day for sixty or seventy years, but, getting at length very frail, and falling into the care of his son and daughter-in-law, he was denied the wonted indulgence, which these relatives deemed pernicious to him, and I remember being one day at his bed-side with my father, when the gaunt old man faintly exclaimed: 'They're killing me, James. No ae drap ha'e they alloo't me this fortnight. Me that has ay had my spark o' speerits mornin and e'enin a' my life. It's a cruel thing – isn't it? Hoo wad they like it theirsells?' The Laird appeared fully convinced that, if he could only get a little whisky once or twice a day, his life might still be prolonged.

I think my father was of the same opinion, remarking that, whatever harm there might be from whisky generally, the sudden abstraction of it from a system which had come to depend upon it, could hardly be wise, any more than humane. I do not know how this might be; but the poor laird certainly did not long survive the stoppage of his grog. Tam, the laird's son, might be supposed from this anecdote to have been a tee-totaller, but in reality he was not much less indulgent to himself than his father had been, and only acted in this matter under the belief that whisky was bad for a sick-bed. He was a blythe hearty man, with an old-fashioned gentility in his aspect, and was a general favourite in the town, which he served for many years in the capacity of bailie. He had a small carpenter's shop and a saw-pit and an appearance of uncut logs about his premises; but I never could connect the idea of either work or business with Bailie Grieve. He continued, however, all through life to have a kind of eminence as a maker of fishing-rods. He was also an excellent angler, in which capacity, and as a mirthful man over a jug of toddy, he was well known to the late Professor Wilson.[6]

It used to be very pleasant, in returning to Peebles as a visitor, to call upon Tam at his neat small white house near the bottom of the Old Town, where, in a miniature terraced garden, I saw tulips for the first time, and thought them the prettiest objects in creation. Being a widower without children, the bailie had an old woman for a general servant and housekeeper; and her reception of us, as she opened the door, and showed us into her master's little low-ceiled parlour, was always of an enthusiastic character. Presently Tam coming in ordered out the case bottles, and, helping himself liberally, was sure to express much concern at seeing how reluctant we were to do honour to his hospitality. Then there would be a gust of kindly and somewhat vociferous talk, Betty standing within the door (but holding it by the handle) all the time, and lending in her word whenever she saw occasion. Dear traits of the old simple world, how delightful to recall you in these scenes of comparative refinement and comparative stiffness and frigidity!

'Aih, dear me, Mr Cham'ers, to think what merry days we've seen lang syne! D'ye mind John Park's house-heating, when we keepit up the country dances till four i' the mornin, and not the half o' the folk in the house could get beds. Tam Summervell had a bed, but it was sae high that he couldna get intill't. He first tried to climb in, but it wadna do. Then he breastit it, as ane does in mounting a high horse, but it was a' in vain, and Tam was found far on in the forenoon sleepin on the floor. And dy'e mind yon nicht at Mr Huntly's inn, where fat John Forsyth was sae far gane that he sat down in a pack measure, and

couldna for the life o' him get out again. What laughin we had at John!
And what a wark we had to extract him, as Mr Oman said! Dear me,
dear me.' So would the bailie go on for half an hour, fighting his battles
o'er again.

'I am afraid, bailie, that yon gentlemen of the old school were a little
too convivial at times, though perhaps most of you lived out your days
like the best of us. Was it true that some of you would be twice
sublimated in one day, and occasionally consume nine tumblers in the
course of four and twenty hours?'

'Oh, I dare say we were all bad enough, but certainly some were
much worse than others, and I must admit I have known nine tumbler
men. The worst among us was John Provand who never went home
but in a *ree* state. Mony a scolding did he get from his wife, but it was
a' of nae use. One night, she had gane to her bed, with a flea blister on
her chest for some illness; but it was sae sair that after half an hour she
took it off, and laid it down on a chair by the bed-side. In the sma'
hours, as usual John came home pretty far gone, and took off his
clothes, and sat down on a seat to get his stockings off, and soon after
that he got into bed, and instantly fell asleep. By and bye, John
wakened up in a very uneasy state, tossing and tumbling, and roaring
and crying, as if he had been frying in a het frying-pan; his wife rase in
a fright, thinking he was going out of his reason, and a' was mystery
for some time, till she *missed the blister from off the chair*. Ye may
guess how it was, I dare say. Aih dear, what fun we had about John and
the blister!'

Chapter IV

My father, though not exempt from the convivial habits of his time, stands in my recollection distinguished from his fellow burghers by a love of information and science, and by a liberality of judgment nearly unique. He was a constant reader of the then infant *Edinburgh Review*, and had purchased a copy of the fourth edition of the *Encyclopedia Britannica*, out of which he had acquired no small store of knowledge. The only fellow-townsman whose mind ranged beyond the common-places of life was a leather-merchant named Smibert, a clever little man who, being inclined to Whig politics, became provost in that interest in 1808. He often spent the evening in our parlour, and in the conversations between him and my father I first heard of the leading facts of astronomy. These made a deep impression on me, which was not lessened when, through a telescope borrowed from a schoolmaster, they showed me the ring and satellites of Saturn, explaining that this was a world like our own, although with some peculiarities. In this way, before my fifth year was expired, before I had even gone to school, a contrast began to be established in my mind between the ideas of the common sort of people, consisting of traditional misapprehensions from the mere appearances of things, and the nobler conceptions of the instructed man, founded on investigation and matured by thought.

It was incidental to a narrow field of life and a limited range of education that men possessing such faculties as Mr Smibert and my father should remain in obscurity. The latter always bore a grudge towards the minister of the parish for having prevented his father from giving him a classical education. The superior ability had come, I believe, through his mother, who was a person of uncommonly vivid intellect and no small amount of originality of character. It was commonly said of this woman that she guided the presbytery of Peebles, and it was explained as coming about in this way. She ruled and guided her husband; her husband, again, being the minister's chief elder, exercised great sway over the minister, who in his turn was autocractical in the presbytery. So everything done in the presbytery was supposed to be ultimately traceable to the white-mutched head of that old lady in the Old Town. She had a good deal of the pugnacious piety of the old-fashioned Scotch people. If the minister's wife indulged in any bit of dress unusually *braw*, Margaret never scrupled to tell the minister the next time she met him, how improper she thought it; nay she once went to the manse on a Monday morning, to enter a serious remonstrance with the minister's wife about a bonnet with primers which the lady had exhibited the previous day at church. The minister was able on that occasion to administer check-mate in a very neat way. 'Well, Margaret,' said he, 'it is your decided opinion that there ought to be no superfluous ornaments on my wife's dress. But here now, I see you always wear a black silk ribbon bound round your mutch. Isn't that a superfluity? How then do you justify it?' She was much abashed, and from that time never again exhibited the black ribbon.

Although Dr Dalgleish was generally regarded as a respectable divine and pastor, he never quite came up either in point of theology or personal conduct to the ideal standard which was created for his cloth in the mind of my ancestress. She struggled on for many years, enduring him with difficulty and only because there was no practicable alternative from attendance on the parish church. As she lived near the manse, I am afraid she must have been a good deal of a thorn in his side, notwithstanding all the palliatives of her gentle-natured husband the elder. At length, pretty well on towards the end of the century, a Secession congregation was formed, with a promising young minister, and her fancy began decidedly to waver. Just about that time, there occurred an incident which determined the old lady's course.

It was a bright summer morning about five o'clock – I rather think a Sunday morning – when Margaret left her husband's side as usual, and went out to see her cow attended to before it should be driven forth to the town pastures. Before three minutes had elapsed, her husband was aroused by her coming in with dismal cries – 'Eh, sirs! eh, sirs! did I ever think to live to see the day! O man, O man, O William – this is a terrible thing indeed! Could I have ever thocht to see it?' 'Lord have a care o' us, woman,' exclaimed the worthy elder, by this time fully awake. 'What is it? *Is the coo deid*?' – for it seemed to him that no lesser calamity could have been expected to produce such ululations. 'The coo deid!' responded Margaret, 'waur, waur, ten times waur! There's Dr Dalgliesh only now gaun hame frae his debusheries at five o'clock i' the morning!' The elder, though a pattern of temperance himself, is not recorded as having taken any but a mild view of the minister's conduct; but the strenuous Margaret joined the Secession congregation next day, and never again attended the parish church.

It has been insinuated that this schismatic movement, in the long run, chiefly concerned the wife of the Secession minister, who, being a much younger woman than the established parson's lady, was fully more open to puritanic criticism. I believe she never after assumed a new ribbon without the fear of Margaret's eye upon her, and really had to submit on one or two occasions to a few strictures from that unflattering tongue regarding both her own dress and that of her children.

I am afraid that the elder (or the Deacon, as he was commonly called, being deacon of the weavers' corporation) was not nearly so firm in all points of faith as his spouse. When on his deathbed, my father spoke to him about the mysterious state into which he was about to pass, and heard him softly whisper, 'After all, it is a leap in the dark.' A candid admission of difficulties was not within the compass of his wife's nature. When my father spoke of obscure or doubtful or inconsistent passages of scripture, she put him down sternly, 'James, dinna *canyill* (cangle) wi' the Bible.' I remember this old matron and her surroundings of forbidding-looking old books by Willison, Flavel, and Ralph Erskine, into not one of which was it ever possible for me to penetrate, omnivorous as my literary taste notoriously was. To recall her figure as she sat in her cottage home, conversing of fate, fixed fate, free will, and foreknowledge absolute, clenching everything she said with texts, seemed to me like looking across some prodigious gulf dividing my own generation from the very *prisca gens mortalium*.

It used to be alleged that the minister himself had a little weak point in his theological cuirass. He had published a brochure on the sonship of Christ, which he was afterwards recommended to withdraw from circulation, as being not quite reconcilable with the standards of the church. I can imagine Margaret launching out strongly on this delinquency.

The minister and his wife never had any children, and their domestic life displayed a good deal of the stingy primness which often appears in childless mansions. The fixed rigidity of the daily picture presented in the manse parlour, the minister at his books, the wife at her knitting, and the one 'lass' spinning at her wheel near the door, being admitted to the room to save a fire in the kitchen, was frequently described in comic terms by my father. Not only did the fire suffice the household during the winter evening, but the minister used to be eloquent in showing how the parlour-fire might be so put on in the morning as to last the whole day without any fresh fuel. The wife had a habit which I never heard of in any other person. When about to travel to Edinburgh or any other place of equal distance, she always lay two days beforehand on a sofa 'to rest herself.' She went upon Horace's maxim, 'Venienti occurrite morbo' (run to meet disease as it comes), without any knowledge of the classical precedent.

The minister's chief elder in my early days was a cart and mill-wright, a substantial citizen, related by marriage to our family, and with whose domestic life I was consequently well acquainted. Language fails me in expressing any sense of the goodness and worth of this old man, though, from the narrowness of his sphere of life, he had never learned to temper his piety with any great share of liberality. He afforded a perfect example of the religious practice of a former age, and would have been considered rather stern by the bulk of his contemporaries. 'The beuks,' – a pyramid of volumes based in a quarto bible and topped with a psalm book – were duly 'taken' morning and evening in Thomas's house, and all through the Sunday there was nothing but church-attendance and pious reading and contemplation. I daresay the young females of the family would scarcely be able to restrain their thoughts at any moment throughout that sacred day, for practically, after all, it is not well possible for a woman to be in church under a perfect unconsciousness of the smart style of her bonnet and the good looks of a few of the young men near her. But all that could be done by mortal man to make the family a sample of holiness on Sunday was done. A female relative of ours came in one Sunday afternoon, and told us she had been calling on this worthy family. 'They were all gathered in the parlour, and Thammas was reading a chapter and expounding it as he went along. Two young men passed the window, and Jessy, seeing them, gave a wee thing of a giggle – just the least in the world. *Thammas looked o'er the specs.* Nothing more was required.' For Thomas to intermit for a moment in reading and cast a glance over the top of his spectacles, was as effective as might have been a locking up on bread and water in another family. Such was old Scotland – the Scotland that now seems passing away.

I could forgive everything in Thomas but the sternness. In the hands of men of his kind, Christianity did not appear as a religion of love; it seemed almost wholly to consist in an imposition of irksome duties and an abstinence from all natural and allowable enjoyments. A strolling company came to Peebles, and the manager went to Thomas, who was acting chief magistrate in the absence of the provost, to negotiate for permission to use the town-hall as a theatre. Thomas was hewing at a log out of doors when the man approached, and stood with his tool suspended above his head while listening to the request. 'I'll oppose it with all the means in my poo'er, sir!' explained Thomas fiercely. 'Not with the hatchet, I hope, sir,' responded the son of

Thespis. He had to set up his scenes in a public-house, and met with a fair share of encouragement. I can imagine Thomas contemplating this theatrical visitation in the spirit of a fanatic at Jedburgh, who, on a similar occurrence there, composed the following verse:

> Oh what a toon wad Jethart be,
>   Wad they but read their bibles,
> Wi' half of the alacrity
>   That they do read the pley-bills!

Thomas was on one occasion nominated as one of the elders to represent the presbytery in the General Assembly, and before he set out on that business, Dr Dalgliesh said to him, 'Let me tell you one thing, Thomas; ye'll go away a much better Christian than ye'll come back.' It was a most shrewd and true remark. What Thomas saw behind the scenes in that clerical parliament, was always understood to have had a disenchanting effect upon him.

The only other elder was a rough-looking old man who often worked in Thomas's yard; and this reminds me that I have seen the elderhood of Peebles engaged at the long saw there, Thomas being of course the top-sawyer. 'Dauvit', while equally a professor, was less of a Christian in practice than Thomas. By the most niggardly economy, he had become proprietor of a house with a garden, and the assiduity he displayed all through life would have been credited to him as an honour, if it had only been accompanied with a little humanity. He had an ailing wife and a large family, and he was not either a kind husband or father. The wife wanted to have tea; but Dauvit regarded the Chinese leaf as an insidious luxury, and never would allow it to show face within his doors. It was said that the poor woman at last managed to take it standing in front of a press, on one of the shelves of which the apparatus was arranged, ready to be shut up if her husband should unexpectedly enter the house. Strong religious professions were certainly presented in a most unamiable form in this instance. Dauvit was the type of a character very common in the lower walks of life in Scotland – combining full conviction of all the doctrines of Christianity with an utter absence of everything like its real spirit and an entire neglect of its sublime precepts.

The minister and his elders constituted the equivalent of the modern parochial board and its inspector of poor. The parish funds, consisting mainly of the halfpence collected at the church-doors on Sunday, had comparatively few depending on them in those days. When any poor person applied for relief, there was a rigorous inquisition to determine the reality of the claim and what amount of pension should be granted. The elders exercised an almost irresponsible power in this respect. A poor widow, mother to my affectionate nurse Nanny Hunter, had become a claimant, and our friend Thomas went to examine the circumstances. Finding two cats in the house, he pointed out to the old woman that, while she supported two such unnecessary dependants, it was not proper, nor was it to be expected, that any weekly relief should be extended to her. The younger woman heard of this decision with the utmost indignation, and, denouncing the worthy elder for his inhumanity, said 'Fient nor the twae cats were at the bottom o' his stamack!' – which I must confess was rather strong, even if there had been clearer justice on the side of the old woman. There was no chance that Nanny had ever heard of the case of Mr Thomas Burdet in the time of Edward IV, who was said to have been tried and convicted for wishing a favourite buck of his, which the king had killed in hunting, horns and all, in the king's belly. I feel very certain that she would have been the last person to actually hurt the respected elder, for, to my experience, there never breathed a more kindly disposed creature.

In strong contrast to the hard character of the elder Dauvit, was that of two women living in the Old Town, in whose house I often spent an hour. There was Bet Stewart, the mother, and Hannah Muir, the daughter, who were both to my apprehension old women; but one was frailer than the other. In one end of their cottage, where they usually lived, they had an *awmry* (French, *armoire*) containing a variety of grocery goods, also two or three barrels for various kinds of meal, and a little counter surmounted by scales for weighing. A small business in tea, tobacco, meal and barley, supported these two good women, and enabled them besides to dispense no small amount of charity. Piety was here united with contentment, gentleness, and many active virtues. Their life was not accommodated to the approbation of the world; it was an unending psalm sung in the presence of their Maker. Such kindness of disposition, such purity of heart, even let me deliberately state such genuine politeness, I have never met as in these two humble women. At the distance of fifty years, it affects me sensibly to think over their singular worth and gentleness. Hannah had had some sad domestic trials. She and her husband had unluckily commenced their married life in a newly finished cottage, ignorant of the harm it would do to their health. They were both struck with rheumatic pains, and so severely that they had to be sent home to their respective parents to be nursed. They parted on this occasion, never to meet again; Hannah was soon after both a widow and a mother. This, however, and all other trials, were accepted with pious resignation as designed for her good, and one querulous word never passed her lips. What a contrast between the ennui and discontentment of the wealthy, and the cheerful poverty and resignation of Hannah Muir.

Chapter V

In the middle of the last century[7], the farm of Jedderfield situated on the hill face above Neidpath Castle, a mile from Peebles, the property of the Earl of March, was occupied at the rent of eighteen pounds by an honest man named David Grieve. He reared on that small bit of his lordship's domains, a family of fourteen children, most of whom floated on by their own merits to much superior positions in life – one to be a merchant in Manchester, two to similar positions in Edinburgh, one to be a surgeon in the East India Company's service, and so forth. Their family afforded an example of the virtuous frugal life of the rural people of Scotland previous to that extension of industry which brought wealth and many comforts into our country. The breakfast was oat-meal porridge, the supper a thinner farinaceous composition named sowens; for the dinner there was seldom butcher-meat: the ordinary mess was a thin broth called *Lenten kail*, composed of a ball of oat-meal kneaded up with butter, boiled in an infusion of cabbage, and eaten with barley or pease-meal bannocks. Strange as it may seem, a people of many fine qualities were reared in this plain style, a people of bone and muscle, mentally as well as physically – 'buirdly chiels and clever hizzies', as Burns says. There was not a particle of luxury in that Sabine life; hardly a single article of the kinds sold in shops was new. The food was all obtained from the farm, and the clothing was wholly of homespun. I cannot be under any mistake about it, for I have often heard the household and its ways described by my maternal grandmother who was David Grieve's eldest daughter. Even the education of the children was conducted at home, the mother giving them lessons while seated at her spinning wheel.

The eldest girl was wedded at eighteen by a middle-aged farmer named William Gibson, who rented a large tract of pasturage belonging to Dr Hay of Haystoun. This farm, called Newby, was not less than seven miles long; it commenced near Haystoun, about two miles from Peebles, and at the other extremity bordered in Blackhouse in Selkirkshire, where the Ettrick Shepherd spent his youthful days. The Gibsons were a numerous clan in Tweeddale, and some of them, including the tenant of Newby, were comparatively wealthy. William Gibson had never less than a hundred score of sheep on his farm, and such was the abundance of ewe-milk, that for a part of the year, his wife made a cheese of that material every day. There was a much less frugal style of life at Newby than at Jedderfield. Although the homestead consisted of only a cottage, containing a *butt and a ben* – that is, a kitchen and parlour – with the usual appendages of a barn etc., it gave shelter every night to groups of the vagrant people, the multitude of whom was a matter of remark and lamentation a few years before to Fletcher of Salton[8] and other patriots. On a Saturday night there would be as many as twenty of these poor creatures received by the farmer for food and lodging till Monday morning. Some of them who had established a good character were entertained in the farmer's *ha'*, where himself, his wife, and servants ordinarily sat, as was the fashion of that time. The family rather relished this society, for from hardly any other source did they ever obtain any of the news of the country. One well-remembered guest of this order was a robust old man named Andrew Gemmell, who had been a dragoon in his youth, but had long assumed the blue gown and badge of a *king's bedesman* or licensed beggar, together with the meal-pocks[9] and long staff. A rough and ready tongue and a picturesque if not venerable aspect had recommended Andrew in many households superior to my grandfather's. Sir Walter Scott, who commemorates him under the name of Edie Ochiltree, tells how a laird was found one day playing at draughts with Gemmell, the only mark of distinction of rank presented in the case being that the laird sat in his parlour and the *blue-gown* in the court outside, the board being placed on the sill of the open window between. I can corroborate the view which we thus acquire of the old beggar's position, by stating that the gudewife of Newby learned the game of draughts – commonly called in Scotland the *dam-brod* – from Andrew Gemmell, and often played with him at her hall fireside. Somewhat to his disgust, the pupil became in time the equal of the master, and a visitor one day backed her against him for a guinea, which the old man did not scruple to stake, and which he could easily have paid if unsuccessful as he carried a good deal of money about his person. When it appeared, however, that she was about to gain the game, Andrew lost his temper, or affected to do so, and, hastily snatching up the board, threw the 'men' into the ash-pit. Andrew circulated all through the counties of Peebles, Selkirk, and Roxburgh, going from house to house, and getting an *awmos* (alms) with lodging if necessary at each, appreciated as an original wherever he came, everywhere civilly and even kindly treated. It must have been on the whole a pleasant life for the old man, but one that could only be so while the primitive simple style of farm life subsisted; that is, while the farmer, his wife, and children, still herded in the same room with their servants, and were not above holding converse with the remembered beggar. Perhaps poor Andrew found at last that things were taking an unfavourable turn for him, for he died in an *out-house* at a farm in the parish of Roxburgh, in the month of February too (1794).

When *The Antiquary* was brought out as a play in the Edinburgh Theatre, about 1823, I endeavoured to induce my grandmother to go with me to see it. I felt that it would be a curious sensation to see the representation of Edie Ochiltree in the presence of one who had familiarly known the prototype of the character more than half a century before. But she had never been in a theatre, and nothing could prevail upon her to enter one at that advanced period of her life.

My grandmother was wedded, and went home to her husband's house at Newby, in 1768. She was a remarkably good-looking portly woman, bearing a considerable resemblance to a profile portrait of Madame Roland, the famous heroine of the French revolution. The 'leddies' of Haystoun, sisters and daughters of the landlord Dr Hay, felt an interest in the pretty young wife, and put themselves on familiar terms with her. They would send a message to her on Saturday, asking if she designed to go to church at Peebles next day, and, if so, making an appointment with her to join their party. The five or six 'leddies' and the young guidwife of Newby, might have been seen next morning, picking their steps along the road to Peebles, each wearing her pretty checked plaid or mantilla over her head, such being the old Scottish succedaneum for a bonnet; a most interesting group it must have been, for the Hays were all handsome people, and the young guidwife was reckoned the bonniest woman in Peeblesshire in her day. A lively gossiping conversation was kept up. The 'leddies' would be telling their young rustic friend of the assemblies they had been attending in Edinburgh, where Miss Nicky Murray (sister of the Chief Justice Earl of Mansfield) was in the height of her authority; the guidwife probably telling them in turn of the results of the lambing season, or some bit of country news. In the second year of my grandmother's matronhood, one of her Haystoun friends, the daughter of Dr Hay, was married and taken to a permanent residence in Edinburgh by Sir William Forbes, the banker, – a man who enjoyed as much of the public esteem in Scotland as any man living during his time, whose memory has been embalmed in the verse of Scott, and whose autobiography I had much pleasure in editing a few years ago through the impression made upon me regarding him by my grandmother's recollections. The unmarried Misses Hay, who survived to an extreme old age, always kept up their intimacy with my grandmother, and I remember 'Miss Ailie' calling upon her in Edinburgh about 1851. Miss Ailie was understood to be above ninety at that time, but she never seemed to admit or acknowledge the progress of time; and time really seemed to have very little to do with her. A question about somebody's age arose, and I recollect the old lady saying, rather snappishly, and with the air of one whose words admitted of no reply, 'As to age, it's a subject that was never mentioned in my father's family.' Misses Ailie and Betty Hay spent their latter days in a *flat* in West Nicholson Street, Edinburgh, and only once during a great number of years revisited the ancient paternal mansion in Peeblesshire. I was at Newby not long after, and heard from the farmer how the old ladies came and wandered about the place, lingering fondly in every romantic nook which they had known in former years, and declaring that they thought they could have recognised the place by the smell of the flowers. I feel impelled here to remark the pleasant old fashion of calling ladies by some familiar form of their Christian name. The world was full of Miss Bettys, Miss Peggys, and Miss Bessys long ago – nay, the daughters of Dukes and Earls were Lady Madies, Lady Lizzies, and Lady Kates. There was something very endearing in the custom. It brought high and low together on the common ground of family fireside life. Your Miss Elizabeths and Lady Catherines seem a people in a different sphere, beyond the range of our sympathies. I have heard a gentleman say that, in the family of which he was one, all went well while they continued to call each other by the pet names of their nursery days, and that, on a resolution being formed to exchange these for the formal Christian names, there ensued a marked diminution of their mutual affection, and they never afterwards were the same thing to each other that they had been. This fact seems to me one well worth bearing in mind.

My grandmother and her maids were generally up at an early hour in the morning to attend to the ewes, and their time for going to rest must have consequently been an early one. There was always, however, a period called 'between gloaming and supper-time', during which another industry was practised. Then it was that the wheels were brought out for the spinning of the yarn which was to constitute the clothing of the family. And I often think that it must have been a pleasing sight in that humble hall, – the handsome young mistress amidst her troop of maidens, all busy with foot and finger, while the shepherds and their master, and one or two favoured gaberlunzies[10], would be telling stories or cracking jokes for the general entertainment, or some one with a good voice would be singing the songs of Ramsay and Hamilton. At a certain time of the year, the gudewife had to lay aside the ordinary little wheel, by which lint was spun, and take to the 'Muckle Wheel', which was required for the production of woollen thread, the material of the gudeman's clothes, or else the 'Reel', on which she reduced the product of the little wheel to hanks for the weaver. Even the Misses Hay were great lint spinners, and I suspect that their familiar acquaintance with the gudewife of Newby depended somewhat on their common devotion to the wheel.

Chapter VI

It was on this farm of Newby, while in the possession of Mr Gibson, in the year 1772, that there occurred a case of the sagacity of the shepherd's dog which has often been adverted to in books, but seldom with correctness as to the details. A store-farmer in another part of the country had commenced a system of sheep-stealing which he was believed to have practised without detection for several years. At length, a ewe which had been taken amongst other sheep from Newby, re-appeared on the farm, bearing a *birn* (Anglice, brand) on her face in addition to that of her true owner. The animal was believed to have been attracted to her former home by the instinct of affection towards the lamb from whom she had been separated, and her return was the more remarkable as it involved the necessity of her crossing the River Tweed. The shepherd James Hislop did not fail to report the reappearance of the ewe to his master, and it was not long before they ascertained whose brand it was which had been impressed over Mr Gibson's. As many sheep had been for some time missed out of the stock, it was thought proper that Hislop should pay a visit to Mr Murdison's farm, where he quickly discovered a considerable number of sheep bearing Mr Gibson's brand B, all having Mr Murdison's, the letter T, superimposed. In short, Mr Murdison and his shepherd Miller were apprehended, tried, convicted, and duly hanged in the Grassmarket – a startling exhibition considering the position of the sufferers in life, and made the more so by the humbler man chusing to come upon the scaffold in his 'dead-clothes'. The long continued success of the crime of these wretched men was found to have depended on the wonderful human-like sense of Miller's dog Yarrow. Accompanied by Yarrow, the man would take an opportunity of visiting a neighbouring farm and looking through the flocks. He had there only to point out certain sheep to his sagacious companion, who would come that night, select each animal so pointed out, bring them together, and drive them across country, and, moreover, across the Tweed, to his master's farm, never once undergoing detection. The story was that the dog was hanged soon after his master, as being thought a dangerous creature in a country full of flocks; but I would hope that this was false rumour, and my grandmother, who might have known all the circumstances connected with the case, never affirmed its truth.

Mr Gibson built a handsome house in a conspicuous part of Peebles, and retired thither with a moderate competency about 1780. There were born to him in succession a girl and a boy, and here he soon after died, little over sixty years of age. The daughter grew up an uncommonly pretty creature, and being in some small degree an heiress was 'the cynosure of neighbouring eyes' long before she had reached a marriageable age, or attained the ability to judge for herself as to her disposal in marriage. She had one or two admirers, who, if successful in obtaining her hand, would have carried her away to a distant part of the country, and one who, in the same event, would have retained her in her native place. This conjuncture of affairs led to a transaction of an extraordinary nature, an elopement favoured by the mother of the fair one. I am not sure how far the young lady's predilections were consulted in the arrangement: perhaps her own views were not of a very decided nature, for she was only seventeen, and in Joanna Baillie's phrase, 'less of a bride than a bairn'. However this might be, the public one day received the astounding information that, through favour of the mother, and without knowledge of the young lady's guardians – indeed, in order to elude possible opposition from these persons – Jeanie Gibson had gone off to Edinburgh in a post chaise with James Chambers to be married. Married they were, immediately on their arrival there, by the Rev. Ian Moodie of St Andrew's Church – an act on his part which I suppose would now subject him to the censure of the church courts. The young pair speedily returned to Peebles, and commenced married life in the neat mansion which I have already described. Although married in the month of May (1799), they were thought to have very good worldly prospects. The public only smiled at the way in which the pair had effected their union, and this perhaps had some effect in inducing other lovers to follow their escapade. Certain it is that, soon after, a youthful uncle of the bride succeeded in inducing the daughter of a wealthy farmer in the neighbourhood to elope with him to Edinburgh in order to be married – a couple whom I remember as very grave and staid-looking people, so that I was always at a loss to imagine their having been guilty of such an escapade. Another pair committed a similar irregularity, and it was the more surprising in that case, that the gentleman was son of the Commissary of the province, the officer who had jurisdiction in matters pertaining to marriage. The minister of Peebles was unable to overlook such delinquencies. My parents and their friends the young Commissary and his bride had to appear in the session-house and receive a censure from the minister, before they could obtain 'tokens' entitling them to partake of the next parochial communion. Many a laugh they had afterwards about this business along with the reverend pastor, when he came to baptise their children and partake of the festivity which always followed the ceremony.

The furthest retrogression which any one can make in memory presents him a few obscure little matters starting out, as it were, from a back-ground of clouds and darkness. I can recall the little parlour with its concealed bed, and a few of its decorations; an alabaster time-piece on the mantel-shelf, with a coloured picture below representing a negro in chains kneeling and a legend proceeding from his mouth, 'Britannia, set me free'; two circular alabaster-framed pictures to match, on the wall above, one of them containing a view of Pope's villa at Twickenham, and the Thames with swans sailing on it in front. Likewise a once favourite and very widely diffused print, representing a woodman walking through a winter scene; item, a print delineative of a shepherd boy, with a verse inscribed below:

See the shepherd's cheerful air,
Mark his looks serene and mild,
Grateful love is painted there –
Simple nature's happy child.

The prominent person in the parlour was a young woman, of elegant petite figure, and delicately beautiful small features, having one white cambric handkerchief crossing on her bosom, with a lozenge-shaped gold brooch at the crossing, and another tied (as a man's used to be) round her neck; a figure of lady-like grace and expression, and scarcely yet in her twenty-fourth year, though already the mother of three children, of whom I was the second. Next to her in distinctness as a figure of the memory was the husband of this lady, a neatly made rather short man, in the prime of life, with a handsome cast of face and a cheerful intelligent look; much given to reading and to music, being a tolerable performer on the German flute, fond of scientific conversation, kindly to children and to every body. There was but one servant – dear kind clever Jeanie Forbes, who used to charm my infant ears with old Scottish songs and ballads in wonderful abundance, and sung with a melodiousness that I have never heard surpassed. It was a delightful atmosphere for me, for of my father's music and of Jeanie's songs I never could tire – they were a very mother's milk of the soul. It was considered something of a wonder that I so readily came to distinguish the various airs, and I remember something of a competition which was instituted in my third year, between myself and a female cousin of precisely the same age, as to

which would name the greatest number of tunes; when it was carried
hollow in my favour, as I was found to be acquainted with no fewer
than sixty. Another familiar figure of these early days was that of
Nanny Hunter, who, acting as an occasional servant, had had a sort of
charge of me in my babyhood, and continued ever after to regard me
with the most intense affection. It seemed to be her supremest pleasure
to feel me all over, with infinite cuddlings and kissings, and a profusion
of fond apostrophisings – the purest nonsense of course to bystanders,
but to me ineffably pleasing.

   Amongst occasional figures presented in the home scenes, besides
visitors of the well-bred and well-off classes, there were individuals of
the opposite end of the scale, who came about us under the encouragement given by my parents' good nature. An old woman, a relative,
who through an unfortunate marriage had sunk into poverty, was
frequently at our fireside, where she regaled us young people with
those legends of the spiritual world of which Burns acquired such
store through a similar channel in his early years. Brownies, fairies,
witches, wraiths, and warnings were as familiar to her as the persons
and things at her own fireside, and equally believed in. She had also
very old traditions of matters of fact – for example, one regarding a
provost of Peebles of old times, Provost Dickison, who, she said, had
been *stickit* (i.e. poinarded) at the back of the Dean's Mill; a fact which
I have since ascertained to be true and to have happened so far back as
the year 1572[11]. Her own household was a poor one indeed: she
described it to us one day in a picturesque bit of cant language which
has stuck to my memory ever since – 'There's naething yonder but the
cat licking the dog's mouth, and the mouse in the press[12] wi' the tear
in its ee.' On the whole, with her abundant folk lore, her numberless
old songs and ballads, and the quaintness of her general conversation,
she was to us young people both an entertaining and instructive
acquaintance.

Chapter VII

A person who lived four or five doors from us, and who smacked of an ancient and by-past world, was James Ritchie, the Piper of Peebles, the last person who held the office. Every Scotch town long ago had its piper, and such officials are the subject of several of the comic poems of Ramsay and his contemporaries – Halbert Simpson for instance, the piper of Kilbarchan in Renfrewshire, who was so noted that a statue of him was erected in front of the parish church. Ritchie had been the Piper of Peebles from the year 1741, so that in my childish days he had become a very old man. It was part of his duty to march through the town every evening between nine and ten o'clock, playing on his pipes, as a warning to the inhabitants to go to their beds. He dwelt in a small cottage, where he had brought up a family of ten children upon an official salary of a pound a year, the gains he derived from playing at weddings and other festivities, and the little gifts it was customary to give him at the New Year. I remember the old man calling at our house on New Year's Day in the course of the round of visits he then paid to the principal citizens, dressed in his official coat of dark red and his cocked hat – rather merry by the time he came to us, in consequence of the drams given him along with the shillings and sixpences. My father had a liking for him, through the sympathy in his nature for everything musical, and one evening he took me with him into Ritchie's cottage, that I might hear some of the old man's tunes. The instrument was not what is called the Great Bagpipe, the bagpipe of the Highlands, blown by the mouth, but the smaller bagpipe inflated by a pair of bellows under the left arm. I suspect that Ritchie had tunes of his own composition, since lost, for there were three called 'Salmon Tails', 'Lyne's Mill Trows', and 'The Black and the Grey' – a racing tune, I suspect – which are not to be seen or heard of now-a-days. He was fond of rallying my father upon a ridiculous notion he was understood to entertain, that the world went round. This seemed to the Piper a heresy unworthy of a sensible man. 'Here's my house, Mr Cham'ers, that I have lived in for mair nor sixty years – it's standing noo exactly as it stood at the beginning. Never tell me.' But, though unenlightened on philosophical matters, the Piper was not without a share of wit. Having invested some little savings in lint, which was carried away by a flood of the Tweed, he consoled his wife

with a joke – 'It cam wi' the wind, let it gang wi' the water.' When I sat
listening that evening to the strains of his pipe, I knew not what my
brother has since brought to notice in his *History of Peeblesshire*, that
the instrument had a history. It was a present from the member for the
burghs, a Sir James Cockburn, in 1773, transmitted through Sir Walter
Scott, W.S., father of a young advocate, who at the time of my visit to
the Piper, was just commencing the series of literary works by which
he so bewitched the world. Poor Ritchie died in July 1807, when I was
five years old, and my first pair of trowsers was put on that I might
attend his funeral. Since his demise, Peebles has contrived to exist
without a piper.

Another of our near neighbours was an equally old man commonly
called Deacon Kerr, for he had once been deacon of the weaver
corporation, but during many years had lived in idle retirement,
mainly supported by a clergyman of the neighbourhood who was his
brother-in-law. As to this friendly assistance, by the bye, the deacon
would never allow that it was anything considerable, and a saying of
his, 'What do I get from Mr B – but my meal, and my flesh, and my
coals?' was often quoted by his neighbours as an amusing instance of
insensibility to what constituted, in their conceptions, the prime
elements of ordinary subsistence. The old deacon was very good-
natured toward me and, finding that, after my assumption of mascu-
line attire, I became extremely interested in metal buttons, he was kind
enough to bring a large one from an old George-the-Second coat of
his, and sew it on the front of my dress, where it shone like a moon, to
my infinite delight for many a day, though no more relative to any
useful purpose than those like ornaments which Mr Lauder, in his
Niger travels, describes as exhibited on the tunics of some of the
African chiefs. The deacon had had an unfortunate venture in life; he
had built a house in the parish of Quothquan in Lanarkshire, and, as
it proved that he had no proper title to the land on which he had reared
this structure, it became to him a matter of pure perdition and loss: the
only consequence of which amongst his friends in Peebles was that the
deacon got a new sobriquet – he was called from that time forth
'Quothquan'. One son of the deacon, who had studied for the church,
was a parish minister in the county, a most respectable man. Another
was thought by the fond parents to be even a more promising youth.
'Isn't he a canny ane?' asked his mother one day, in the pride of her
heart; and from that time 'The Canny Ane' became his recognised
name, – a term, I may remark, which does not signify cunning and self-
interested, as English people generally suppose, but, on the contrary,
gentle and amiable. It was told of the Canny Ane that, being engaged

in field sport one day, his companion by accident sent the contents of a gun through his hat, narrowly missing his head; whereupon, on his return home, and telling the adventure to his mother, she exclaimed, 'Aih Jamie, ma man, what would you have said if you had been shot, and your father frae hame?' The Canny Ane had sufficient sense to remark that probably in that case his words would have been few, whether his father was at home or not. He was not, however, destined to realise the hopes of maternal affection, for, having obtained a situation in the Register House in Edinburgh, he foolishly threw it up, and thenceforward lived the life of an idler and sot. I often wonder, if I now lived in the Old Town of Peebles, whether I should find there such queer quaint neighbours as Deacon Kerr and the Canny Ane of sixty years since.

One not less queer was an old woman called Mrs Scott, whose sole dependence in life was a pension of twenty pounds a year which had been settled upon her by Grant of Rothiemurchus, in whose family she had served as housekeeper. On this trifle the poor woman lived, I may say, genteelly, though she was far from being too proud to accept an invitation to a comfortable dinner from a more affluent neighbour. She was a tall gaunt woman, with a huge black silk bonnet not unlike a hearse, and this association of ideas appears to me the more appropriate when I remember hearing her tell how she had long prepared her dead-clothes, and took care to air them once a month, that everything might be found ready and in good order at the last. Mrs Scott had been three times married, and yet was now a widow. Her first husband was a near relation of Mr Lindley Murray, the celebrated grammarian. The second was a man named Scott, who came to Peebles, bringing her with him, and there commenced a culture of peppermint which might have perhaps succeeded if he had not been cut off by an early death. Mrs Scott, being thrown upon the Peebles world as a widow with a pension, became an object of affection to an old widower, a weaver, named William Dods, a close-fisted miserly fellow of habits and ideas totally different from hers. Being led to suppose that he was rich, and able to keep her in comfort, she married him, but soon found that no woman ever committed a greater mistake. The refined tastes she had acquired in the mansion of Rothiemurchus met a dreadful check when she entered the house of William Dods. All her nice little habits were there scoffed at and condemned. A cup of tea, which had been her mainstay of comfort through all the troubles of life, was no longer to be had. She was anxious as far as possible to conform to the rigorous ménage of her new husband; but it was no easy matter. One day the following colloquy was heard to take place between the ill-matched pair:

'I'm sure I do everything in my power to please you. For instance, do I not now take porridge constantly to my breakfast?'

'Aye, parritch,' was the response, 'parritch made wi' butter, and sweet 'ream on them!'

From this it will be evident that Mrs Dods had very little chance of ever coming into a true conformity of habits with her husband. She was indeed truly miserable under the Dodsian regime. Fortunately, it did not last long, and when she became for the third time a widow, such was her disgust at the old man's memory, that she resumed the name of her second husband, which was that under which we knew her. Poor old woman – I could almost have said lady – your part in this troubled existence must have closed many years ago, the long provided dead-clothes put to their use through the help of the strangers around you, and few besides myself can have any remembrance of you.

Chapter VIII

Simple and primitive as our community was, it possessed within its bosom a regular criminal, – a subject of no small interest to his neighbours. Ostensibly, Jamie Scott was a labourer, and his family, occupying a cottage near our dwelling, seemed in no respect different from the ordinary families of that class. But Scottie (such was his common appellative) did little regular work, and was, indeed, little seen abroad by day. During the night, while the entire community was asleep, this queer little man went prowling about, seeking to possess himself of any outlying pieces of loose property which could be turned to account; and as there was no watch or patrol in those days, he pursued this course for a long time in comparative security. Now and then a sheep was missed from the stocks of the neighbouring farmers; but the thief remained undiscovered. In reality Scottie, after appropriating the animal, was accustomed to bring it home to his cottage in the Old Town, and there kill it, taking good care always to burn the skin, so as to defy identification. One night, the cellars of Provost Kerr were broken into, and a considerable quantity of grocery goods abstracted; a criminality most unusual and surprising, and about which the people generally indulged in endless surmises. So did Scottie go on for a number of years, suspected, but never detected; but at length an act of theft was brought home to him, and he was clapped up in the prison. This was a very simple establishment consisting mainly of one apartment on the ground floor, in which the town-officer and gaoler resided, and another up stairs for the incarceration of offenders. Only one locked door intervened between the prisoner and the open stair-case communicating with the court below, which in its turn was always open to the street. It was the winter time, and the country was covered with deep snow. The gaoler's wife went up in the morning to the prisoner's room, with a bowl of porridge which she had made for Scottie's breakfast. The moment she entered, Scottie thrust her aside, and plunged down the stair, through the court, into the street. The cry arose, 'Scottie's broke the prison!' but his movements were so quick, that no one had an opportunity of laying hold of him. While the few stragglers on the street were still bewildered by the suddenness of the outcry, Scottie was off like a deer along the Tweed bridge. I was in the garden behind our house at the moment, and remember the rush of people into it to try if they could catch a glimpse of the fugitive. A boy was watering a horse at Tweedside to the west of the bridge, and was startled by the sudden apparition of a wild half-dressed figure (with stockings, but no shoes, for Scottie had not completed his toilette at the moment of escape), who snatched the horse from his hand, and in a moment had mounted and ridden off along the road to Manor. So here was another felony, that of horse-stealing, added to the already teeming catalogue of Scottie's offences. The town was in the greatest excitement all that day to learn what could be learned about the escape and the course of the fugitive. It was surmised that the horse might have been there by connivance; but that idea could not be substantiated. Next day, it was learned that Scottie, after getting two or three miles from the town, had left the horse and taken to his own feet, shoeless as he was, and it was said there were some bloody footsteps to be observed for a certain distance in the snow. Here, for the time, all traces of the fugitive were lost.

There was something very dreary in the idea of this poor outlaw wandering about the snow-covered hills and dales of the south-west district of the county, and people wondered whether he would receive any sort of succour or harbourage from the store-farmers and shepherds whom he had so often robbed. Every effort was made to trace and lay hold of him, but in vain. Three weeks after his escape, while the snow still lay upon the ground, Mr John Ramage, the tenant of Whitehaugh, a mile from Peebles, was awakened by a tapping at his bed-room window. He listened for a while to assure himself that the sound was a reality, and then aroused his wife (my grand-aunt) to consult her as to what should be done. It was resolved that they should rise and look out to ascertain who was causing the disturbance. Probably their thoughts turned on some of those incidents of nocturnal courtship which were once so familiar in rural Scotland. Their feelings were greatly roused when they beheld a poor tattered miserable-looking man, and heard a faint and piteous voice, telling them who he was, reminding them of old acquaintance, and intreating for God's sake some food and clothing. It was the hapless Scottie. Mr Ramage, who was the kindest of good men, could not resist this appeal, but went and got some bread and an old blanket which he handed through the window to the wretched petitioner, commanding him, however, to leave the place and trouble them no more.

Weeks passed on, and spring advanced; but nothing was ever heard of Scottie. It was suspected that he occasionally got home by night, and that his wife, if she had chosen, could have told a tale as to his whereabouts and means of life. She denied all knowledge of his movements, and seemed with her family in the last stage of wretchedness. Meanwhile, Mr Ramage began to send in last year's grain to market, and one day, on a particular stack being taken down, a curious *exposé* was made. The hollow in the interior showed unmistakable traces of a human being having recently lived there. There were bones and other remains of food, feathers of fowls, and a couch or lair composed of straw. They could even ascertain that access and escape had been obtained through an aperture formed by the abstraction of a single sheaf. No doubt was ascertained that this had been for a considerable time the Patmos of the unfortunate Scottie. Encouraged by the benevolence of Mr and Mrs Ramage, he had made them his hosts for the time, and subsisted on the fowls and eggs of their farmyard. They were too generous to feel anything but wonder at the ingenuity of the poor creature, and pity for the sufferings which he must have undergone while harbouring at their place.

Scottie was ultimately tried at Jedburgh for sheep-stealing, and transported to Australia.

Chapter IX

The means of subsistence in my native burgh were generally small. One notable way of eking out the ordinary gains was to keep a cow. Almost every body kept a cow. The municipality had been accustomed from early and primitive times to rent a pasturage farm called Edderston, a mile from the town, for the daily support of the townsmen's cows, charging from each a mail or rent. Every morning, about six, the cowherd walked through the town, blowing a horn, literally a cow-horn, to call out and assemble the cattle. The *mugitusque boum* was heard pervading the burgh for an hour, as this man led them forth for their day's pasturage on the brown slopes of Edderston. They had their morning ground, their mid-day ground, their afternoon ground, and over these in succession they were led each day; finally, in the evening, they were driven back into town, when each animal would be seen unpromptedly diverging into its own door, as the crowd marched along, until all were housed. The time 'when the kye came hame' was the Sabbath of the day. Then would be seen the shopkeepers chatting at their doors. Then were the servant maidens seen tripping about, in their neat dimity short-gowns (an attire now as much out of fashion and as much lost sight of, as fardingales and stomachers) and with their hair in tidy ringlets, subjects of admiration to infinite journeymen and apprentices. Then were the boys most vociferously joyful over their sports. Then were planned the meetings of burgesses in Miss Ritchie's, for toddy and talk. This bucolic feature of the old burgh life is now a thing of the past. It has been found that to attend to a cow, to provide food for it in winter, and to risk all its occasional ailments, is not worth while for the sake of any good derived from it. The keeping of cows is left to people who make a business of it. Edderston is no longer the pasture ground it once was, but a well cultivated farm.

Our little burgh was nominally under the care of a council of seventeen persons; but in those days of unawakened intelligence, before people learned that they were so miserably oppressed as they afterwards discovered themselves to be, the provost was generally able to carry every thing his own way. The chief medical man, Dr John Reid, who enjoyed a high professional reputation, was the provost for a long course of years, and it was alleged to be customary at the council board for the inferior men to ask, 'What does Dr Reid say?' and to give their votes in accordance with that dictum, without further question. Not but that there were occasional inlets of Whig light into the dark recesses of the council. Not long before my time, there had been a provost of a liberal complexion, a thriving brewer named Ker – of whom, by the bye, it was told that, being in London, he was induced to attend a public dinner presided over by Charles James Fox, when, the toast of 'the Majesty of the People' being given, the worthy provost, who was a little deaf, thought it was 'the Magistrates of Peebles', and straight-way rose and gravely returned thanks. My father's intimate friend Mr Smibert was another example of the liberal sort of provost. Under his influence, the Magistrates and Town Council petitioned for an enquiry into the conduct of the Duke of York, when that became so mercilessly exposed by Colonel Wardle; and it was alleged by the wags that some curiosity was expressed in the House of Commons as to the situation of Peebles and the reality of its existence, upon which points there was some difficulty in obtaining information. The judicial functions of the magistrates were performed in an off-hand and simple manner. If a set of boys were detected breaking into an apple-garden, the one town-officer (also jailer), a fussy little man commonly called Pisty Walker, dragged them into the shop of a bailie, where, in the midst of old women buying soap and candles, the worthy magistrate would dispose of the young culprits with that brevity and directness which one admires so much in the Cadi in the Arabian Nights Entertainments, and at once cause them to be clapped up in prison, though usually only for a few hours. On these occasions, the gravity of the magistrate – interrupted in the ordinary work of his counter – the very scales of justice arrested in his hand – and the officious forwardness of Pisty Walker, together with the howls of the repentant and blubbering boys, and a commenting crowd like the chorus of the Greek tragedy pressing in at the door, formed a *scena* to which I should vainly endeavour to do justice.

It was a popular story that, a quarrel which had arisen about a disputed will having led to an unpleasant breach of the peace, the case came before one of the bailies for adjudication; when one of the parties, a glib-tongued person, set forth that the defunct had dictated so and so. The defunct had done this; the defunct had said that. Till at last the magistrate fairly lost patience, and burst out with: 'What's he aye funk-funking about? Canna he bring forward the Defunk and let him answer for himsel'?' It was the same dignitary who had to settle a matter of damages for a kangaroo, which had been allowed by the master of a vessel bringing it home to leap overboard. 'Ye should ha' clippit its wings,' said the bailie sternly to the owner of the lost animal.

'Bailie,' said a well meaning bystander, 'the kangaroo is a quadruped.'
'Quadruped, or no quadruped,' rejoined the bailie, 'he ought to ha'e
clippit its wings.' And so the claim was dismissed.

The great and pressing duty with Scottish municipalities in the
early part of this century was to manifest loyalty. It had been so all
along from the time when the house of Brunswick acceded to the
throne. It seemed as if it would take all that a body of magistrates and
a town-council could do in the way of outward demonstration by
drinking of the royal health with three times three at the cross or in
their town-house, and getting all other people engaged in the same
vociferous processes, to maintain the reigning family upon the throne.
Thus alone were 'the liberties of the people' preserved from Pope and
Pretender under the first two Georges: thus alone, under the third king
of the name, were 'the precious institutions of the country' saved from
the sapping influence of French politics. The burgh authorities of
Peebles in my childish days appeared to be under a strong and abiding
sense of the necessity of continually drinking old King George's
health, as a measure indispensably required for the stability of life,
property, religion, and generally whatever men held most dear. Accordingly, the 4th of June, his Majesty's birthday, was a festival held
in honour and respect to a degree of which the present generation can
form no adequate idea. The provost, bailies, and councillors met
solemnly over wine and cake in their town-hall, in company with all
the citizens of any account or importance, and there, with eloquent
speeches and vehement acclamations, honoured the loyal toast of the
day. At one time, they did this in the open street at the Cross, each man
flinging his glass over his head after he had emptied it; but latterly it
was found more convenient to perform the ceremony within doors,
and to spare the crystal. The truth is, the outer public, and particularly
that important part of the community, the Boys, had grown more and
more troublesome to the celebrators as the demand for loyal demonstration had increased, till at last there was a Junius, and Johny Wilkes,
and Horne Tooke spirit abroad, and a disposition to the utterance of
opprobious truths, combined with a tendency to the flinging of dead
cats, previously dragged through gutters, which made the open performance of the ceremony next to impossible. As it was, the crowd
which besieged the door of the town-hall while the ceremony was
going on within, manifested a spirit only too strongly marking the
necessity under which every loyal citizen lay of drinking the king's
health to the utmost extent of his power. It was a spirit much akin to
that which caused a seceding minister at Kilmarnock to pray for 'our
puir fulish benichted king and his regardless faimily.'[13] Perhaps a sense

that the wine and cake were for others and not for them might give it pungency. But, any how, the dispersion of the company was always more or less a scene of political martyrdom; and it was all that loyalty and good port could do to nerve the gentlemen for the encounter. What was one Pisty Walker among so many?

It is rather odd, and I cannot pretend quite to account for it, that the Multitude had all the time a way of celebrating the King's birthday of its own. Whether there was a feeling of loyalty at bottom, or whether it depended purely on the profound interest which humanity finds in gunpowder, I cannot tell. But there it was – the entire mass of the common people inspired, as it were, with a notion that the king's birthday, in the nature of things, inferred a continual cracking of rusty pistols and Lilliputian artillery, and a flinging of squibs, and a setting off of *pee-oys*,[14] all through that long, long day. You heard them in the morning before getting up, and they disturbed your rest after you had gone to bed. Towards dusk – as far as there was such a thing as dusk in Scotland at that season – the whole community was out in the streets, and the explosion of powder in various ways, here, there, everywhere, had become deafening, indeed bewildering. A quiet citizen suddenly found some infernal fiz-gig going off in his coat pocket. A servant lass who thought she was safely looking on from her master's door was suddenly set a-screaming by a pistol fired close beside her ear. It was a sad time for any body lying ill, or whose nerves were habitually delicate.

A relative of mine, finding himself in the midst of a scene of this kind in a Scotch burgh, stepped into the shop of a man whom he knew, a sort of general dealer.

'How are you to-night, Mr Sandison?'

'Oh, I'm vera weel mysell, Mr William; but O man, the mistress (i.e. his wife) is dreadfully distressed wi' the nerves. And there's thae rascals on the street, makin sic a noise. Every crack o' their pistols gangs to her heart like a knife.'

Enters a boy hastily from the street. 'A penny worth o' pooder, Mr Sandison!'

'Aye, aye, my man,' exclaims Mr S. briskly, and bustles away round the counter to serve out the demanded article.

Mr William cannot resist making the remark that, Mrs Sandison being so ill, and so sorely harassed by the pistols, it was somewhat inconsistent conduct on Mr Sandison's part, that he should be selling gunpowder to the boys.

'I wonder to hear ye, Mr William,' quoth Sandison, 'when there's Thamas Johnston on the other side o' the street – were I to refuse the laddies' custom, *he* wad sell them joost as muckle as they likit or had bawbees for.'

Chapter X

Amongst the greatest trials and troubles of the Peeblean magistracy, in my youthful days, was the enforcement of what are now called sanitary regulations. Nobody dreamed of such a thing as a connection between dirt and disease in those days; but, from some dim sense of the το πρεπον,[15] or what was in the sixteenth century called *civility in burghs*, there was a wish more or less clearly pronounced, even in those simple times, that filth might not unnecessarily be accumulated on the street or anywhere near the dwellings of men. But there was also a well understood connection between *knicken moddings*[16], stored behind houses and in closes, and *rigs* of potatoes on the Kirklands; and it became somewhat dangerous to meddle with a matter in which the public felt that its bread and butter were so deeply concerned. A newly introduced bailie would now and then make a strenuous effort to get acts of council on this subject enforced; but there was always sure to arise some village Hampden who, with dauntless breast, would stand up for the natural right to domestic accumulations of manure, and who, from the extensive backing he was sure to have, could scarcely fail to defeat the innovator. Or, failing a Hampden, there was sure to be a Jenny Geddes to take the field, and by mere screaming and obloquy carry the day. One of these reforming magistrates, from a habit acquired in childhood, and which he could not refrain from even when sitting in the magistrates' *loft* in church, had acquired a certain nickname; and one of my earliest reminiscences was seeing this worthy dignitary walking along the street, while a virago named May Ingram, whose midden had been (vainly) ordered away, went after him with violent gesticulations, and a face inflamed with passion, calling, 'Sook-thoombs yet – Sook-thoombs yet!'

To be a bailie or even a provost in my native burgh was, generally speaking, a thankless office. Although they marched every Sunday to church, with the town-officer and the town drummer parading with halberts before them, and planted themselves in a prominent and special gallery, I could never see that they were held in real honour, such as might have partly compensated the trouble they took in ruling the town and conducting its affairs. Only now and then an occasion would arise when the provost emerged as a man of some consequence. For example, when the Forty-second regiment passed through the town on its return from services in Egypt in 1802, the colonel and other officers were entertained by the magistrates with much ceremony and no small amount of hospitality, at the expense of the corporation: it was almost incessant Saturnalia for three days. The Royal Company of Archers would now and then come from Edinburgh to shoot for a silver arrow which Peebles had possessed as an object of toxophilite competition for two hundred years; and of course the magistrates had to give the company a dinner, likewise at the public expense. Or some single distinguished person would visit the town, and it became necessary to elect him as an honorary burgess, and celebrate his inauguration with the traditionary 'riddle of claret'; that is, a riddle with as many bottles of Bourdeaux as could be stuck into it, all of which it was essential to consume on the spot – for the honour of the town; and I never heard that there was any difficulty in paying the town this indispensable compliment. When the new burgess had been well primed with wine, he was led out by the provost, with his burgess ticket fixed in his hat, to call upon the chief magistrate's wife, from whom he was privileged to receive a kiss (or rather to take one if he could get it,) and the evening usually closed in a shower of toddy. These were the proceedings of the old merry days, when to find fault with any doings or expenditures of persons in authority was to be a *black-neb* and a Jacobin dangerous to society and to all its most cherished institutions.

I never heard, indeed, that the Peebles magistracy was ever so much or so constantly regaled at the public expense as that of the 'honest town' of Musselburgh, where it is on record that three convivial meetings were held to deliberate on the question whether there should be a new bell-rope in the town-house, and where it was customary, when any of these burgh magistrates chanced to meet of an evening in the inn, for the landlord to ask the provost at the close of the festivity, 'The mussel and the anchor?' (a reference to the town's armorial bearings,) meaning, 'I suppose this is to be put down to the town's account.'

The town-drummer, Will Moffat, was almost as curious a relic of old times as Piper Ritchie. He was a sturdy old man, who had spent his youth in the army, had served all through the American war, and wore a red coat with those white facings, turned up upon the breast and skirts, which you see in pictures of the military of George the Second's time. Will's main business, besides carrying a halbert before the magistrates, was to go through the town advertising it of any such business as a letting of grass parks, a roup[17] of furniture, or an arrival of certain provisions at some particular shop. In this business, however, which might be called the substitute for a native newspaper in Peebles, he was rivalled by a tall old woman, who called attention to her oral advertisements by rapping on a timber platter with a porridge-stick, for which reason she passed by the name of Clap Meg. Meg, I suppose, required a smaller fee than Drummer Will, and was therefore a good deal employed for announcements of a comparatively trivial nature. Her mode of drawing an audience has a melancholy associa-tion connected with it, for persons afflicted with leprosy in the sixteenth century used the same means for calling the attention of the charitable, as they sat a little apart from the wayside, severed from their fellow-creatures under pain of death.

There was still another official, one little seen or heard of, but an object of no small interest to the boys – Charlie Rodger, the hangman. In reality, Charlie, though always thus designated, never got anybody to hang: his highest range of practice was limited to a public whipping or the exposing of an offender on the cross. He wore a dark-blue coat with white facings, provided for him by the magistrates; and there is an entry in the council record under April 1803, granting him a suit of new clothes for his marriage. Charlie's salary being small, he and his wife lived very poorly in general; and an occasional half guinea for a whipping was a prodigious windfall to him. On the first such occasion after his marriage, he and his wife sat down to deliberate as to what they should have by way of a really good, if not luxurious dinner, and the result was – a mess of beef-steak and gingerbread! They calculated, in their ignorance, that beef-steak was the most choice part of butcher meat, and that gingerbread was a superior kind of bread, and so, by a very natural process of reasoning, came to decide upon a feast of beef-steaks and gingerbread.

A number of persons in Peebles were generally recognised as 'Characters', on account of some peculiarity either in their persons, their manners, or their circumstances. There was a family in humble life, named Brunton, several of whom were persons of weak mind, though not all to the same degree. Jamie was a thorough imbecile, who went about under his mother's care, dressed in a blue petticoat, with bare legs and feet, his faculties being insufficient to enable him to manage the attire belonging to his sex. Now-a-days, such a person would be put aside in a pauper lunatic asylum; but in those days there were no such institutions, and so the poor idiot boy was kept in his parents' house, – a constant figure at their fireside, or seated on a stone at the door in good weather, smiling vacantly to the passers by. His brother Adam, commonly called Edie, was scarcely fatuous – only silly – not fit for any regular trade or business, but yet able to go about without tendance, and even to earn a little money by running messages or acting as a porter. Edie was a general favourite, on account of his harmlessness, and a certain drollery which occasionally appeared in his conduct. Everybody knew him, and was kind to him. It was wonderful how, with such defective judgement, he possessed a more than usually tenacious memory – of which peculiarity I can relate an anecdote which came under my own observation. A relative of mine, a young man of some fortune, being destined to be a cotton-manufacturer, was put into a weaver's shop to learn the processes of the business – a most unsuitable course of life for him, as it proved, for he was wholly destitute of industrial faculties, and had not been long at the loom, when, dressing the web one day, he lost his balance, and fairly tumbled into it. About twenty-five years after this event, during all which time he had been absent from Peebles, I was walking with him in one of the streets of the ancient burgh, when we met Edie Brunton. 'Edie,' said I, 'do you know this gentlemen?' 'Ay,' said Edie, after only a momentary hesitation, 'he ance fell through a wob.' I consider this a remarkable illustration of the independence of the mental faculties upon each other.

There were several oddities of whom I remember only the names – for example, a cobbler called Kookoo Kippy; a man who lived by keeping a horse and cart and passed by the name of Puddle-Michty; a woman of miserable appearance and wretched reputation, known as Scanty – why I cannot imagine, except it was that she was very scanty of attire. There was also a queer rough fellow, of morose habits, who was employed to keep down the breed of foxes, and bore the appellative of Tod-hunter Will: a down-looking mysterious man, always going about the country in pursuit of his vocation. The character Gibby in Guy Mannering bears a considerable resemblance to the Tod-hunter.

Chapter XI

There were several stages or eras in the history of childhood. First there was the well-recognised *mud-pie stage*. Little creatures, newly allowed to leave the arms of mothers and nurses, were to be seen on the street or in bye lanes, amusing themselves with those constructive works, raised out of the dirt, which so strongly mark out man as an engineering animal. Carrying *glaur*[18] in my *daidly*,[19] to be used as mortar in a house-building by a senior companion, is about the oldest of my reminiscences. Then there were cruises of little creatures into fields two or three hundred yards off, under the conduct and encouragement of some one rather above our age, or who was previously a traveller to that extent himself; into fields where we made our first acquaintance with gowans and buttercups, or along hedges supposed to contain the mystic wealth of birds' nests, a few of which had been detected by certain big boys, and were the theme of profound speculation, as to whether they contained eggs or *gorbs*,[20] whether the mother bird was likely to 'forsake', whether she had forsaken, whether, if taken by us, the young ones could be brought up at home, and so forth. The May blossom and dog-rose were a treasure in early summer; the haws and hips and brambles at a later season. A furlong from our house were the ruins of a church of Red Friars. To wander thither, to climb the mouldering walls, to peep into a sepulchral vault of the Earls of March, and watch for the ripening of wild apples on a tree amongst the ancient cloisters, were favourite pastimes of those pinafore days, while the sun of our third or fourth July shone strong upon our heads, and everything in heaven and upon earth was new. There was also a meadow beside Eddlestone water, with plenty of rushes, whereof to weave conical bonnets and rattles, or construct millwheels to be set a-going on some detached bit of the stream. Little girls often formed part of our vagrant companies, and I am ashamed to reflect how little gentleness or consideration we usually showed to that weaker part of creation. I am afraid that chivalrous feelings towards the fair are in a sadly undeveloped state during the mud-pie period.

I describe the next stage as the *See-Saw* period, being the time when we began to invade wood-yards for the gratification of *shooing* upon deals; also the time when we assembled at dusk to play games at

Ho-spy or Hide and Seek. There were rhymes, from time immemorial traditional among the boys, for determining by a kind of lottery who was to hide and be sought for, or who, in the game of the honey-pots, was first to be treated as the pot. There was nothing fine among us: it was corduroy all over, with only some differences as to the condition of the draperies. The sleeve of every one of us, from an unmentionable use it was systematically put to, might have served as a mirror. In summer, every one of us was eager to get quit of shoes and stockings, and go paidling in the waters from morning sun till dine. Nor were bonnets of any more account than shoes. Many boys had no acquaintance with that part of dress, but presented an undaunted front (garnished perhaps by the *coo's lick*[21]) to the Jovian influences, alike indifferent to summer's heat and winter's cold.

There was nothing that could be called property among us at this era. One boy, indeed, would have an eel-skin of his own capture tied round his ankle – a trophy analogous to the scalp decoration of the North American savage. Another might have a handful of cherry-pips or an old button, to be employed in games. But to possess anything that had required money to obtain it was rare. What, then, were the feelings of the boys in some particular street or district, when suddenly one of them appeared in possession of – a knife! – ye gods, a twopence halfpenny knife, (for such, I remember, was the price,) a gift probably from some relative come on a visit from a distance! To be allowed to see this precious article – still more to be allowed to handle it – or to see its quick execution in the whittling of sticks – were great favours. All looked on with admiration, and beheld the happy owner with envy. I remember a clever member of our fraternity getting a knife, and becoming a kind of king of the corps through that cause alone. He immediately set himself to put the implement in use in paring the nails of his companions, and soon had them all down to the very quick. It was rather a trial to the general fortitude under the infliction of pain; but, though some winced, none complained. Some time after, a shoemaker, father to one of the patients, seeing the mother of the experimentalist at her door, accosted her thus: 'Eh Mrs –, that's an extrornar laddie o' yours. D'ye ken, he's lately got a knife, and has pared the nails o' a' the other laddies sae sair, that oor Ian, for ane, has na been able to scart[22] his head for a week past!'

The parish school of our ancient burgh was a long low building situated on the green near the Tweed, and was divided into two parts, one for the junior classes under a 'helper', the other for the more advanced classes under 'the master'. The person holding the chief office in my childish days was Mr James Gray, a teacher of some repute, author of an excellent arithmetical textbook and also of a spelling-book, both of which were at one time extensively used in Scotland. There was, near by, a grammar-school, where Latin was taught, and the teacher of which, Mr James Sloane, had generally forty boarders under his care, besides the native youth. My first two years were spent amidst the crowd of children attending Mr Gray's seminary, where, owing to a small endowment from the heritors (after the usual Scottish arrangement), the charge for each young person was only two shillings and threepence per quarter. On these easy terms I was well grounded by the master and his helper in English. The entire expense must have been only eighteen shillings – a fact sufficient to explain how Scotch people of the middle class appear as so well educated in comparison with their southern compatriots.

It was prior to the time when the intellectual system was introduced. We were taught to read the Bible and to spell the words. No attempt was made to enlighten us as to the meaning of any of the lessons. The most distressing part of our school exercises consisted in the learning by heart the catechism of the Westminster Assembly of Divines, a document which every child in presbyterian Scotland has to learn, though it is impossible for any person under maturity to understand it, or to view it in any other light than as a torture. Some of the phrases of this catechism stick to my memory, but only to raise associations of pain and disgust; and such must be the case of many. As a means of opening the mind of a child to the relations he bears to the mysteries out of which his life has sprung and into which his pleasing anxious being is finally to be resolved, nothing could be more unsuitable. Viewing the severe, taxing way in which it is taught and the penalties connected with it, I deem the *Scottish Inquisition* a good name for it. Yet, strange to say, this catechism, with one preliminary page containing alphabets and ranges of monosyllables, was at one time the only initiatory book used for instruction in English in Scotland.

It was a strange, rough, noisy, crowded scene, this burgh parish school. No refinement of any kind appeared in it. Nothing kept the boys in any sort of peace and order but the tawse, and when the master's back was turned, an uproar took place, accompanied by showers of bibles and spelling books, that was truly dreadful. The master sat in a desk, keeping an eye upon his rebellious subjects, and when any two boys were observed to be indulging in a little idle conversation, the instrument of flagellation would suddenly alight between them, – a signal to them to come up to the desk, bearing that lash with them, each holding one of its dread filaments, and there submit to a series of *palmies* in proportion to their offence. Mr Gray, however, was a meek and simple-minded man, comparatively little addicted to cruel inflictions upon his pupils. Many people thought he did not punish enough. This idea in part was the cause of an act of wild justice which I saw executed one day in the school.

The reader must imagine a drowsy summer afternoon, and the school hum going on in a dull monotone, when suddenly the door burst open, and in walked a middle-aged woman of the humbler class, carrying her right hand under her apron. The school sank into silence in an instant. With flashing eyes and excited visage, she called out, 'Where is Jock Forsyth?' Jock had maltreated a son of hers on the green, and she had come to inflict vengeance upon him before the school. Jock's conscious soul trembled at the sight, and she had no difficulty in detecting him. Ere the master had recovered from the astonishment which her intrusion had created, the fell virago had pounced upon the culprit, had dragged him into the middle of the floor, and there begun to belabour him with her own domestic tawse, which she had brought for the purpose under her apron. The screams of the boy, the anxious intreaties of the master, with his constant, 'Wifie, wifie, be quiet, be quiet,' and the agitated feeling which began to pervade the school, formed a scene which defies words to paint it. Nor did Meg desist till she had given young Mr Forsyth reason to remember her to the latest day of his existence. She then took her departure, only remarking to Mr Gray as she prepared to close the door, 'Jock Forsyth will no' meddle with my Jamie again in a hurry.'

Chapter XII

Boys for whom a superior education was desired were usually passed on at the beginning of their third year to the Grammar School – the school in which the classics were taught, but which also had one or two advanced classes for English and Writing. This was an example of an institution which has affected the fortunes of Scotsmen not much less than the parish schools. Every burgh has one, partly supported out of public funds. For a small fee – in the Peebles grammar-school it was only five shillings a quarter – a youth of the middle classes gets a good grounding in Latin and Greek, fitting him for the university; and it is mainly, I believe, through this superior education, so easily attained, that so many of the youth of our northern region are inspired with the ambition which leads them upwards to professional life in their own country, or else sends them abroad in quest of the fortune hard to find at home. I observe, while writing these pages, the advertisement of an academy in England, where, besides sixty pounds by way of board, the fees for tuition amount to twenty-five. For this twenty-five pounds, a Scottish burgher of my young days could have five sons carried through a complete classical course. The difference is overwhelmingly in favour of the Scotch grammar school, as far as the money matter is concerned. And thus it will appear that the good education which has enabled me to address so much literature of whatever value to the public during the last forty-five years, never cost my parents so much as ten pounds. Mr Sloane for thirty-five or forty pounds a year took youths from a distance into his house and fed alike their minds and bodies without further charge.

He was an excellent pains-taking teacher, but severe after the fashion of his day. The lash was pretty constantly in exercise among the idle, the stupid, and the ill-behaved. The end of a desk formed an altar of immolation, and rarely did a day pass without an instance of the sacrifice. Palmies (lashes upon the extended hand) fell fast and thick. Some boys never seemed to understand what it was all about, or what end was in view, in this incessant hammering of their brains with unintelligible Latin rules and equally incessant affliction of their bodies with stripes. They would have willingly seen all the Latin books in the school thrown into the Tweed which flowed past the play-ground, and abandoned all the hopes professedly derived from education for ever. It always seemed to me as if fully two thirds of the boys were incapable of learning, and as if their attendance at school was, in a great measure, a nugatory ceremony. Perhaps their ages – from eight to thirteen – partly accounted for this. Usually there were three, or so, at the top of each class, who, from natural aptitude for the instruction, were what might be called good scholars; and to them, as a very natural though unfortunate result, came a large part of the teacher's attention, for it was not wonderful that he preferred the painting of lilies to the washing of Ethiopians. And so the Ethiopians remained a dead weight in the lower part of the class, only going through the forms of education, and obtaining nothing of the reality, till the time came for their entering upon such lines of business as might be open to them, in which, by the way, many proved sufficiently clever, notwithstanding their bad scholarship.

The castigatory part of the teacher's exertions formed a subject of careful observation and no little discussion among the boys. They always considered it a bad sign when he came to school in the morning with his night-cap on, for they had learned from experience that any little personal illness did not improve his temper. They watched the wearing out of a pair of tawse, and the coming on of another, with great anxiety, curious to know whether the change would be for the better or the worse. There were speculations as to the processes to which tawse were subjected to make them effective. Some thought he burnt the ends of them; some had an idea that they were steeped in some chemical composition of an indurative tendency. There were equally serious discussions as to means of mitigating the sharpness of the pain. Some boys had great faith in a lick with the wet tongue before holding out the hand. I found a noted victim one day in a tannery, prone beside one of the pits, with his hands inserted in the tanning liquor, under an idea (I need not say how false) that the living fibre might be thickened and strengthened as well as the skins of dead animals, so that he might deceive the master in the amount of suffering inflicted. I cannot but rank it among the improvements of our age, that this old system of instruction by brute force is no longer practised by any teacher worthy of the name, and that the tawse now threatens none but the positively bad boys of a school.

What was thought and felt by the boys in general regarding education as practised in those old days was pretty clearly evinced by the burst of hilarious excitement with which they poured from the school into the green when the penitential part of the day was past. The joyous outcries, the wild romps, the glowing faces, were a practical condemnation of the system, if the master could have opened his eyes to it. There was no lack of healthful play for my young compatriots. Hockey, called in Scotland *shinty* – I suppose from the danger into which it puts the shins – furnished the *certaminis gaudia* above all other games. Crooked sticks from the hedgerows, and any bit of wood round or square, were all the apparatus required. There was, however, a round of games in connection with the seasons; marbles (called with us the *bools*), cherrystones (the *paips*), pitch and toss, and kite-flying (the *dragon*), predominated in succession, according to what appeared a fixed order, though I never could see how any such was maintained. At the beginning of June, there were Saturday expeditions to the Tor Wood three miles off, 'to herry the crows'; that is to obtain the fledgling rooks, wherewith to make pies. All through the summer, the beautiful waters of the Tweed afforded sport, and no small amount of it. Bathing was a matter of course; but boys who could obtain any thing like a rod and line, with a few 'buskit[23] flies', and for this only a few pence was necessary, could go a-fishing. Or even where such means were denied, the young piscator could pull up his trowsers (the obstruction of shoes and stockings presumably did not exist), and wade in, to search for eels under the stones or beneath the overhanging grassy banks. To fling a *ramper*[24] out upon the sod, was a great triumph. I was very fond of fishing, but never could catch anything but *smouts* or par, which surprised me a good deal, till, a man taking my rod one day for a few minutes, and having in that time hooked a good trout, which he gave me, the philosophy of the matter became clear to me, namely that, from the nature of things, little fish were taken by little people, and big fish by big people, and all I had to do was to acquiesce in the arrangement.

In my family the first four children were all born with a superfluity of fingers and toes. My elder brother, William, had a sixth finger on each hand, and a sixth toe on each foot – only connected, however, by a small tendon and artery which were divided without any inconvenience. In my instance, there were the same extra members, but connected, in the case of the toes, by means of a substantial bone, which projected at a right angle from the neighbouring metatarsal group. The surgeon, reputed to be a man of skill for his sphere, appears to have been afraid to amputate these members at the root, and he accordingly contented himself with cutting off the upper joint only, which he did, in the most cruel and unprofessional-like manner, by means of a pair of scissors. Thus while my hands retained hardly any mark of this extraordinary bounty of nature, my feet were left with each a stump projecting from its side, that of the right foot measuring half an inch in length. The consequence in adult life was a pain in walking, which shook my whole frame, and effectually disposed me for sedentary, rather than active amusements. Throughout the whole of my early years, it was impossible to induce any shoemaker whom we had an opportunity of employing to diverge so far from the routine of his occupation as to fabricate a shoe applicable to my extraordinary case; and hence I never experienced the least ease for twenty years, except when my shoes were become so loose with long usage as to be on the point of dropping from my feet. It may seem absurd to allude so minutely to this mean and personal matter. I would have thought so too, if it had not in reality operated in the most powerful manner upon my character and life, as will afterwards appear.

Happening to be of a very pacific disposition, more given to study than to rough sports, and disqualified for these by almost constant suffering from my feet, I acquired from my experiences with boys a strong sense of the prevalence amongst them of ungentle usages. They appear to me to form a type of primitive society. Cruelty – cruelty to innocent animals, to weaker and inoffensive companions, to dotage and fatuity, to whatever cannot resist – is the leading feature of their moral nature. Their very play is tinctured with it. Might, not right, avails with them. The boy who can thrash certain others has the rule over them. To others who can thrash him he has to submit. Any doubt that may exist as to the comparative power of any two has to be settled by a fight. Such was the custom at the schools of the old burgh; and, strange to say, though it is pure barbarism, there are grown people of our day who profess to think it a fitting rule in the public schools of England. It is only when boys verge upon puberty that they begin to feel the beauty of mutual courtesy and gentle words and deeds, as opposed to quarreling, interchanges of foul and contemptuous language, and daily fisticuffs. Only then do they cease to represent the savage condition of mankind.

Chapter XIII

There was a bookseller in Peebles: a great fact. There had not always been one; but some years before my entrance upon existence, a decent man named Alexander Elder had come to the town and established himself as a dealer in intellectual wares. He was a very careful and sober man, and in the end, as was fitting, became rich in comparison with many of his neighbours. It seems a curious reminiscence of my first bookseller's shop, that, on entering it, one always got a peep of a cow, which quietly chewed her cud behind the book-shelves, such being one of Sandy's means of providing for his family. Sandy was great in shorter catechisms and what he called *spells*,[25] and school bibles and testaments, and in James Lumsden (of Glasgow)'s halfpenny coloured pictures of the World Turned Upside Down, the Battle of Trafalgar etc., and in penny chap-books of a coarseness of language that would make a modern Scotsman's hair stand on end. He had good stores, too, of school slates and *skeely*,[26] of paper for copies, and of pens, or rather quills, for 'made' pens were never sold then, – one of which he would hand us across his counter with a civil glance over the top of his spectacles, as if saying, 'Now, laddie, see and mak' a gude use o't.' But Sandy was enterprising and enlightened beyond the common range of booksellers in small country towns, and had added a circulating-library to his ordinary business. My father, led by his strong intellectual tastes, had early become a supporter of this institution, and thus it came about that by the time we were nine or ten years of age, my brother and I had read a considerable number of the classics of English literature, or heard our father read them, were familiar with the comicalities of Gulliver, Don Quixote, and Peregrine Pickle, had dipped into the poetry of Pope and Goldsmith, and indulged our romantic tendencies in books of travel and adventure, which were to us scarcely less attractive than the works of pure imagination. When lately attending the wells of Hombourg, I had but one English book to amuse me, Pope's translation of the *Iliad*, and I felt it as towards myself an affecting reminiscence, that exactly fifty years had elapsed since I perused the copy from Elder's library, in a little room looking out upon the High Street of Peebles, where an English regiment was parading recruits raised for Wellington's peninsular campaign.

There was certainly something considerably superior to the com-

mon book-trader in my friend Alexander Elder, for his catalogue
included several books striking far above the common taste, and
somewhat costly withal. There was, for example, a copy of a strange
and curious book of which Sir Walter Scott speaks on several occasions with great interest, a metrical history of the clan Scott, written
about the time of the Revolution by one Walter Scott, a retired old
soldier of the Scottish legions of Gustavus Adolphus, who describes
himself unnecessarily as 'no scholar', for in its rhyme, metre, and
entire frame of language it is truly wretched, while yet interesting on
account of the quantities of its ideas and the information it conveys.
Another of Sandy's book treasures – and the money value of them
makes the term appropriate – was the *Aeneidos of Virgil* translated into
Scottish verse by Gavin Douglas, Bishop of Dunkeld; well known as
a most interesting product of the sixteenth century, and gratifying to
our national vanity as prior to any translation of Virgil in English. On
beginning to read the Aeneid under Mr Sloane, I bethought me that
Sandy had put a 'crib' within my reach, and eagerly flew to his shop
for old Gavin's volume, which I remember, startled me at first sight by
its folio size and its black letter. Hugging it as a stolen treasure, I bore
it home to my chamber, and there opened it in the full belief that it
would enable me to get over all the difficulties of my school tasks. But,
alas, for human hopes! Gavin's Scotch proved scarcely more intelligible than the Latin of the original poet. Who was to translate that
translator? So, after more ineffectual efforts to understand the fine old
book, I had to bear it back to the library, *re infecta*.

In a fit of extraordinary enterprise, Sandy had taken into his library
the successive volumes of the fourth edition of the *Encyclopedia
Britannica*, and had found nobody but my father in the slightest
degree interested in them. My father made a stretch with his moderate
means, and took the book off Sandy's hands. It was a cumbrous article
in a small house; so, after the first interest in its contents had subsided,
it had been put into a chest (which it filled) and laid up in an attic beside
the cotton wefts and the meal ark. Roaming about there one day, in
that morning of intellectual curiosity, I lighted upon the stored book,
and from that time for weeks all my spare time was spent beside the
chest. It was a new world to me. I felt a religious thankfulness that such
a convenient collection of human knowledge existed, and that here it
was spread out like a well-plenished table before me. What the gift of
a whole toy-shop would have been to most children, this book was to
me. I plunged into it. I roamed through it like a bee. I hardly could be
patient enough to read any one article, while so many others remained
to be looked into. In that on Astronomy, the constitution of the

material universe was all at once revealed to me. Henceforth, I knew – what no other boy in the town dreamed of – that there were infinite numbers of worlds besides our own, which was by comparison a very insignificant one. From the zoological articles I gathered that the animals, familiar and otherwise, were all classified into a system through which some faint traces of a plan were discernible. Geography, of which not the slightest elements were then imparted at school, here came before me in numberless articles and maps, expanding my narrow village world to one embracing the uttermost ends of the earth. I pitied my companions who remained ignorant of what became to me familiar knowledge. Some articles were splendidly attractive to the imagination – for example, that entitled Aerostation, which illustrated all that had been done in the way of aerial travelling from Montgolfier downwards. Another paper interested me much, that descriptive of the enquiries of Dr Saufsure regarding the constitution and movement of glaciers. The biographical articles, introducing to me the great men who had laid up these stores of knowledge, or otherwise affected the destinies of their species, were devoured in rapid succession. What a year that was to me, not merely in intellectual enjoyment, but in mental formation! It appears to me somewhat strange that, in a place so remote, so primitive, and containing so little wealth, at a time when the movement for the spread of knowledge had not yet been thought of, such an opportunity for the gratification of an enquiring young mind should have been presented. It was all primarily owing to the liberal spirit of enterprise which animated this cow-keeping little bookseller in the Old Burgh.

Chapter XIV

This part of Robert's reminiscences ends in full flight, and I fear that a portion may have been lost. However William's *Memoir* can fill the gap, and the following two chapters from his account of this period of their lives continue the story.

With Elder's field of literature laid open to us, my brother and I read at a great rate, going right through the catalogue of books without much regard to methodised study. In fact, we had to take what we could get and be thankful. Permitted to have only one volume at a time, we made up for short allowance by reading as quickly as possible, and, to save time, often read together from the same book; one having the privilege of turning over the leaves. Desultory as was this course of reading, it undoubtedly widened the sphere of our ideas; and it would be ungrateful not to acknowledge that not a few of the higher pleasures experienced in life are due to Elder's library in the little old burgh.

My brother and I had another source of self-education when we were boys, on which it is agreeable to reflect. The schools we attended, as has been said, were devoid of maps, and no instruction whatsoever was given on physical geography. Nor did the parents of the pupils seem to make any complaint on the subject. By a fortunate circumstance we were able to make up for the deficiency. When I was about ten years of age, Mr Oman, an old and retired keeper of a boarding-school, died. He had, in his day, been a good teacher, with enlarged scientific views, and left no successor of a like quality in the town. At his decease, his effects were sold off by auction. Among other articles offered to public competition were a pair of school-globes, twelve inches in diameter, which my father was lucky in securing for the modest sum of five shillings.

I can remember the delight with which the globes were received in the family circle, and exhibited on a table for general admiration. Old and dingy in the colours, they had not the polished sprightly look of modern globes, but when cleaned and brushed up, no fault was found with them. We did not even care much about a severe injury that had been sustained by the terrestrial globe, consisting of a hole the size of a crown-piece in the middle of the Antarctic Ocean. There were, likewise, shortcomings on the score of recent discoveries. Of Australia, there were only a few fragmentary outlines, with large intervening spaces, marked 'unknown country'. It was satisfactory, however, to see the track of Columbus in his discovery of America, and the routes respectively pursued by Anson and Cook in their memorable circumnavigations.

We flew with avidity on these poor old globes. By poring over them, we learned how to find out the latitude of places, to comprehend the signs of the zodiac and their relative positions, and to attain a correct idea of the ecliptic or great circle in the heavens, round which the sun seems to travel in the course of a year. From the celestial sphere, that had been less injured, we gained a knowledge of the constellations and situation of the principal fixed stars, of which, along with the planetary bodies, we had already received some information from my father in his observations with a telescope. Mostly engaged at school during the day, we occupied ourselves in a study of the two globes early in the morning, or in the evening when candles were lighted in the parlour. My mother was glad to see us interested in these recreations, instead of rambling idly about the street at night, and suggested that we should begin to fix the leading facts in geography and astronomy in our minds, by means of notes. The advice was taken. Having no money wherewith to buy paper, I was permitted to make a note-book from a number of blank leaves torn from an old ledger. To give the little book a decent exterior, I covered it with strips of marble paper pasted together, that Elder had pared off in his binding operations, and which he kindly allowed me to carry home. The note-book so formed was somewhat miscellaneous in contents, for we wrote down all sorts of useful facts that came in our way – an exercise in composition, if nothing else, and which could scarcely fail to be beneficial in connection with the subsequent duties of life.

Passing from these reminiscences of boyish days, something may now be said of the circumstances which, in a strangely unexpected manner, sent my brother and myself adrift in the world that lay beyond our hitherto limited horizon.

The calm tenor of my father's affairs was at length abruptly ruffled. The introduction of the power-loom and other mechanical appliances had already begun to revolutionise the cotton trade. Down and down sank hand-loom weaving, till it was threatened with extinction, and ultimately the trade was followed only as a desperate necessity. Happy were those who gave it up in time, and betook themselves to something else. Moved by the declining aspect of his commission business, my father bethought himself of commencing as a draper. For this purpose, he alienated the small property in which my brother and I were born, and removed to a central part of the town. Here he began his new line of business, for which, excepting his obliging manners, he had no particular qualification. As, however, there was then little of that eager striving which is now conspicuous everywhere, matters would perhaps have gone on pretty well, but for one untoward circumstance, shortly to be mentioned.

At this period – 1808 to 1812 – the country at large was in the heat of the French war. My reminiscences bring up the picture of universal soldiering, marching to and fro of regiments, drums beating, colours flying, news of victories, and general illuminations. There was an active demand for recruits for the regular army, and hardly less eagerness in procuring men to fill up the militia regiments. Of various regiments of this class stationed at Peebles I have some interesting recollections. The officers gave an intellectual fillip to the place. Some of them were good artists. Others brought with them books of a superior class, about which they conversed in the houses they visited. They received London newspapers, which were prized for their original and copious news of the war, also for comments on public affairs not to be found in the timid provincial press of that day. The militia officers were still more popular in making the natives acquainted with English outdoor sports, until then unknown. I first saw cricket played by officers of the Cambridgeshire militia on the green margin of the Tweed. Melodies, which few had heard of, were introduced at private evening parties. Some of these I listened to with ravished ears – one in particular, the charming air, *Cease your Funning*, which was exquisitely played on the octave flute by Carnaby, a young and accomplished officer in the Ross-shire militia. In wakeful nights, even at this long-distant time, I think of Carnaby and his flute.

The militia, as is well known, consisted of men drawn by ballot – a kind of modified conscription; for substitutes were accepted. By paying a small sum annually to an insurance club, a substitute was provided from the general fund. In the fiercest period of the war, the pressure for substitutes grew intense. The bounty to be dispensed for one was occasionally as large, if not larger, than the bounty paid by government for enlisting into the army. On a particular occasion, I knew of fifty pounds being given for a substitute. There were some interesting circumstances which impressed it on my recollection.

A substitute was in urgent demand. Advertisements were issued. Nobody would go. Thirty pounds were offered. Forty pounds were offered. At length the offer rose to fifty. A poor man of middle age presented himself. Sandy Noble, for such was the name of this true-hearted person, was by trade a cotton-weaver. He was a widower, with a grown-up family, but they had left him to pursue their own course in life; so he was in a sense alone in the world. The wages realised by his peculiar species of labour had materially declined, and he was now only able to make both ends meet. Not even that. He had become responsible for a number of petty debts, caused by the long and expensive illness of his lately deceased wife. These debts hung round his neck like a millstone. The thought of never being able to liquidate them was acutely distressing.

One day as he sat on his loom, meditating on the state of his affairs, a neighbour came in to announce the intelligence that fifty pounds had just been offered for a substitute. Making no remark on this piece of news, Sandy, when alone, took a slate, and calculated that fifty pounds would clear him. His mind was instantly made up. For two days and a night he worked with desperation to finish the web he was engaged upon. Having executed his task, and settled with my father, his employer, he walked off to the secretary of the insurance club, and coming in the nick of time, was thankfully accepted as the required substitute. The militia authorities were in a fume at the delay, and a sergeant had been despatched to bring the man who had been balloted for, otherwise he would be treated as a deserter. As the recognised substitute, Sandy, in a few quiet words, pacified the sergeant. 'Just gie me half an hour,' said he, 'and I'll be ready to gang wi' ye.' The half-hour was given, and devoted to a noble act of integrity such as, we fear, is rarely presented in matters of this nature. With the fifty pounds in his pocket, Sandy went from one end of the town to the other, paying debt after debt as he went along – fifteen and sixpence to one, three pounds eleven and threepence to another, and so on, not leaving a single shilling undischarged. When all was over, he mounted a small bundle on the end of a stick, and, in a calm, self-satisfied mood, he trudged away with the sergeant to headquarters. The name of Sandy Noble deserves to go down in the roll of honour with many of greater distinction.

The war, as we see, with its innumerable horrors, was not all bad. It evoked endurance, courage, manliness, a disposition to make a sacrifice of even life itself for the public good. To take the obscure incident just recorded, there was a grandeur in the honesty and disinterestedness of Sandy Noble, that gives dignity to human nature.

Chapter XV

As an out-of-the-way country town, Peebles had been selected by government as a place suitable for the residence of prisoners of war on parole, shortly after the recommencement of hostilities in 1803. Not more, however, than twenty or thirty of these exiles arrived at this early period. They were mostly Dutch and Walloons, with afterwards a few Danes – unfortunate mariners seized on the coast of the Netherlands, and sent to spend their lives in an inland Scottish town. These men did not repine. They nearly all betook themselves to learn some handicraft to eke out their scanty allowance. At leisure hours, they might be seen fishing in long leather boots, as if glad to procure a few trouts and eels, and at the same time satisfy the desire to dabble in the water. Two or three years later came a *détenu* of a different class. He was seemingly the captain of a ship from the French West Indies, who brought with him his wife and a negro servant-boy named Jack. Black Jack, as we called him, was sent to the school, where he played with the other boys on the town green, and at length read and spoke like a native. He was a good-natured creature, and became a general favourite. Jack was the first pure negro whom the boys at that time had ever seen.

None of these classes of prisoners broke his parole, nor ever gave any trouble to the authorities. They had not, indeed, any appearance of being prisoners, for they were practically free to live and ramble about, within reasonable bounds, where they liked. In 1810, there was a large accession to this original body of prisoners on parole, to whom I must specially refer.

Memory carries me back to a particular Sunday evening. Having gone through the day in a perfectly constitutional manner, the inhabitants of the town felt that, towards evening, they might, in a mild and quiet way, indulge in a little recreation – not amusement by any means, only a smell of the fresh air. All depended on slowness and quietness. Anything like laughing, whistling, singing, walking hurriedly, or boisterous behaviour, was proscribed. You might do almost what you liked, provided it was done slowly and quietly, as if you were not doing it. The impropriety consisted in making a noise.

On Sunday evenings, from the proceedings of the day, everything was agreeably calmed down to an unchallengeable quietude. People who had gardens walked out quietly – if by back-doors so much the better – and with their hands in their pockets made their observations quietly on the growth of the cabbages and gooseberries. Others took a sauntering sort of walk quietly to the river, and in a manner not to provoke discussion, spoke of the prospects of fishing for the season; perhaps introducing a somewhat playful anecdote about catching a salmon, but always in a subdued tone of voice, and never venturing beyond a smile. Some took a fancy for going a little more afield, and, leaning over gateways, made remarks quietly on the crops, and threw out speculations as to the probable price of meal and potatoes after next harvest. A number, otherwise bent, took a fancy for visiting the churchyard, where an hour was quietly and pleasantly spent in making observations on 'the poor inhabitant below', in the respective newly made graves. To all this there may be fault-finders. As long as human nature is what it is, I can imagine nothing more decorous or reverential than these modest and leisurely Sunday evening musings.

My father had no garden to speak of. His tastes did not lie in that direction. At all odd hours he fastened on books, reviews, and newspapers. The only newspaper of which I have any familiar remembrance at this early period, was *The Edinburgh Star*. It was a twice-a-week journal, and, as things went, had a good circulation. My father could not afford to subscribe for *The Star*. All he could do was to be a member of a club to take in the paper, which was handed about to one after the other, each member being allowed to have it in turn for a certain number of hours. Such, in the days of taxed and dear newspapers, was an almost universal practice, and in our community it was no way singular.

By some chance, which I am unable to explain, my father's tenure of the Friday's *Star* began on Sunday evening, at six o'clock, when the natives generally were out on their quietly sauntering perambulations. For three days he had heard nothing satisfactory of the war, and in his anxiety had watched the face of the alabaster time-piece on the wall of our little parlour, to see when the paper could with propriety be sent for. The hands on the dial having at length pointed to a quarter to six, I am requested to go for *The Star*. At the time, I am seated at a window trying to commit to memory that Scripture paraphrase of matchless beauty, which my mother prescribed to me as a study:

Few are thy days, and full of woe,
O man, of woman born.

Laying the book aside, I obey the command to go for *The Star*, and, on the whole, being glad to get into the open air, I hurry off with a leather cap on my head, and a crisply plaited frill down my back, in quest of the paper. I knew all about the mission, for it was not the first time I had been so employed.

The person to whom I was sent was a respectable candlemaker – his surname of no consequence. He was a short, stoutish man, who filled the office of Dean of Guild, which contributed to give him a certain dignified position in the town. Ordinarily, however, he was best known as 'Candle Andrew'. As a bachelor, though advanced in life, Andrew lived with his sister, who acted as housekeeper and shop-woman, and was usually called 'Candle Nell'. It was altogether a successful arrangement. The brother and sister made no sort of show. The business was conducted cheaply and quietly.

On the present occasion, being Sunday, the shop was shut, and entrance to the premises was by a side-door, the first on the right-hand in going down the close as you went to the candle-work. To that door I proceeded. It was opened by Nell, and I was ushered into the kitchen until she announced the object of my visit. All was quiet and decorous. I was invited to step into the room. Here sat Candle Andrew in his Sunday's best, with an under red-silk waistcoat, and his bald head lightly powdered. Before him, lay a large open folio volume of Matthew Henry's Bible, covering nearly the whole table. Above it, and just about the same size, lay *The Star*. Candle Andrew, whom I esteemed to be a great man, as Dean of Guild, with his powdered head and red under-waistcoat, was so kind as to speak to me, and what he said (while folding up the newspaper) was momentous. 'Great news, my man – terrible battles in Spain – thousands o' French prisoners – a number o' them brought to Leith, and I shouldn't wonder if some were sent here. However, there's *The Star*; and please to give my compliments to your mother.' Little did I think that what Candle Andrew had hinted at, was destined to shape the whole existence of my brother and myself, indeed the whole family, father and mother included.

Inspired by the notion that there was something important in the intelligence, I hastened home, but before I arrived, my father had received a glimmering of the news. A neighbour had called to say that there was to be immediately a great accession to the present French prisoners of war on parole. As many as a hundred and eleven were already on their way to the town, and might be expected in perhaps a day or two.

There was speedily a vast sensation in the place. The local militia had been disbanded. Lodgings of all sorts were vacant. The new arrivals would on all hands be heartily welcomed. On Tuesday, the expected French prisoners in an unceremonious way began to drop in. As one of several boys, I went out to meet these new prisoners of war on the road from Edinburgh. They came walking in twos and threes – a few of them lame. Their appearance was startling, for they were in military garb, in which they had been captured in Spain. Some were in light-blue hussar dresses, braided, with marks of sabre-wounds. Others were in dark-blue uniform. Several wore large cocked-hats, but the greater number had undress caps. All had a gentlemanly air, notwithstanding their generally dishevelled attire, their soiled boots, and their visible marks of fatigue. Before night, they had all arrived; and through the activity of the agent appointed by the Transport Board, they had been provided with lodgings suitable to their slender allowance.

This large batch of prisoners on parole were, of course, all in the rank of naval or military officers. Some had been pretty high in the service, and seen a good deal of fighting. Several were doctors, or, as they called themselves, *officiers de santé*. Among the whole there were, I think, about a dozen midshipmen. A strange thing was their varied nationality. Though spoken of as French, there was in the party a mixture of Italians, Swiss, and Poles; but this we found out only after some intercourse. Whatever their origin, they were warm adherents of Napoleon, whose glory at this time was at its height. Lively in manner, their minds were full of the recent struggles in the Peninsula.

Through the considerateness of an enterprising grocer, the prisoners were provided with a billiard-table, at which they spent much of their time. So far well. But how did these unfortunate exiles contrive to live – how did they manage to feed and clothe themselves, and pay for lodgings? Thereby hangs a tale, which we will by-and-by come to. The allowance from government was on a moderate scale. I doubt if it was more than a shilling a head per diem. In various instances two persons lived in a single room, but even that cost at least half-a-crown a week, which made a considerable inroad on revenue. The truth is, they must have been half-starved, but for the fortunate circumstance of a number of them having brought money – foreign gold pieces – concealed about their person, which stores were supplemented by remittances from France; and in a friendly way, at least as regards the daily mess, or *table d'hôte*, the richer helped the poorer, which was a good trait in their character. The messing together was the grand resource, and took place in a house hired for the purpose, in which the cookery was conducted under the auspices of M. Lavoche, one of the prisoners, who, as is not unusual with Frenchmen, was skilled in cuisine. My brother and I had some dealings with Lavoche. We cultivated rabbits in a hutch built by ourselves in a back-yard, and sold them for the Frenchmen's mess; the money got for them, usually eightpence a pair, being employed in the purchase of books.

Billiards were indispensable, but something more was wanted. Without a theatre, life was felt to be unendurable. But how was a theatre to be secured? There was nothing of the kind in the place. The more eager of the prisoners managed to get out of the difficulty. There was an old and disused ballroom. It was rather of confined dimensions, and low in the roof, with a gallery at one end, over the entrance, for the musicians. In the days of yore, however, what scenes of gaiety had it not witnessed! Walter Scott's mother when a girl, I was told, had crossed Minchmoor, a dangerously high hill, in a chaise from the adjacent county, to dance for a night in that little old ballroom. Now set aside as unfashionable, the room was at anybody's service, and came quite handily to the Frenchmen. They fitted it with a stage at the inner end, and cross-benches to accommodate a hundred and twenty persons, independently of perhaps twenty more in the musician's gallery. The thing was neatly got up, with scenery painted by M. Walther and M. Ragulski, the latter a young Pole with artistic tastes. No licence was required for the theatre, for it was altogether a private undertaking. Money was not taken at the door, and no tickets were sold. Admission was gained by complimentary billets, distributed chiefly among persons with whom the actors had established an intimacy.

Among these favoured individuals was my father, who, carrying on a mercantile concern, occupied a prominent position. He felt a degree of compassion for these foreigners, constrained to live in exile, and besides welcoming them to his house, gave them credit in articles of drapery of which they stood in need; and through which circumstance they soon assumed an improved appearance in costume. Introduced to the family circle, their society was agreeable and in a sense instructive. Though with imperfect speech, a sort of half-French, half-English, they related interesting circumstances in their career. My brother and I, desperately keen to learn, but with poor opportunities of doing so, listened with greedy ears to the discourse of the Frenchmen, which had the double advantage of increasing our stock of facts and improving us in the knowledge of the French tongue.

How performances in French should have had any general attraction may seem to require explanation. There had grown up in the town, among young persons especially, a knowledge of familiar French phrases; so that what was said, accompanied with appropriate gestures, was pretty well guessed at. But, as greatly contributing to remove difficulties, a worthy man of an obliging turn, and genial humour, volunteered to act as interpreter. Moving in humble circumstances as a hand-loom weaver, he had let lodgings to a French captain and his wife, and from being for years in domestic intercourse with them, he became well acquainted with their language. William Hunter – for such was his name – besides being of ready wit, partook of a lively musical genius. I have heard him sing *Malbrouk s'en va-t-en guerre*, with amazing correctness and vivacity. His services at the theatre were therefore of value to the natives in attendance. Seated conspicuously at the centre of what we may call the pit, eyes were turned to him inquiringly when anything particularly funny was said that needed explanation, and for general use, he whisperingly communicated the requisite interpretation. So put up to the joke, the natives heartily joined in the laugh, though rather tardily. Dear old William Hunter, with his ready demonstrations of Scottish humour, how my brother and I in later years regretted his loss! As for the French plays, which were performed with perfect propriety, they were to us not only amusing but educational. Life, to be worth anything, is made up of happy recollections. The remembrance of these dramatic efforts of the French prisoners of war has been through life a continual treat. It is curious for me to look back on the performance of pieces of Molière, in circumstances so very remarkable.

My mother, even while lending her dresses and caps to enable performers to represent female characters, never liked the extraordinary intimacy which had been formed between the French officers and my father. Against his giving them credit, she constantly remonstrated in vain. It was a tempting but perilous trade. For a time, by the resources just mentioned, they paid wonderfully well. With such solid inducements, my father confidingly gave extensive credit to these strangers – men who, by their position, were not amenable to the civil law, and whose obligations, accordingly, were altogether debts of honour. The consequence was what might have been anticipated. An order suddenly arrived from the government, commanding the whole of the prisoners to quit Peebles, and march chiefly to Sanquhar in Dumfriesshire; the cause of the movement being the prospective arrival of a militia regiment. The intelligence came one Sunday afternoon. What a gloom prevailed at several firesides that fatal evening!

Part 2

EDINBURGH AND BOOKS

Chapter XVI

William's account may be left at this point, because Robert has covered the same ground in a notebook written much earlier. I have, however, inserted a few paragraphs by William where they could conveniently help the story.

The prisoners departed, leaving at least two Peebles girls pregnant. Agnes Fleck subsequently produced a son, naming the French surgeon César Fougues as the father. The baby was baptised Etienne by Mr Reid, the Catholic priest from Terregles. In other parts of Scotland similar dramas were being enacted; at Penicuik one girl, advised by her friends to put the blame on a local man, declared, 'What wad I say when the bairn began to speak?' Another young girl, Mary Paterson, a waitress at the Tontine Inn where some prisoners had been billeted, had to appear before the Peebles Kirk Session to be rebuked for fornication, and to discuss how she might claim maintenance.

But getting money out of departed French prisoners was probably no easier for Mary Paterson than it was for James Chambers, who was now in serious trouble. During the year in which the French had stayed in Peebles he had foolishly advanced them a vast amount of credit equal to almost his whole capital. They had promised to pay as soon as their allowances came through, but the following letters show the predictable outcome:

> Mr James Chalmers
> Merchant
> Peebles
>
> Dumfries
> 28th January 1812
>
> Dear Sir,
> I have received your letter in date of 16th of this month, I have made known the contents of it to Mr Mauvoisin who after having heard the perusing of your letter said to me that he would answer to you and would expose all his reasons for having behaved so.
> As for the note from Mr Casson i advise you to send it back to Mr Mauvoisin in saying to him to try himself if he can be paid with it.

The two frenchmen whom you have spoken me of, have paid nothing till now. Messrs Bonnecarere e Chapelain have i think not you received their money.

I have nothing more to mention to you meantime.

> I remain
> your friend
> L. Motin
> S.Lt 1er Leg.

On the back of this letter is written another one to Mrs Chambers:

Madam

I have received your kind letter by Mr Duffour, I am very sensible of the interest you take to my health, I am pretty well just now and i thank you for your kind attention. I was not at the ball of friday because my acquaintance being in mourning could not go there but i hope to attend it when i please. The persons who have told you that many Frenchmen had made their escape were not well informed, for three only of us have broken their word, of whom Mr Cauvet has been taken in London and has got his parole again. Messrs Baudoin and Sutheny have got away one month ago and we have heard nothing about them. as for me, the fancy of breaking my word never till now entered into my mind.

I know nothing worth of your attention I pray you to excuse me – if I have been so long without writing. Adieu madam, I remain your friend

> L. Motin

Two months later the following arrived:

Mrs Chalmers
Peebles

> Dumfries
> 30th March 1812

Madam,

I have received your last by Mr O Conor, i wish you to excuse me for having delayed so long to return you an answer. I hoped every day to have the pleasure of sending you some money of your debtors but unluckily these many weeks we have received neither money nor letters, i am as unfortunate as the rest –

We have lately lost our friends Walther, O Conor, etc –
who have been removed from this town to a dirty place
named Sanquar, I heard some days after their departure that
they were extremely uncomfortable, such kind of people as
the inhabitants have no room to spare, the greater part of the
Frenchmen are lodged in barns and kitchens, they can get
neither beef nor mutton; nothing but salted meats and eggs –
they have applied to the transport office in order, i was told,
to be removed to Moffat –

As i have many acquaintances i am obliged to speak
English incessantly i improve every day, i can express myself
tolerably well just know; but that is not very wonderous for, i
must tell ye that since my arrival to this i have got a professor
to Whom i give lessons of French in return –

As for Mr Chalmers coming to Dumfries i think it should
be quite useless just now, he must expect some while and if
any money comes i'll let you know the sum and if it be necessary to take such a step –

Adieu, Madam, I am

Your most humble servant and friend

L.M.

My best compliments to Mr. Ch.

However the prisoners were all repatriated in 1814, and in fact
James Chambers only received a tiny fraction of the money he was
owed. Let Robert take up the story.

My father was doomed to experience in full bitterness the proverbial
want of principle which, with all their gallantry and enthusiasm,
characterises the French nation; and being thus reduced to a state of
great embarrassment, he was at length obliged to declare at least a
temporary insolvency. It would have been very easy with half the
management often shown in such cases to get over all the existing
difficulties; for it was clearly ascertained that his stock and heritable
property were more than equal in value to all existing debts. All that
was at first contemplated was a composition with the creditors as to
time. Unfortunately, however, the largest creditor was an uncle of my
mother, a merchant in Edinburgh, a man of great sagacity in business,
and whose general character was such, that, putting his influence as a
creditor out of the question, he naturally became my father's chief
adviser. Partly through the threats, and partly by the persuasion of this

individual the original plan was changed for the more expensive and less honourable process of a sequestration under which my grand-uncle became trustee. The stock was then brought to sale, and pur-chased by emissaries of the trustee, at a low price, every competitor holding back from an understanding which was diligently conveyed, that it was bought for my mother. In short, the trustee, by a course of chicanery for which I hope he has obtained forgiveness elsewhere, contrived to render himself a large gainer by the transaction, while my father whom he had betrayed was left not only destitute of a farthing in the world, but with the stigma of having paid his creditors no more than six and eight-pence in the pound, while his estate had originally appeared equal to all the demands that could be made upon it.

To a person of my father's upright disposition – who was advanced, moreover, beyond that period of life when the world can be counte-nanced with unbroken spirit – this calamity was one of the most severe and most fatal that could have happened. He now had no resource but to fall back upon his cotton agencies; a line of business in which he had latterly had many rivals, and which was of course less productive than formerly. Even if this could have supplied the means of subsistence, there was now but little comfort to be expected in his native burgh. Bankruptcy, however innocently occasioned, is always regarded in a rural district as a very heinous crime. Let the causes be never so obvious (and they were sufficiently so in my father's case) other reasons are always looked for in the personal conduct of the unfortu-nate individual, who, like the lamb in the fable, seems as if it were not in the nature of things that he could do any thing right. My father had always been a man of social disposition, and, under the temptations which beset a man of enterprising and speculative character in a dull country town, was perhaps as remarkable as any of the better class of citizens for convivial indulgences, though to an extent that would never have been remarked if he had not been unfortunate from other causes. This, however, was regarded by the prejudicial vulgar, as bearing a large share in the causes of his misfortunes. My mother, on the other hand, had always dressed herself and her children in a way which, though by no means expensive or such as was not justified by her rank in life, was yet superior in taste to the general appearance of our neighbours; and this of course supplied material for many ungen-erous remarks. In fact, as it always happens in such cases, all who, from whatever good cause, had lived in a meaner style than we, now took it upon them, in the more unhappy spirit of envy, to characterise our former mode of life as extravagant, and to point to our present situation as only the natural and deserved result of our personal conduct. Of course, it was soon found that some decided shift of situation was necessary for our future comfort.

In December 1813, the whole family, excepting myself, was removed to Edinburgh, where my father had prospects of prosecuting the business of an agent for the cotton manufacture, upon a much larger scale than at Peebles. I was permitted to remain, in order that I might conclude the current school year with Mr Sloane, who had kindly proposed to commute the payment of fees for such assistance as I could render in occasionally superintending some of the junior classes. I accordingly remained at this academy till August 1814, being lodged in the house of my maternal grandmother.

To my inconceivable distress my father was obliged to part with the *Encyclopedia Britannica*, and the loss was never repaired. I had then no resource but an occasional volume afforded by my scanty pocket-money from the circulating library, or a book of juvenile instruction borrowed from the better class of boarders at the academy. Some of these last, containing pleasing and simple expositions of science, made an impression on me which will never be effaced. They were cheaply purchased by the surrender of 'pieces', (Anglice, crusts of bread) of which I could generally command an extra supply at home, while the boarders were more sparingly, or rather I should say more systematically provided. One way and another, I certainly read a great deal before I was twelve years of age, and of this quantity of reading had fixed no small portion in my mind.

In August 1814, I was removed to Edinburgh, where my father's prospects were already becoming even more clouded. The operative cotton-weavers in that city were not many in number; neither were they so well principled a class of men as at Peebles. He accordingly failed entirely to realise that profit which he expected and which was necessary to our maintenance. My devotion to learning had already pointed me out to my parents as one qualified to study for the church; and even amidst the clouds of their present distress, a hope still prevailed that I might be able to fight my way, like many others, to a distinction for which they could supply little of the means. I was therefore placed in October at a private academy in the new town, then taught with extraordinary success by Mr Benjamin Mackay. It was supposed that, after I should have finished the full course of five years, I might be able to contend successfully for a bursary at the university, and so advance myself in some measure by my own means. I was placed at the bottom of Mr Mackay's fifth class, which I found to contain boys very much upon the same level with those amongst whom I had lately been. Accordingly two days had not passed, when

I ascended to my proper level near the top. There was this essential difference between my late and present master that the latter exercised his boys more upon the actual rules of syntax than in the rendered method of translation which was the chief feature of Mr Sloane's system. This at first put me about, and I had also some trouble in changing Ruddiman's for Adam's grammar; but, having made myself equal in these respects, I found a great superiority over my companions in my more familiar acquaintance with translation and version making, and in a certain command of diction which was probably derived from my general reading. At the end of the first quarter, it was found that the circumstances of the family were not such as would longer justify my being kept at school, and I was accordingly withdrawn. A friend, however, who was acquainted with Mr Mackay, having ascertained the cause of my removal, employed himself to such kind and good purpose between the parties, that the teacher was prevailed upon to request, and my father to permit my gratuitous attendance at the school for the remainder of the year. There was a kindness in this, and at the same time a compliment to myself, that I can never reflect on without pleasure, notwithstanding the many painful reminiscences with which it is associated.

During this year, I read Ovid, Virgil, and Livy, and also made a little progress in Greek. As in the former year, I settled at the third place in the class, the two first being occupied by boys who were considerably my seniors, and were moreover better acquainted with the minutiae of the peculiar system followed at the academy than I could make myself in such a short time. My habits of assiduous private study and abstinence from play were now, if possible, increased; and for a considerable time, before becoming known by name, I was distinguished only as 'the fellow who takes his books home in the forenoon'; a circumstance which I dare say appeared very affected or very singular, as the most of the boys employed the interval in amusement. At this time I began to compose verse in English and Latin; but from a specimen of the latter, which happens to have been preserved, I can see that correct prosody was, as usual in such juvenile exercises, my only attainment. In Latin composition, I was put to great straights for want of an Anglico-Latin dictionary; however, there was a copy of Ainsworth on a stall in the next street, and to it did I use to resort, several times a day, in order to ascertain the best Latin for certain words in my own language. I shall never forget the rapture with which these literary stolen pleasures were enjoyed: I never see the proprietor of the book since, without an emotion of grateful feeling which he neither claims nor is aware of, but which I still feel to be his due.

I may remark that in writing these verses, I was not urged by any principle of imitation. Neither English nor Latin versification formed a part of our school exercises, and I am not aware that any other boy in the academy distinguished himself by similar acts of supererogation. If I am not mistaken, my first inspiration was derived from an enthusiasm which I conceived in favour of the doctrines of the metempsychosis, as detailed in Ovid. The humane part of the argument of Pythagoras made so deep an impression upon me, that for nearly a twelvemonth period after reading it, I resolutely abstained from every kind of animal food which had been obtained by the sacrifice of a life. I looked upon it as most disgraceful to man, that he should deliberately deprive other creatures of existence, merely for the purpose of pampering an appetite which I conceived might be satisfied with the simple fruits of the earth. Nor could either the ridicule or the arguments of those who were informed of my principles in the least shake them, till at length they gave way of their own accord before some other access of boyish conceit.

After eighteen months' residence in Edinburgh during which the industry and economy of my mother alone counteracted the current of declining circumstances, my father obtained what appeared at first a good situation, in the superintendence of a salt-work near Musselburgh. In August 1815, after I had concluded my year at the academy, the family was removed from a neat house which we occupied in the southern suburbs of Edinburgh, to a small lodging in the very centre of the salt-work, where we were almost constantly enveloped in dense smoke. A more disagreeable or distressing residence could hardly have been found; and I have often wondered since how it was endured. Nothing I am persuaded but the sense of an emancipation from the immediate pressure of poverty could have reconciled us to such an abode.

My elder brother had now for upwards of a year been apprenticed to a bookseller in Edinburgh, that being the business which our common propensity to reading had pointed out to him as the most likely to be agreeable. Amidst all the distresses of the family, the prospect of my attaining to a learned profession had still been seen as a star of hope; and humble, and precarious, as was the income to which my father lately acceded, it had sensibly brightened the prospect. It was arranged that I should attend a sixth year at Mr Mackay's academy, which would be equivalent to an attendance at the Rector's class in the High School, and that on the opening of the university in November, I should be matriculated there for the first humanity class; a double course of instruction from which it was hoped I would derive great advantage. Accordingly, at the commencement of the school year in October, I was sent to reside in Edinburgh in the same lodging with my elder brother, in order that I might be near the academy. I remember proceeding to this humble abode, on a Sunday evening, in company with William, who had been spending the day as usual with the rest of the family. He was then fifteen while I was thirteen; but adversity had given us reflection beyond our years. We conversed freely about the reduced circumstances of our parents, and of the difficulties which consequently must obstruct our path in life. We resolved, however, that, as far as fortitude in endurance and frugality of living could go, we should struggle manfully against them. William had already, during the short interval since the removal of the family to the salt-work, established a system of economy which I regarded with admiration and resolved to imitate. He lodged with an aged widow whom we had known at Peebles, from which town she had removed about the same time with ourselves, in order that her sons (two industrious young men) might obtain a better kind of employment in the capital. This poor, but decent and honest woman, lived in the upper part of a tall house in the suburb of Portsburgh almost next door to that since polluted by the murders of Burke – and such was the parsimony of her style of life, rather than the humility of her accommodations, that she could give my brother a room to himself, and prepare his meals, for the small sum of eighteen pence a week. This, with Sunday at home, left him two shillings and sixpence of his weekly wages to himself; and out of this small sum he had hitherto contrived to support himself, without requiring anything at home except a dinner on the Sundays. His daily expenditure stood thus:

Breakfast – porridge, three farthings; butter-milk one farthing	£0-0-1
Dinner – broth, three farthings; bread, three farthings	£0-0-1$^{1}/_{2}$
Supper, same as breakfast	£0-0-1
	£0-0-3$^{1}/_{2}$

The same room and bed which accommodated him, now also accommodated me; but as the trouble was in every other respect doubled, I was also to pay the same sum for lodging. I remember we grumbled dreadfully about this; and, cheap as our apartment was, my brother kept me almost incessantly on the hunt for three or four months, through all the lanes and suburbs of the city, after one which might be still cheaper. It may be readily supposed that this extreme frugality was not practised without much self-denial and even suffering. Dictated as it was by stern necessity, and partly supported by a kind of pride which we took in its exercise, it was nevertheless a severe trial to two young persons, who had been heretofore accustomed to all the comforts which generally prevail in the middle ranks of life.

Our abode, the uppermost floor in Boak's land, was more elevated than airy. The back of the tall edifice overhung a tannery and a wild confusion of mean enclosures, with an outlook beyond to the castle, perched on its dark precipitous rock. The thoroughfare in front was then, as it is still, one of the most crowded and wretched in the city. The apartment assigned to us was a bed-closet, with a narrow window fronting the street. In the evenings, when mason and carpenter lads dropped in, the conversation turned chiefly on sermons. Each visitor brought with him experiences as to how texts had been handled on the preceding Sunday; on which there ensued discussions singularly characteristic of a well-known phase in the Scotch mind.

'Weel, Tammie,' inquired the widow one evening of Tammie Tod, a journeyman mason lately arrived from the country, 'what was the doctor on last Sabbath afternoon?'

'He was on the Song' – meaning the Song of Solomon.

'Eh, the Song! that would be grand. He's a wonderfu' man, the doctor; and what was his text?'

'It was a real fine text,' said Tammie, 'the deepest ever I heard – "For my head is filled with dew, and my locks with the drops of the night"; fifth chapter, second verse, the second clause of the verse.'

'I ken that text weel,' responded the widow. 'I heard a capital discourse on it thirty years syne; but how did the doctor lay it out?'

'He divided it into five heads, ending with an application, which it would be weel for us a' to tak' to heart.'

And so Tammie, who had a proficiency in dissecting and criticising sermons, proceeded to describe with logical precision the manner in which his minister had handled the very intricate subject; his definitions being listened to and commented on with extraordinary relish.

Till the college opened it was fully intended that I should go to it, as formerly arranged, and accordingly when the day arrived I proceeded to that illustrious seminary of learning, along with other boys who ranked with me at Mr Mackay's, and was present at the first meeting of the humanity class for the season. The fees, however, were found to be an insurmountable difficulty; and, with feelings I shall not attempt to describe, I was obliged to turn back from a course in which I saw so many of my companions about to start with every advantage in their favour, though I was sensible that hardly any of them cared so much for the pleasure of the race, or was so ambitious of its eventual honours as myself. I have reason to believe that my worthy master regarded my misfortune with the kindest sympathy, considering his past exertions as now rendered in a great measure useless. I nevertheless continued to attend school, but with no trust as far as I recollect, except in the chapter of accident. At length, in the month of April or May 1816, I quitted the school for ever, my parents having at length perceived that, since I was not to go forward in a learned career, it was necessary that I should apply decidedly and immediately to something else.

Chapter XVII

Now commenced the truly dark age of my history. The prospects which had induced the proprietors of the salt-work to employ my father not having been realised, they were obliged, about the time just mentioned, to give him a discharge. We were therefore left, in a strange land, far from the place where we had any friends, to begin the world anew, and that without the least capital or stock of any kind whatever. Besides William, who lived upon his little wage, there were four children to be supported; and after the ensuing term of Whitsunday, it was not to be imagined from what quarter the food was to come. Of all these domestic distresses, young as I was, I became in a great measure aware; and my heart yet bursts with anguish when I reflect on the situation of my mother in particular, a woman born to the finest prospects, courted in early life as a kind of goddess, and now, while still young and beautiful, condemned by an inevitable fate to find herself, her husband, and her children threatened with the speedy and absolute want of the necessaries of life. Nor was this the sum of her calamities. The greatest of all consisted in the uncertain dependence that was to be placed on my father's disposition or power to exert himself. Ever since his unmerited misfortunes at Peebles, he had manifested a kind of indifference, which, though not absolutely dis-qualifying him for any duty imposed upon him, had given him a disinclination to encounter any difficulty that stood in his way, and rendered him particularly unfit for pushing forward in the world. Even by nature he was a soft and easy man; and adversity, instead of erecting his character into something more firm, as it ought to do, had increased his disposition to self-indulgence, and rendered his practice a sad commentary on the philosophical maxims and extensive moral observation, for which he was remarkable. It was obvious, that henceforward the support of the domestic establishment must depend chiefly upon its mistress rather than its master.

It is a curious fact in married life, though I never saw or heard it remarked, that, where there is either a deficiency or excess of power on one side, there is apt to be a corresponding excess or deficiency on the other. As my father declined in ability to exert himself, my mother rose in proportion, and in time altogether absorbed the masterly character which once belonged to her husband. At her instigation one of a neighbouring cluster of houses, which stood by the wayside, was taken on lease, with the view of opening a shop for the sale of miscellaneous articles, amongst which, I regret to say, it was found indispensable that liquors should be included. I well remember the struggles of the spirit which preceded this step, the unavailing reflections on past and happier days, the irrepressible breathings of execration at the man who had been the cause of our ruin. Necessity, however, while it urged, at the same time justified the measure; and there was a great consolation to a Scottish bosom, in the remoteness of the scene of our degradation from the place where we were known in the time of our better fortune.

The expedient succeeded better than had been hoped. Notwithstanding the paucity of the neighbouring population, and the existence of other small depots of goods at no great distance, custom was found to no inconsiderable extent; and, for a time at least, absolute destitution seemed to be kept at bay. Perhaps some part of our success was owing to the sympathy which even uncultivated rustics and operatives could not help feeling towards a family which had evidently seen better days, and which still bore a genteel appearance – strangely discordant with their occupation. My mother, I am sure, excited a large share of the interest with which we were regarded. In spite of all her cares and distresses, among which a weak state of health was not the least, and though latterly obliged to perform almost every household duty unassisted, she was almost as fair, as handsome, and as neat in her personal appearance as ever. It was impossible, moreover, to view her noble exertions for her family – for noble they were morally, however mean in detail – without feeling an anxiety for her welfare. There were not wanting some circumstances to alleviate the unfortunate situation of my parents. So far as I could save their feelings from a painful contact with the public, or from humble drudgeries, I did so without a murmur, though my recollection of better days was still fresh, and triumphant scholarship was not the best preparative for a servile office. William, also, came home every Saturday night, with some book (perhaps a Waverley novel) which he had been permitted to take from his master's shop, and which we could not otherwise have seen; and thus, through this means, we were enabled to keep up a kind of communication with the superior world which we had left. Good health, that crowning blessing which still remained to the family, completed the sum of these advantages. My own peculiar situation became in time the most distressing circumstance with which my parents had to deal. I was advancing to fifteen years of age, without either being able to go forward to my original destination, or finding any other course accessible. Many attempts had been made to obtain me a place as an apprentice in the shops of druggists, booksellers, music sellers and other traders, but no good had ever come of them. No doubt, I was useful in the meantime at home; my continuance there, however, threatened to carry me beyond that period of life when I could be received into any profession whatever; and then there was some danger lest I should fall altogether to the ground and remain forever a useless member of society. It will be considered as something curious, that one who before thirty has written nearly as many volumes, was looked upon at this time as a person destined by circumstances, and by natural character, for a life of inglorious sloth. Scholarship and an appetite for information were conceded to me, but it was contended that these very peculiarities unfitted me for exerting myself to obtain my daily bread, and almost every one of my friends predicted that I would be a 'downdraught' to the family.

My time, I must confess, was spent more exclusively in reading than was to be wished in one who had to push his way in the world. I procured a copy of Smollett's *History of England*, in thirteen volumes, and went steadily through it in the course of a few weeks. Other books I devoured at the same rate; and it must have been really difficult to see how this propensity was to be turned to any account in gaining my subsistence.

Scientific experiments now began to attract the attention of both my brother and myself. William had become acquainted with an aged porter, named James Alexander, who lived in an obscure court or alley at the back of Calton Street, and chiefly subsisted by his ingenuity as a mender of old china. Jamie, as we called him, had been in his earlier years servant to one of the Tytler family, and had picked up a few crumbs of knowledge from the table of that learned savant. He was great in electricity, and had once actually fabricated a machine for producing that fluid. His house, which resembled the den of an alchemist or a magician – so full was it of all kinds of odd and unaccountable implements – was also resorted to by two young men of the name of King, one of whom was shopkeeper to a seedsman, while the other was a draper, and who were really most ingenious young men. Alexander and the two Kings were our first instructors and inspirers in science. Janet, the mistress of the mansion, did not greatly encourage our visits. Her chief concern in life seemed to consist in nursing a small and ingeniously made-up fire, which was apt to be seriously deranged by King's chemical experiments – such as the production of coal-gas in a blacking-bottle, used by way of retort – the proposal of lighting the city with gas having suggested this novel experiment. For a special reason, this old woman was not more favourable to electric science. Under King's advice and directions, my brother and I contrived, out of very poor resources, to procure a cylindrical electrifying-machine, with some apparatus to correspond. Having one night given Janet an electric *shock*, slily conveyed to her through a piece of damp tobacco, she ever after viewed the machine with the darkest suspicions. In these apprehensions her gray cat had some reason to join; when the Leyden jars were placed on the table, she fled to the roof of the bed, and there kept eyeing us during our mysterious incantations.

I was also at this time still more devoted to astronomy. The globes had remained with us through all our misfortunes, and I now studied them with such zeal that, in a short time, I could perform every problem contained in a treatise on the subject, of which I had more lately become possessed. Astronomy led to dialling, in which I became so great an adept that I could make the most complicated kind of instruments in that science – at least the most complicated kind which I ever found described in any book, and which could be constructed of wood. It was at this time that Dr Chalmers's astronomical sermons were published; I read them with enthusiastic pleasure, but surprised my father by several corrections which I pointed out in the reverend author's calculations. Mathematics also engaged my attention; but without a master to explain and urge my way, I could make little progress in this grand department of scientific culture. In all my proceedings, I was put to infinite difficulty by the want of books and instruments.

It was about this time that William and I, who were at all times each other's chief companions, began to show a disposition to make remarks upon the ways of the world, and upon human character. At all times when we were walking together, our discourse was framed in a spirit of sarcastic observation, and we greatly encouraged each other by a religious agreement to laugh at each other's sallies. William was from the first dawn of character more cold and severe than I, and it suited my father's philanthropic disposition to like me the best of the two, and take the most pains in unfolding to me his views of life. By our own frequent intercourse, however, every thing that either William or I knew or thought became a common property. We used to join cordially in the most merciless ridicule of all common-place ideas and common-place people, and appeared determined that, whatever should be our fortune in life, our own careers should not be of a tame or ordinary kind.

The impression produced upon me at this time by reading the

earlier novels of Sir Walter Scott was of a very decided kind, and I remember entertaining the design, all inadequate as was my knowledge of past times, to attempt the composition of a similar work on the story of Montrose – a subject subsequently taken up by my great inspirer himself. The bent of my mind was not however towards fictitious composition: I was more ambitious of writing on scientific subjects, and actually did contemplate throwing some little branch of knowledge which I had mastered into a new literary modification. No project of this kind was ever really attempted; but at the beginning of the year 1817, I commenced a journal into which I find incorporated (for it is still in existence) a kind of view of the political state of the country at the opening of the parliament of that year.

In the summer of 1817, accident enabled my brother to recommend me to a Russian merchant residing in Pilrig Street, Leith Walk, who wished to have a young person to copy his letters. My hand-writing being found suitable, I was appointed to the situation at a salary of ten pounds a year, and, as I was not required to attend after four in the afternoon, I resolved rather to lodge at home than in Edinburgh. For six months I trudged patiently every morning to Pilrig Street – a walk of five miles – whence, after working at a desk for six hours, I as patiently repeated my walk homewards, seldom requiring more than a half-penny-worth of any kind of victuals between the hour of eight, when I left home, and six, when I returned. A misunderstanding with my employer about salary eventually lost me this place, at the beginning of the year 1818, and I never was again in the service of any man, except for about three weeks in the following spring, which I spent in the counting room of a merchant in Leith, who, finding at the end of that time that he had hardly enough of employment for me, gave me a polite discharge, accompanied by a small present. It seemed to my parents and other friends, as if I were doomed to indecision and idleness for life; and I began to suffer so severely under the imputations which no generosity could prevent being thrown out upon me, that I became fitted for any desperate adventure which could give me an object to work upon, and an independent, however scanty subsistence.

A thousand expedients were suggested; all kinds of trades and professions were again thought of; and I was so often shown out before shopkeepers in their back-rooms that I had some thoughts of breaking away from all existing ties, and commencing any kind of traffic, however humble, which would only rescue me in the meantime from the ignominious reputation of a broken down scholar. I must not, however, forget to mention that I had had a regular but partial employment in teaching or attempting to teach a family of young children at Portobello, the most wayward and uninstructible creatures I ever met with. The few pounds which were the reward of this and other exertions, taught me the sweets of industry, and inspired a still more eager solicitude for that independence which the sense of living by one's own labours so universally gives. I had thus grown up to sixteen years of age - a studious, awkward, and apparently energetic youth, full of eccentricities in thought and action, and as yet unconscious of an aim in life; but yet, it would appear, possessed of a secret vein of enthusiasm, which was ultimately to lead me through many difficulties, and place me in a respectable station. On subsequently reading the life of Burns, I have been struck with the resemblance which existed between our respective situations at this period of existence. I was placed like him in a remote and unfavourable situation, and to all appearance doomed to abject servitude and toil. I felt the same ambitious impulses, resembling, to use his fine expression, the gropings of the blind Cyclops round his cave. Unlike him, however, I did not despise any means which might present themselves, for redeeming myself from my unhappy position. My ambition, like the fairy tent in the Arabian tale, could expand itself when required over a whole army; but it could also be collapsed into a handful, and carried in the pocket of the possessor. This is the more remarkable a difference, when it is recollected that my early nurture was far more likely to have inspired me with a disdain of lowly expedients than was that of Burns. The difference on my part was to be traced to a Jew-like patience of contumely, a quite steady endurance of all kinds of injuries that could be offered to my self love, which I had been taught by repeated disappointments, and which I persuaded myself by a powerful exertion of the understanding, to be necessary for my eventual rise. I felt, in reality, like one acting in an incognito, who is not expected to take amiss any slight that may be put upon his apparent rank. My present situation, as well as that of my immediate relations (thus ran my reflections) was not that for which our dispositions and habits of life were fitted; it was, however, the result of unavoidable misfortunes, and must therefore be endured in the best manner possible. Neither, thought I, does it matter what method I may assume of gaining my own livelihood, provided that it promises, in time, and after a period of suffering, to restore me to the enjoyment of that station in life which was my original destiny and is still the secret object of all my care. Any contamination to which I might be exposed in the passage from the larva to the butterfly state, I feared not to resist; for reading had rendered me independent of all companionship, and I have never hitherto felt the least temptation amidst mean circumstances to act in a plebeian or unworthy spirit.

I must confess, at the same time what seems requisite to give a natural tinge to this picture, that I did not uniformly maintain my philosophical temper throughout these distresses, but occasionally abandoned myself to something approaching to despair. How to proceed under such circumstances, was too trying a question for a person of my years, however tempered heretofore in the school of adversity. Sometimes the future would appear so gloomy that I would shrink from it with fear, and wish that I had rather never been, or could cease to be, than thus be loaded with an existence for which all proper provision was wanting. I well recollect spending a whole evening by the fireside, in a state of minute sorrow, resembling that of Burns in the introduction to his 'Vision' but without the self-reproach which formed a part of that picture. I thought of the past, of the present, and of the future; and the mortification and torture which the comparison inflicted upon me were only relieved by the wellings of a softer spirit, arising from I know not what subjects of reflection, and which gushed unbidden and almost unnoted to my eyes. At that time, I had frequent walks of considerable extent, and often performed by night, many of them being undertaken in the vain hope of obtaining employment. On one occasion, having left Edinburgh at nightfall after some disappointment of this kind, my sensations were of so morbid a nature, that without regard to the rain which was beginning to descend, but rather catching sanction for my mood from the corresponding state of the elements, I threw myself upon the sward in the King's Park and with bitter tears felt as if I could have been glad that I should never more rise in possession of life. My manner was so like that of a desperate outcast as to attract attention from a gentleman who soon after passed that way, and who conceived it his duty to come up to me, and enquire why I thus exposed myself. The intrusion was seasonable, for it disturbed me with a different train of ideas, and I immediately rose and proceeded towards home.

Illustrations

2. The house, 'modern' (1796) and 'sklatit' (slated), where William and Robert were born, beside the Eddlestone Water in Peebles.

Mr Chalmers, Merchant, Peebles,

To James Sloane

For Education to his Sons Wm & William and
Robert from March 1810 to Whitsunday 1811 ... £13..4

Ditto 1 Quarter to Mr William at the
Evening School in Winter ... 5..0

For a Copy of the Rudiments to Mr Robert
on 4th October 1810 ... 1..3

For Ditto to Mr William on 30th Jany ... 1..3

For Grammatical Exercises to William
on 30th April ... 1..3

£1..1..9

Mr Robert from Whitsunday to March 1811 ... 10..0

£1..11..9

Peebles 9th October 1811 Received payment

James Sloane

3. Mr Sloane's account for William's and Robert's attendance at the
Grammar School, Peebles, 1810 - 1811. His addition is faulty and
he robs himself of fourpence. He taught classics and English but
not arithmetic.

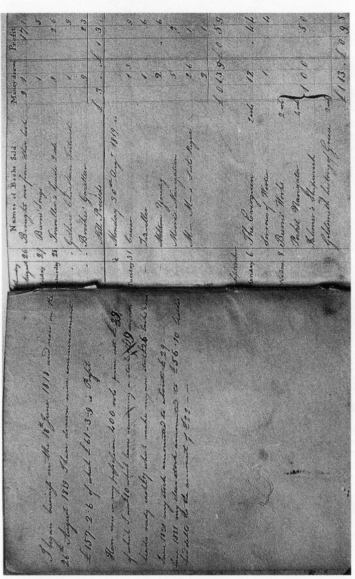

4. The struggling bookseller. In Robert's salesbook for 1819, the summary on the left shows that his first 14 months in business produced a profit of £61-3-9. But in the daily account on the right it is clear that there were many days (probably rainy days) when he sold nothing at all.

TO

SIR WALTER SCOTT, BART.

OF

ABBOTSFORD

THESE SPECIMENS

of

minute

Penmanship

ARE

respectfully presented

BY

AN Admirer OF

HIS

GENIUS.

5. Robert's faultless penmanship. This title-page was written out by hand, although you would scarcely know it. It is from the book which Robert presented to Sir Walter Scott, and which marked the turning-point in the fortunes of the Chambers family.

6. Anne Kirkwood, wife of Robert Chambers, and mother of their fourteen children. There is reason to think that this old photograph has been printed the right way round, and therefore that Anne was left-handed. Sadly, her letters replying to Robert's have not been found.

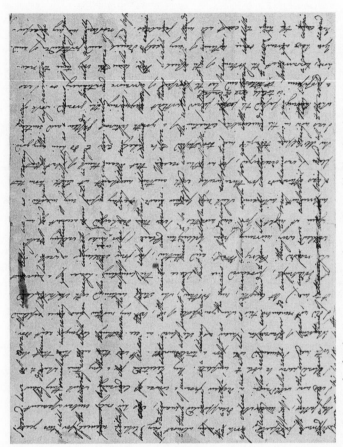

7. An example of Robert's cross-written letters. He used both sides of thin paper, writing twice on each side.

VESTIGES

OF

THE NATURAL HISTORY

OF

CREATION.

LONDON:

JOHN CHURCHILL, PRINCES STREET, SOHO.

MDCCCXLIV.

8. The anonymous title-page of *Vestiges*, the book that shocked
Britain and America in 1844 and paved the way for Darwin's
Origin of Species fifteen years later.

9. No 1 Doune Terrace, Edinburgh, the home of Robert Chambers from 1844.

10. Anne Chambers and family about 1844. From left to right they are James (3), Amelia (6), Anne (9), Mary (11) with William (1), Anne Chambers at her harp, Janet and Eliza (8), and Nina (14). Robert, the eldest son, is missing, presumably away at school. Three children had already died in infancy. Phoebe and Alice were yet to be born.

Chapter XVIII

Sharp misery at length so far wore down my spirit, that I became fitted for any species of employment, were it ever so humble. In a state of feeling which I can now hardly recollect, I resolved to take all the books which I had myself collected, together with all those belonging to my brother, and all that misfortune had left to my father – the whole including Horace and other school-books amounting in value to two or three pounds – and expose them for sale in a small shop in Leith Walk, where there were already several similar dealers. From my first arrival in Edinburgh I had been a zealous student in small and out-of-the-way bookshops, and I was not altogether so inept in mercantile matters as not to perceive that many of those depositories of offcast literature increased and prospered. I had also seen, in the memoirs of the celebrated Lackington, how apt the smallest beginnings in that trade were to expand to something respectable. My brother's actual acquaintance and connection with the business of bookselling furnished me with additional encouragement; and if any more had been wanting, it would have been found in my personal appetite for books, which was promised, by this trade, a larger measure of indulgence than it could have hoped for in any other. I therefore in July 1818 presented my little stock to the notice of the public, in a shop which by an immense stretch of daring I had taken at the rate of six pounds a-year. To my own infinite surprise, I drew eleven or twelve shillings the first day, thereby receiving for the first time in my life the delightful assurance that there was a chance of regularly obtaining sustenance by my own exertions. When I went home and showed the actual money, the reluctance which my parents had expressed to my taking so odd a step was sensibly staggered; and William who took a keen interest in my project, was completely overjoyed. It was speedily resolved that my brother should live with me in the little back apartment connected with my shop, so as to assist me regularly with his advice in all the intervals spared by his business, and at the same time spare all expense for lodging. So miserably was the place furnished, that at first we had no bed, but lay on the floor, with a rug for covering, and a bundle of books for pillow. Afterwards, a bed stuffed with chaff made things a little easier, and, rolled up during the day, the bed with its rug answered as a convenient sofa.

Leith Walk may be described as a broad kind of Boulevard, stretching nearly a mile in length between Edinburgh and the seaport, and as being constantly used as a thoroughfare by merchants, clerks, strangers, and seafaring people. It was then the daily resort of a multiplicity of odd-looking dependants on public charity – such as old blind fiddlers, seated by the wayside; sailors deficient in a leg or an arm, with long queues hanging down their backs, who were always singing ballads about sea-fights; and cripples of various sorts, who contrived to move along in wooden bowls, or in low-wheeled vehicles drawn by dogs – which personages reckoned on reaping a harvest of coppers in the week of Leith races – that great annual festival of the gamins of Edinburgh, which has been commemorated in the humorous verses of Robert Fergusson. Besides its hosts of mendicants, the Walk was garnished with small shops for the sale of shells, corals, and other foreign curiosities. It was also provided with a number of petty public-houses; but its greatest attraction was a show of wax-work, at the entrance of which sat the figure of an old gentleman in a court-dress, intently reading a newspaper, which, without turning over the leaves, had occupied him for the last ten years.

The oddest thing about the Walk, however, was an air of pretension singularly inconsistent with the reality. The signboards offered a study of the definite article – *The* Comb Manufactory, *The* Chair Manufactory, *The* Marble Work, and so forth, appearing on the fronts of buildings of the most trumpery character. At the time I became acquainted with the Walk, it owned few edifices that were worth much. Here and there, with intervening patches of nursery-grounds and gardens, there was a detached villa or a row of houses with flower-pots in front. But the majority of the buildings were of a slight fabric of brick and plaster, with tiled roofs, as if the whole were removable at a day's notice. There being no edifices, however mean and inconvenient, which do not find inhabitants, these frail tenements were in demand by a needy order of occupants, whose ultimate limit in the article of rent was ten to twelve pounds a year.

My success at bookselling was to myself astonishing. In a very short time, my original stock comprehending many old smoked volumes of divinity was almost entirely changed, and from two or three pounds, it soon reached fifteen or twenty in value. During the single week preceding Martinmas, I had actually cleared as much profit as I originally had capital, and within a few shillings of what sufficed to pay the rent of the shop up to that period. I used to increase my stores chiefly at the winter auctions in the Old Town, and, as there were then no cheap new books, I used to find the chief difficulty of the trade to consist in getting a sufficiency of old ones to supply the demand. Before the end of the first year, I had had so many through my hands, and studied this traffic so effectually, that I could readily assign a value to almost any tolerably well known English book – besides having immensely increased my knowledge of their contents.

The condition of the weather was an important element of consideration. In fine days, the Walk was thronged with foot-passengers, a number of whom found some recreation in lounging for a few minutes over my stall. If there was a prospect of rain, they hurried on; and when it became determinedly wet, business was over for the day. I might as well bring in my books at once, and try to find something to do indoors. When the stall was not in operation, sales were almost at a stand-still. Hundreds, I found, as Lackington had done before me, would buy books from a stall, who would not purchase them equally cheap in a shop. The advantageous peculiarity of the stall is, that it secures those who have formed no deliberate intention to buy. Lying invitingly with their backs upward, the books on a stall solicit just as much attention as you are pleased to give them. You may look at them, or let them alone. You may, as if by chance, take up and set down volume after volume without getting compromised. The bookseller, however, is perfectly aware of what is likely to ensue. When he observes that the lounger over his stall is not satisfied with a casual glance, but goes on examining book after book, he is pretty certain there is to be a purchase. Continued inspection excites an interest in the mind. There is perhaps no intention at first to buy, but gradually the feelings are warmed up, and it is then scarcely possible to resist asking the price of some book which more particularly strikes the fancy. Asking the price is equivalent to passing the Rubicon. After that, the desire for purchasing becomes nearly irresistible. Going into shops to buy books in cold blood is quite a different thing. Before entering, there must in general be a distinct intention to purchase.

Stall-keepers of all varieties know the value of the obtrusive principle; and it may be doubted if the modern shop system is in most cases an improvement on the old practice of exposing wares in open booths along the sides of the thoroughfare. The original *Stationarii*, who exposed their books at the gateways of universities, immediately after the invention of printing – what were they but stall-keepers? Did not also many booksellers of good repute last century set up stalls for the sale of their wares on market-days? There is something, therefore, like a classical authority for book-stalls. They remind us of the infancy of printed literature and the usages of an olden time.

The Walk offered uncommon facilities for the traffic in which I was engaged. Long stretches of the footway from thirty to forty feet wide, admitted of stalls being set outside the doors without obstructing the thoroughfare. Some might think that they were an attraction to what was otherwise a pleasant promenade. The book-stalls, four in number, were all situated on the shady side of the road, forming at proper distances from each other a series of literary lures, likely to be visited *en suite*. Interesting from the diversity of their wares, they to a certain extent were mutually helpful. There was nothing like a feeling of rivalry among us. Accustomed to discuss professional matters, we were able to cultivate a few jocularities as a seasoning to a too frequent dullness. We learned how to distinguish habitual nibblers, who never bought, but only gave trouble, from those on whom we could reasonably reckon for a purchase, and knew how to act accordingly. The stall offered a study of character. There was not a little perversity or stupidity to be amused with. Some stall frequenters would buy nothing but books which had been used. Defective in judgment, they could not imagine the possibility of getting a new book as cheaply as an old one. The stall-keepers on the Walk found it necessary to humour purchasers of this sort. It was not difficult to do so; they had only to cut up the leaves, and soil the outside of a book, in order to make it thoroughly acceptable.

Having been trained by adversity to a degree of prudence almost odious in a young person, I was never tempted by the possession of money or by the gains I had made, into any indulgence beyond the most simple necessaries of life. If there was at all an exception, it was in my taking it upon me about this time to treat myself, perhaps once a month, to a seat in the theatre; an indulgence scoffed at by my more ascetic brother, and which I have since learned to hold in indifference, but in which I then certainly experienced a great and, as far as I was myself concerned, an innocent pleasure. Every penny I possessed I looked upon as part of the means which was to work my redemption, and perhaps that of my parents also, from the unfortunate circumstances into which we had been thrown. The only thing which ever gave me any pain was being seen occasionally in my little shop by old schoolfellows, almost all of whom had been set forward in the world under infinitely more promising and more respectable circumstances than myself; so that our relative positions were now very different from what they had been at school. I had no refuge from this but to affect non-acquaintance, and so imperative were the ordinary rules of life that I generally found my old friends disposed to second me in this effort.

For one or two years before this period, my brother had employed a great part of his spare time in a peculiar kind of penmanship. A British officer who had been several years in a French prison, and there amused himself by transcribing little volumes in a fine small hand, placed a copy of the *Pleasures of Hope* done in that style in the shop of my brother's master, with a view to its being disposed of by raffle; and the sum realised was near twenty pounds. To the most of those who saw it, the style of writing seemed a wonder and a mystery, not only on account of the taste necessary for guiding the pen so neatly, but on account of the patience and the acuteness of sight which were still more obviously requisite for practising it. William, nevertheless, resolved to attempt something in the same style, and it was amazing how well he succeeded in a very short space of time. After having attained to what appeared to him the ultimatum of the art, he wrote off the poem entitled *Prisoner of Chillon* in neat octavo pages, and had the whole bound up at the conclusion. The volume astonished all who had the opportunity of seeing it, and I was frequently twitted by my father for my inability to perform any similar wonder. For my own part, I looked upon my brother's proficiency with the despairing wonder which it seemed to excite every where around me, and had hitherto made no attempt at rivalry, however humble. One day, however, when suffering a little pique on account of my father's raillery, I took a piece of paper, ruled it in the proper manner, and with one of my brother's crow-quills commenced writing a small poem, in imitation of a piece upon which he was then employed. To my own wonder, I found that there was hardly any difficulty in the matter. The few scraps which I wrote that day passed off easily with my father at night as of William's execution; and when he again remarked how disgraceful it was to me that I could do nothing of the sort, I had the triumphant satisfaction of informing him that *these* were of my doing – an allegation which he would scarcely believe, till my brother assured him of its truth. Thereafter, I practised small writing very industri-ously, and, having much more spare time than my brother, I soon outstripped him so completely that he gave up the art entirely and took to something else. The chief peculiarity of this species of calligraphy was its resemblance to print, or rather to the lettering in which engravers generally give a poetical motto at the bottom of the print. Many of the pieces which I wrote were so minute and fine, that the paper hardly seemed at a cursory glance to be charged with ink. The larger writing for titles and signatures was in Norman, German, and Old English, and was done with equal care, and so far as I recollect equal neatness. It was, however, a useless and unprofitable way of spending time. Hardly anything could be made of it but a mere show.

It was a mad attempt to revive an art which the invention of typography had for ever laid to rest.

In May 1819 William, who had just concluded his time, set up a shop similar to mine and at no great distance, and thus the extraordinary circumstance presented itself, of two brothers rivalling each other in business in the same street. This step, however, never appeared to me as one in the least likely to prove injurious to my interests; and so far were we from feeling any jealousy of each other, that my back-room still continued to be our common abode. There every evening, when the shops were closed, did we sit at our frugal meal conversing of matters of business (if they could be so called) or of matters of literature, in which we were now beginning to be more interested than in science, or of our general prospects in the world, which like starry skies seen from a pit, looked all the brighter that my immediate atmosphere was one of poverty and hardship. I can never reflect on this period of my life without pleasure. All lowly as I then was, and out of the observation of the world, my days were spent in innocence and moral improvement; I had also so much hope within me, that I failed in a great measure to feel the real meanness of my circumstances.

It was about the date just mentioned, being then about to complete my seventeenth year, that I commenced, or rather recommenced the composition of poetry. The mind was then bursting into manhood, and began to be acted upon by sentiments and passions to which I had hitherto been a stranger. My verses, therefore, though by no means what I would now consider tolerable, were inspired with a feeling and a sense which in no degree characterised the compositions, whether Latin or English, of my school-boy days. I sometimes wrote them out in the neat hand just alluded to, and they were then sure, for one cause or another, to excite admiration. I had now for the first time become acquainted with modern English literature, particularly the works of Campbell, Byron, and Scott, and, as usually happens at a period of life when we are apt to be more replete with the ideas of other men than our own, my compositions were in a great measure created out of the writings of those poets, with an admixture from Burns, with whom I had been longer acquainted. In a few months, however, I improved considerably in the art, becoming, above all things, more original. Having every day many hours of leisure, all of which I dedicated to calligraphy or to poetry, I could not fail to make advances in both.

In the winter of 1819-20, a new pursuit opened upon me. I found that, while in poetry there was a perpetual sacrifice of ideas to rhymes, I could write much more freely, and consequently much more to purpose, in prose. The discovery was made in writing letters to my friends, and I eagerly took advantage of it. In January 1820 I began a historical novel on the adventures of Charles the Second in Scotland, designing to make the duke of Buckingham one of the principal characters, and to throw romantic interest on a love affair between the well known Colonel Montgomery and a Lady Henrietta Livingstone, daughter of the earl of Almond. About half a volume was written, and I then threw it by in despair though, on dipping into the manuscript lately, I found far less occasion to be displeased with it than I expected.

Among the humble but ingenious persons with whom my brother and I became acquainted at this time, was John Denovan, a grocer's apprentice about our own age, who, though entirely self-educated, wrote remarkably good poetry, and had even made some ventures in the more difficult field of prose. Denovan was the illegitimate and neglected son of a citizen of Edinburgh – reared by a mother little above the condition of mendicancy – totally unacquainted with the interior of any school – had been the drudge, since early boyhood, of a slavish trade; and yet he read with enthusiasm the works of modern poets, and, to use an expression of Burns, kindled at their flame. His verses, through of course written on the model of Byron and other eminent bards, were animated, and to my ear excellent; only, from want of an acquaintance with the rules of prosody, he never knew when his lines were correct and when they were not, and they were almost as often erroneous as otherwise. My superior musical ear and better education enabled me to do him some good in this respect. Denovan was a violent *radical*, and persuaded my brother and myself, though we knew nothing of politics, to join him in equal shares of a weekly sheet, which he was anxious to start, in the style of Wooler's *Black Dwarf*. This work made its first appearance in October or November 1819, under the title of *The Patriot*, and the whole affair was then and has ever since been to me as a kind of dream. Eight numbers were published, containing, I believe, bitter diatribes against the existing government and all connected with it; the whole of which were the composition of Denovan, and carried to me hardly any meaning, seeing that I had neither knowledge nor sentiment on the subject. One of its leading articles, I remember, began with the portentous words, 'Day follows day, and chain follows chain.' All that I received in compensation for the few pounds which I disbursed to make up the general loss was the pleasure of seeing for the first time a few of my verses in a printed shape. I have never since seen a single copy of the work. Denovan afterwards sought employment in London as a grocer but, having lost his testimonials, was unsuccessful in his object. Having soon expended all his money he was obliged for several nights to lie in the open air; but afterwards, by what means I know not, found his way back to Leith, where I recollect his arriving in a state verging on starvation, having walked in one day from Berwick on threepence halfpenny. After many struggles for a comfortable means of subsistence, during which he was cheered with much kindness from Sir Walter Scott, he sunk under the severity of his toils, and died in great wretchedness about the year 1827.

In May 1820 I removed to a much better shop than any I had hitherto occupied, and my brother, having now a back room of his own, left me to live by myself. My stock of books was by this time much improved, and I began to add a circulating library and an apartment of stationery articles to my other stores. So far as I can recollect, my profits must have now averaged from six to eight pounds a month, while the expenses of subsistence did not exceed a third of either sum; I had thus the means of slowly but constantly increasing my capital. As little time was required by business, I had a great deal of leisure, which I divided between literary composition, calligraphy, and reading. Not a day passed without something being done in one or other of these pursuits. It will thus be observed that, if I improved, it was only under such favourable circumstances that not to have done so would have been disgraceful. There was but one drawback, and that consisted in an exclusive taste which now possessed me for books of fancy, to the neglect of the works of science and information in which I delighted at an earlier age. This I have since had great occasion to regret, as it caused me to miss an opportunity which has never returned in nearly so large a measure, of storing my mind with useful facts.

Throughout the years 1820 and 1821, I wrote a considerable quantity of prose, and several small poems, but made no attempt to publish till the latter part of the second of those years, when my brother, who had set up a small printing-press, at which he wrought himself, urged me to join him in the publication of a weekly literary sheet, under the title of *The Kaleidoscope*, and proposed that I should chiefly contribute the necessary matter. To this I consented, and the work was accordingly started in November, almost the whole being of my composition. To describe the flashy extravagancies, the injudicious satires, and the juvenile improprieties in general, of this little work, would be doing it too much honour. Suffice it to say, that it sunk deservedly at the eighth number, the sale having been quite inadequate to pay the expenses. There was hardly one article in this work which could be considered unexceptionable in point of taste, except the poetry, which was at least free of the wretched affectations that beset my prose, and in some instances was honoured with considerable applause. I am tempted to believe that my mind and whole manner of writing had about this time suffered a temporary vitiation from the reading of certain periodical works, of brilliant, but by no means pure lustre, with which I had become captivated, and of which I could imitate the vices, while I could not rival the real talent and ability.

Chapter XIX

At this time there dwelt in Leith a good-natured middle-aged man, a shipbuilder, by name Mr Alexander Sime. He had been educated at Peebles, and retained some vivid recollections of the old burgh and its inhabitants. One of his agreeable remembrances related to the dancing-school, at which shone a pretty and lady-like girl, Jeanie Gibson, the noonday of whose married life had been clouded by a series of misfortunes in saddening contrast with the bright anticipations of her early morning; and now, as he learned, her two elder sons were pushing their way on as booksellers in Leith Walk. Sime's best feelings were interested. He made himself known to us, and a cordial intimacy ensued. Through him we became acquainted with Mr William Reid, a well-known bookseller in Leith, and a person of singularly genial disposition. Reid acted as a true friend. He occasionally looked in upon us to offer a word of advice and encouragement, and was much pleased with a specimen of calligraphy which consisted of extracts of Sir Walter Scott's poetry. Reid carried off the specimen to show to his friend Constable, then in the zenith of his power. This circumstance immediately led to an interview with the great publisher.

It was proposed that I should write something of the same kind in the shape of a volume, which I should myself present to Sir Walter, with an introductory letter from his publisher. The matter proposed by Mr Constable was the songs in *The Lady of the Lake*, which he seemed to indicate as the poet's pet compositions. In the course of a few months I had finished my little volume, with a neat title page, and it was sent to Mr Constable at his own request in order to be bound. The great bookseller was now in London on account of his health, and it was not till February 1822 that it was returned, along with the promised letter of introduction. Furnished with that document, I proceeded next day to the poet's residence in Castle Street, where I had the good fortune to find him in his study. He received me, as he received every one who approached him, with a homely kindness of manner, which at once placed me at my ease; and having had the volume in his possession for some hours, he was able to express his surprise, and also that of his wife – for so he designated Lady Scott – at the extreme neatness and minuteness of the writing. He said he would place the book in his library at Abbotsford, and he was sure it would be considered as not the least curious of the many curiosities there deposited. He then made inquiries respecting my occupations, and having been informed that I dealt partly in old books, requested that I would let him know when I happened to possess any of particular rarity or value. After some further conversation, I took my leave astonished at the gentle and easy manner of a man whom I had been accustomed to regard as of a superior order of beings, and delighted with the reflection that I would ever have it to say, perhaps many years after he should be dead and gone, that I had seen and talked to him.

Whether business had now taken a different turn, or my other pursuits interfered with mercantile concerns, I began to find myself in a less prosperous state than formerly. I was anxious to remove to some respectable shop in a central part of the city, but not possessing the necessary capital, was obliged for another tedious year to continue where I was. Literature and calligraphy still were my chief employments. In the former department, I compiled a small volume which was published in Autumn 1822, entitled *Illustrations of the Author of Waverley, or Notices of Real Characters, Scenes, and Incidents Supposed to be Described in his Works*. Though it met with little encouragement, and was monstrously deformed by bad taste, it certainly contained some writing of a better character – *more to purpose*, if I may so express myself – than any I had formerly given to the public. My connection with the southern district of Scotland, to which Sir Walter himself belonged, gave me a facility in ascertaining the prototypes of many of his characters, and also in gathering information respecting them; and I have since had the satisfaction to read in his notes to the uniform edition of the Waverley Novels, that I was generally correct in my assumptions. In August this year George the Fourth paid his visit to Edinburgh; and Sir Walter Scott, as president of the Royal Society, was able to put some lucrative employment in my way. The address of that society, written by himself, and expressed with as much brevity as elegance, was sent to me by his recommendation to be drawn up in my best style of penmanship. For this duty, which occupied me two days, I was paid five guineas. Three other societies, the Wernerian, the Medical, and the Caledonian Horticultural, hearing of me from some members of the Royal Society, brought me their addresses to write also; and I cleared about eighteen pounds in little more than a week. To crown all, I was apprised that the King, at a private inspection of the addresses in Dalkeith Palace, was pleased to remark the curious neatness of hand with which mine were written. It is, however, but justice to myself to observe, that young as I was and little accustomed to praise, I never felt in the least flattered by any compliments paid to me on the score of my calligraphic exhibitions. I not only entertained a secret contempt for the accomplishment, but believed that many others would have excelled in it to as great degree as myself if they had only tried. Often, when my specimens were shown in my own presence, and wondering looks were directed to the individual who could so well command his eyesight and his hand, I felt a conscientious shame at receiving praise on such an account, both because I knew that the wonder was not properly founded, and because I hated to be thought only a cunning workman in the art of writing, when I was in reality ambitious of the moral honours of the pen.

My employment in the autumn of 1822 was to transcribe into a volume similar to the songs in *The Lady of the Lake* the best of the poetical effusions which had been poured forth on the occasion of his Majesty's visit. This had been ordered by Sir Walter Scott, and I was led by a person in his confidence to expect the sum of twenty pounds for it. Upon the strength of this expectation, I removed in December to a shop in the outskirts of the New Town, the rent of which, though cheaper than usual (£20), would have otherwise deterred me from taking so ambitious a step. I calculated that the chief difficulty of the first year would be thus got over, and trusted to good fortune and industry for what should follow. This new place of business had no den of refuge in which I could lodge, and I was therefore obliged after four years and a half of house keeping to take up my nightly abode at a hotel in the Old Town, which, after various intermediate stages, my parents had recently begun to occupy. I may remark that during these four and a half years, and for nearly a twelvemonth after, I never got dinner except on Sundays; nor tasted animal food at any period of the day, excepting at night, when I generally supped with my mother. My almost sole diet was tea, taken twice a day with bread, butter and cheese. Liquors – except very rarely a bottle of porter – were totally excluded from my domestic system; and I hardly ever tasted them on any other occasion. The slenderness of my stock, and the rarity of the population around me, combined to render my business at first very small and unproductive. Consternation, therefore, began to come upon me, when months elapsed after months, and no intelligence arrived from Sir Walter Scott. After many misgivings, I found myself compelled to put him in mind of the labour he had imposed upon me, and, with an elaborate apology for the necessity of my circumstances, to request that he would render me any payment he thought appropri-ate. To my ineffable mortification, he enclosed me ten pounds, *as a loan to be repaid, if I ever should be able, without interest,* but to be otherwise held as a gift; and he concluded a polite letter by reminding me that, though a friend might contribute to push a vessel from the shore, it was necessary for those on board to exert themselves afterwards by sail and rudder, to carry it rightly and rapidly on its course. This benevolent man, oppressed by the multitude of his labours, had evidently forgot the order he had given and the volume I had sent him in consequence, and looking only to the statement of necessitous circumstances which I had given as an excuse for dunning him, concluded I was in distress and sent me a sum for my relief. To my regret ever since, the letter in which I returned the money referred more pointedly to my wounded feelings than it ought to have done, considering the beneficence of his intentions. It explained, however, the real nature of my late application, and was promptly answered by an apology for his mistake and a request that I would now accept the sum, as the price of the volume I had written for him. To this I could have no objections, and the matter ended thus; but I feel persuaded that there was some radical misunderstanding between us from the beginning about this volume, which, in all probability, I never shall be enabled to explain. The transaction always appeared to me as having an effect unfavourable to myself. I believe that, in my slender acquaintance with the world, accompanied as it was by a gift of writing a rather showy letter, I must have used expressions which did not accord with the simplicity and plainness of my honoured correspondent; and I rather think that it required his appreciation of the design of my *Traditions of Edinburgh* to reconcile him to me – for till the appearance of the second number of that work, nearly two years after, we had no further intercourse.

It was in July 1823 that I commenced my collections for this fortunate little work. For several years, the idea of gathering all the floating memoranda respecting the former state of society in Edinburgh had been resolving in my mind; but it was not till now that I found myself at leisure to take up the task in a serious manner. The first number of the work appeared in March 1824, and met with so favourable a reception, that a second and a third edition were speedily demanded. So curious a disclosure of the homely manners and domestic accommodations of past ages seemed to make a strong impression on the public mind, even beyond the place which it specially referred to; and I found myself at length surprised in my poverty and obscurity, by something like the honours of successful authorship, and a small share of its profits. Among other advantages, I prized greatly the notice which the work procured me from various literary men of established reputation. Nothing ever gratifies a young aspirant more than a nod of condescending recognition from his seniors, and I often wonder that the pleasure is so penuriously dispensed by the latter individuals, considering that they must in general recollect how much they once enjoyed it themselves, when in the way of needing it, and how grievously they used to be chagrined when it was on any occasion withheld. The renewed friendship of Sir Walter Scott followed, as already mentioned, the publication of the second part of the *Traditions*. He came into my little shop one day with Mr Lockhart, whom I had formerly seen, and sitting down on a form began to discourse familiarly about my publication, the subject of which was so much a favourite with him, that he had intended to write upon it himself in conjunction with Mr Skene of Rubislaw. Having heard that Mr Charles Kirkpatrick Sharpe was among the number of my informants (intelligence which I now confirmed) he concluded that part of the work was written by that gentleman; probably the best parts – and I must own that this was more likely, considering the experience and acknowledged talent of Mr Sharpe, rather than that they came from a person of my unassuming and youthful appearance, and who occupied so humble a station in life. Sir Walter accordingly took up a copy of the newly published number, and saying to Mr Lockhart he would shew him a capital passage, read aloud a somewhat droll account of the many marriages of the earl of Eglintoune. 'I could have told you,' said he, laughing heartily, 'that that was Sharpe's. It is so very like him.' The passage was in reality my own writing, quite independent of the few brief notes I had received from Mr Sharpe; nevertheless, such was either my bashfulness or my modesty, that I could not assert my title to the praise of my visitors till after they had left the shop. In a note which I had occasion to write that evening to Mr Lockhart, I mentioned the mistake of his distinguished father-in-law, which Mr L. assured me in reply, he would take an opportunity of explaining to Sir Walter.

The success, however humble, of this little work was the first ray of prosperity that had fallen upon our unfortunate family for twelve years. It came at a time when the usual amount of our distress was increased by the loss of a law-plea, which my father had instituted for the recovery of a piece of property in Peebles – his own by every thing like right, but declared to be alienated by prescription. The fresh embarrassment occasioned by the unhappy issue of this process, and the mental distress produced by disappointment in what had been a leading idea of his mind for several years, were attended by the most lamentable effects; and this unhappy man, whose prospects in the world were originally of the brightest, as his intellect was among the best, and his honour the most unimpeachable, was now fast sinking at a premature age into the grave. Amidst the griefs of this dismal period, the praise and profit derived from my little work appeared like a sunburst in the morning of a winter day. My father read it with feelings most inappropriate to the naif and gossiping nature of its contents; and whenever anyone spoke of it, more especially if with praise, tears rolled profusely down his cheeks. When taken in conjunction with the steady conduct of my brother and myself, it seemed to hold out a promise that the comfort and honour forfeited by our family so many years before, would not only be restored, but that a lustre of a higher kind might yet be shed upon it. To him, however, the promise came all too late. There are some griefs which bite so deeply into the heart, and wear away so many of the fibres of life, that no consolation even of a more immediate kind than this can reverse their effect. There was, besides, the instant distress of circumstances, against which my slender success could be of little avail. A bilious distemper was pressing sore upon his health, and it seemed a dubious question whether the prison or the grave should first obtain possession of his person, when I accompanied my mother and some other members of the family, to visit him in a lowly lodging, a little way out of town, where he had taken refuge from both of these impending calamities. When he saw me, he took me by the hand, and burst into tears. I can suggest no other explanation of this sensibility than that, anticipating the possibility of my gaining some distinction in the world, and feeling his own end approaching, he wept to think he should never witness a triumph in which he was so much interested – never enjoy what would have gone so far to compensate his own reverses.

Exactly a week after this affecting scene, November 1824, he died – the victim of a broken heart – for I can trace his dissolution to no other cause. Many a time since then, when men have ascribed unsolicited honours, how large a discount did I mentally subtract from them, when I reflected that they had come too late to soothe the spirit of this amiable and injured man, to whom I was indebted for so much of the instruction and observation which had been their bases, and whose life they might have perhaps redeemed.

In the course of the year 1825, besides bringing the two volumes of the *Traditions of Edinburgh* to a close, I wrote a volume entitled *Walks in Edinburgh* for the guidance of strangers to the miscellaneous objects of curiosity throughout the city. This book, composed in three weeks, produced me twenty pounds, and though not free of faults, it advanced the humble kind of literary reputation which I had already acquired in Edinburgh. The number of the *Traditions* first printed in Edinburgh was two hundred and fifty. The impression was then increased to six hundred, and still was found too scanty. All at once, by the advice of Mr Archibald Constable, it was advanced to two thousand eight hundred. This publisher, whose ideas had no fault but that of extravagance, had promised to himself and me that he would secure a large sale for the work in London; and accordingly, by his directions, a thousand copies were dispatched to that market, and placed in the hands of the company with which his own was connected. The London house beheld the consignment with surprise, being of opinion that the local nature of the book forbade the hope of selling a tenth part of that quantity in England; and the whole parcel to my great mortification was returned to my hands. This, however, was eventually found better than if it had been absorbed into the stock of the London company, for this became insolvent in the course of a few months thereafter. Fortunately the effects of Mr Constable's advice, which would have not only deprived me of all profit from the work, but seriously embarrassed my affairs, were done away with by a bargain which I made in October with Messrs Tait of Edinburgh, for a complete transference of the property of the work into their hands. The results of this arrangement were a profit on my part, amounting to about one hundred and fifty pounds, and on theirs, I regret to say, the possession of the stock, which though it soon reproduced its purchase-money afforded only a small and tedious compensation for the trouble of managing it. It is an expressive proof of the enormous ideas of Mr Constable in publishing, that, even in eight years, the utmost activity and frequent advertising have not been able to clear off above two thousand of the quantity he advised to be printed. His advice, I am sensible, was well meant, and involved a high compliment to myself; but I would have been many pounds richer, at a time when a few pounds were of much consequence to me, if I had not regarded it.

The trade of publishing was at this time in a very flourishing state, and, as I had now ascertained that literature promised me a quicker rise in the world than any other employment which lay within my reach, I was easily persuaded by Messrs Tait – two enterprising young men of capital – to undertake the composition of a superior kind of guide-book to Scotland, which they conceived to be then wanted. For this work, which was to occupy two volumes, they proposed to give me a hundred pounds for the first edition, and a certain fee for superintending every subsequent impression. I could have wished, now as well as at an earlier period, to have attempted some composition of a more

ambitious kind, by which any powers I might possess for the ornamental branches of literature would have been fairly tested.

Early in 1826 occurred those distresses in the publishing world,
which so completely altered the prospects of many an author, and,
among others, ruined the greatest of them all. Nevertheless, as the
book I was engaged upon seemed of a sure kind, I was encouraged to
proceed with it, and accordingly commenced a course of reading in
Scottish topography and antiquities. Before proceeding far in this
study, I found that it would be impossible to describe the country with
accuracy or animation from the reports of others, many of which were
rendered incorrect by recent improvements; and, though no such plan
was calculated upon in my bargain with the publishers, I resolved to
acquaint myself personally with my native land by a complete survey
on foot. Having for this purpose taken extraordinary pains to obtain
a pair of easy shoes, which I never formerly had, I began my peregri-
nations in March, and during the ensuing season was fully five months
absent, in which time I travelled upwards of two thousand miles,
mostly on foot, and spent more than half of the sum which I was to
receive for my book. During these walks, I suffered much from the
heat, which it will be remembered was of unexampled intensity, and
from many other causes. I nevertheless persevered with an unbroken
spirit, consoling myself for every hardship by reflecting that the fa-
miliarity I was acquiring with the surface of my native country and the
manners of its inhabitants would perhaps prove of service to me in
subsequent literary undertakings. It was a curious proof of the exten-
sibility of all human powers by use, that though I had previously
feared to encounter a walk of two or three miles, on account of my
unfortunate lameness, I became so hardened before the close of my
travels, as to walk on one occasion forty-one miles (from Douglas to
Edinburgh) in nine hours and forty minutes, stoppages included. At
every considerable place, I delivered one or more letters of introduction, which I had obtained in town, and was favoured with the services
of intelligent individuals in showing and explaining to me whatever
was worthy of general attention. I also collected from the conversations of rustics and others innumerable local anecdotes and traditions,
which, along with the drawings of the principal objects, I carefully
treasured up in my note books. The whole enabled me to compile a
book, which was published at the beginning of the year 1828, in two
volumes, under the title of *The Picture of Scotland*.

The composition of this work was in reality finished early in 1827,
when I commenced a popular history or narrative of the Rebellion of
1745-6, designing to sell it when finished to the best advantage. Mr

Archibald Constable was now beginning his Miscellany of original and selected works, and, on my apprising him of the design, did me the honour to say that he would include my work in his list, and allow me thirty pounds a volume for writing it. This sum I refused, not from any immediate hope of receiving more from another publisher, but from pique at finding that he was more liberal to individuals who had not hitherto written any successful book, and whose superior position in the world seemed their only pretension to a higher recommendation. Mr Constable however died in June 1827, and some months after my *History of the Rebellion* – for so it was called, although I never aspired to higher honour than that of writing a narrative – was purchased by his representatives for one hundred pounds, and published in October. The success of this work was very great: it was three or four times reprinted, and proved, as I have been informed, of some service in recommending the Miscellany in various quarters. By minute research into events, and the charm of local and historical association, I endeavoured to render it a vivid portraiture of the insurrection and all its external circumstances, at the same time that it called for the sympathies of the modern reader on behalf of a gallant prince and a primitive and heroic race of people. In fact, this was a history written with the unction of a poem or an historical romance; and, if it had not been deformed by some extravagancies of reflection and sentiment attributable to my juvenile years and imperfect acquaintance with the world, it would have perhaps attained a higher degree of success than even that which I have so gratefully to acknowledge.

In May of this year, I moved from the place of business in which I had been since 1822, to one of larger dimensions, and more imposing exterior, in the centre of the New Town. The former place remained, however, in the occupation of a younger brother, along with a stock partly made up from those belonging to William and myself, and partly purchased by one of the copyrights of my books. At the former place, I had, as already stated, no apartment besides the shop, which did not in any direction measure above sixteen feet. I had therefore written my *Traditions of Edinburgh, Picture of Scotland*, and other works, in an open place of resort, where I was liable every minute to be called to some trivial duty, or where, if I did not attend in person to my customers, I was at least exposed to hear all that passed between them and my young assistant. To those who write in comfortable and secluded libraries, it may appear almost incredible that a sequence of ideas should have been maintained in such a scene; yet so much do habit and strong necessity to reconcile men to disadvantageous situations that I do not recollect feeling, on any occasion, either annoyance at the interruptions, or a difficulty in resuming a train of thought, however delicate, after it had been broken off by even the most grotesque and incongruous intrusion. I always felt that business, if it did not hold forth the prospect of so quick a rise in literature, was too valuable an auxiliary, and too necessary as a retreat, to be in the least neglected for the sake of study; it would have, moreover, been disreputable to abandon, or appear to abandon, any branch of livelihood which the common world around me was, even from prejudice, disposed to look upon as the surest; and hence my difficulty was not so much to apologise to literature for the ungracious treatment which it received from trade, as to excuse to trade the abstraction of part of my mental energies in favour of literature. Of course I could not in such a situation have been a poet – could not have perhaps written a novel or a philosophical essay, at least not without a far greater neglect of business, and a fretting under its paltry details. So effectually, however, did I command my mind to the species of literature which I had chosen, that I recollect in one day writing twenty-six pages of by no means widely disposed manuscript – attending at the same time to such matters of traffic opposite in subject and character to the matter I had in hand. In my new shop, I not only had a more lucrative kind of business, but was also enabled to sit apart in a back-room, so that I did not require to mingle in the affairs of the shop, except when I thought it indispensably necessary. At all times, however, till the year 1830, I was obliged to write in places more or less the reverse of secluded; and I have only further to remark on this point, that, though I certainly was brought in this way, and by other compulsory circumstances, into a habit of applying to humbler objects than my innate feelings would have dictated, the result has upon the whole been favourable, inasfar as it has enforced upon me that patience under what is distasteful and annoying, which I originally set out with as my only patrimony, and had all along found of the greatest benefit in life.

The gradual improvement of my business and stock in trade, along with a course of (to me) lucrative employment in writing for Constable's Miscellany, enabled me in 1829 to aim, without imprudence, at forming a matrimonial engagement. This was an object which had animated me from my earliest years, even when my fancy had no reigning queen; and I never professed any other sentiment on the subject than that a disinterested alliance should be formed by every individual, as soon as he could rationally convince himself that it was convenient. To this virtuous ambition *before* marriage, and a desire *since* to support my little household in the best manner within my power, are in a great measure to be attributed any industry for which

the world may have given me credit. Early in the year just mentioned,
I become acquainted with a young lady ...

Part 3

MY DEAR MADAM

Chapter XX

The letters that follow have been in the possession of one of Robert's descendants for years, but because of their illegibility have probably not been read within living memory. Robert wrote at great speed and seldom revised anything. Indeed Sir Walter Scott, writing in 1829, said, 'Chambers is a clever young man but hurts himself by too much haste.'

Anne Kirkwood came from Perthshire. Her father, John Kirkwood of Perth, had been a well-known clock-maker and engraver, two crafts which often went together in the days when an engraved face was one of the most important things about a clock. In 1829 Anne was nineteen and both her parents were dead. She seems to have come under the protection of an aunt who lived in Edinburgh, and to have been engaged as governess or companion to an aristocratic family. She was considered a notable beauty, and was certainly an excellent pianist. Moreover her aunt owned a harp, and all accounts agree that Anne played it with great skill and flair.

To make some allusions in the first few letters intelligible, it should be said that a certain Captain Charles Gray of the Royal Marines had been paying his respects to her for some time. 'The Captain', as Robert refers to him, was by all accounts a cheerful and friendly soul, and in poetical terms decidedly an enthusiast. A small volume of his poems had already been published, and he would later write ballads and hearty Jacobite songs. Anne Kirkwood and her harp soon had the Captain in thrall, and she began to be assailed by his sledgehammer verses:

> Gallants a', beware o' Annie!
> Gallants a', beware o' Annie!
> Love's deep wyle lurks in her smile,
> Her ilka glance is far frae cannie! . . .
>
> O ne'er was breathed so sweet a lay!
> Still o'er the notes my memory lingers;
> As swelled the strain – syne died away
> Like harp strings touched by fairy fingers.
>
> Gallants a', etc.

Since that sweet night nae rest hae I –
I think, I speak, I dream about her;
To win her favour I maun try,
For O! I canna live without her!

Gallants a', etc.

Three days before Robert started writing to Anne, the Captain had
composed an 'Address to the Shade of Burns' for the Irvine Burns
Club dinner:

Hail Burns! my native Bard, sublime;
Great master of our Doric rhyme!
Thy name shall last to latest time,
    And unborn ages
Shall listen to the magic chime
    Of thy enchanting pages!

and so on – for fourteen stanzas. The trouble is that to any ear familiar
with Burns the thing trips over itself in the last line where Gray has
unaccountably introduced an extra foot.

The Captain left this poem for Anne to read, and she somewhat
mischievously sent it on to Robert, asking him how she ought to
respond. The first letter contains his reply, but things turn out not
quite as he intended.

To Miss Kirkwood
14 Royal Circus

48 Hanover Street
Jan 27 1829

My Dear Madam,

I'm vexed to the last degree that I missed you tonight, as I
am sure, if I had been here, I would have succeeded in win-
ning the influence. You astonish me by the strange insinu-
ation you hint regarding my dusky and dirty, but innocent
back room; a place which never harboured a malicious
thought against any mortal living, but which rather, like a
certain lady, according to my mother's description, is 'by far
too slatternly to be ill natured'. Possibly, some demon may
have taken up his abode in it, upon the same principle by
which Satan long ago colleagued with the oldest and ugliest of
your admired sex. But if such be the case, I say with a clear
conscience that I have nothing to do with him. He is no

servant or apprentice of mine.

The Captain's Poem is a puzzling matter. It is not good – not even worthy of himself. However, say something like the following: 'Your verses for Burns's Birthday are, in my poor opinion, written in a very fine strain of sentiment. They are a worthy tribute from one poet to another – from a living and breathing man of this world to a brother who has gone before him into the house of death. You have displayed great taste, I think, in adopting Burns's own favourite Doric measure, which is finely suited to the subject; and, if I may venture further criticism on a matter which perhaps lies beyond my proper sphere, I would say that the measure is greatly improved by the Alexandrine innovation which you have seen fit to make in it. The length of the final lines gives a pleasing elegiac tone to the whole poem, which I cannot sufficiently admire. They are like the pedal in the harp and piano.'

This will make the Captain very proud, and yet you do not compromise your sincerity. He is a fine little man, and it would really be cruel to disturb his poetic enthusiasm which is perhaps the only charm of his life. Besides, he does possess a share of that *divinus afflatus* – that inspiration above what this world can bestow, which ordinary mortals like us are called upon by all the gods to regard with veneration. Even a leaf of the chaplet of Apollo is an object worthy of admiration.

I think the other poem very good indeed. It is a pretty little lyric. In expectation of your visit on Saturday, I am,

my dear Miss K.
Yours most faithfully
R Chambers

February 17 1829

My Dear Madam,

I have received your packet, containing Captain Gray's letter and your own, the former of which, in accordance with your request, I return enclosed. The Captain is really an amusing body, with his poetry, and compliment, and self conceit, and good humour. Yet I am almost sorry to laugh at his little foibles, because, after all, he is upon the whole an estimable and worthy man – to say nothing of the poetic talent he professes. I am glad to find that the critiques I dictated for you on his songs have gone off so well. They

never could have done so, I am afraid, had his accustomed
penetration not been neutralised by the praise. – You surprise
me much by what you say of going away with Mr Hamilton
on Saturday. I never thought of considering the thing strange
till you confessed something like conscious guilt on the
subject. I do not even now see that it was strange – unless you
insist upon thinking it so yourself. In that case, I will grant it
to have been strange. And you call Mr H. nobody too! Ah,
Miss K., I'm afraid there is somebody at Musselburgh who
does not think so. In my opinion, Mr Hamilton is a pretty
substantial sort of nobody. But be he what he likes, or what
the world likes, there could be no harm in going away with
him on Saturday. – I am much concerned to hear of your low
spirits and your hoarseness. But I hope they will both go
away soon. As a sort of lenitive for both in the meantime – or
rather by way of a humble attempt on my part to amuse you
in your distress, I enclose the scribble of a ludicrous poem I
wrote the other day.[27] It is an imitation or converse of one
which Mr Bell published on Saturday in his Journal under the
title of 'The Tall Gentleman's Apology'; and I undertook it in
consequence of a request on his part, and with a view to it
appearing in the same paper. It is not nearly as good as his;
but I have been flattering myself with the idea that the
circumstance is chiefly owing to his having gone before me,
and picked up all the best ideas which the subject presents.
Please to pardon my bad manners in sending such a blurred
sheet, instead of writing out a clean copy. My guilt arises
rather from want of time than from anything else; a reason
that you, who are acquainted with the domestic politics of my
back shop, must be prepared to appreciate. – Why, in the
name of the fates, has it happened that your dinner party
takes place, of all the days of the week, on Thursday, seeing
that I am engaged on that date to dine out, and will, I'm
afraid, scarcely be able to return to the shop in time to see
you? This is truly unfortunate for I would have liked so very
much to receive the visit you so kindly design me. Let me see,
however. Suppose you were to call at about half past eight, or
from that to a quarter before nine? I may perhaps be able to
escape by that time. Let me know if you think you can do so,
and I will endeavour to get away. I may at least absent myself
for an hour, perhaps. In such a case, it will not be necessary
that you should wait for me. If I fail to be in the shop at the

time stipulated, you will understand that I cannot get away, and you will therefore only ask if I be at home. Excuse this solicitude about a trifling arrangement. It is altogether owing to my wish that you should not experience the least distress in any matter connected with me – not the least, the very least.

> I remain,
> My Dear Miss Kirkwood,
> Yours most truly
> R Chambers

February 24 1829

My Dear Miss Kirkwood, (for I suppose I must no longer say Madam,)

I was excessively chagrined at receiving your note containing your refusal to go to the Exhibition; and I write this to entreat that you will alter your resolution and go next Saturday. In the hope that you will do so I have all this time denied myself the pleasure of seeing the Scottish Academy, purely that I might see it for the first time along with you. You must really consent to come. I will take it very ill if you don't. Nay, I don't know but I will fall into a passion if you persist in refusing; and you know that would be a terrible thing for a person of my stoical temperament. It would be so much more dreadful in my case than in an ordinary one, as it were more difficult to smoothe over a frozen lake once broken than to tranquillize the surface of the sea which the breeze had stirred a little.

I beg a thousand pardons for misunderstanding you about the Thursday night business. You must think me a vain creature to be always interpreting what you say so much in my own favour. As you, however, are so good as to ask me to forgive you for some fault which you think I might impute you, (although God knows I am unperceptive of any), I beg to propose that we should draw scores and pass a mutual act of oblivion and indemnity. If you will pardon me for my real faults, I will most willingly forgive you for all your imaginary ones.

I had a call from the Captain the other day, and heard him tell with rapture about your criticisms. But the stupid body, would you believe it, had not understood the simile about the pedal, which was by far the best idea in the whole. Any how, he has an exceptionally high notice of you. I don't know but he is absolutely in love with you.

Whenever yet was bard unmoved
When beauty smiled or birth approved,

James Hogg says, and I suspect he's not far wrong. One thing I'm sure of; the shortest road to the Captain's heart is to praise his verses. But, after all, I suspect the Captain's heart is at present on half-pay – laid up in dock – out of commission – something like himself. So you need not be in a flutter.

You speak to me with a great deal of candour in your letter, and I have certainly great reason to be pleased with the kind approbation which you confess for me. It would be an affectation to abstain from informing you how much I am gratified by your good opinion. I *am* excessively gratified – let that be enough. 'A sudden thought strikes me,' as the one democrat says to the other in one of Mr Cummings' satires; 'let us swear eternal friendship.' You must look upon me as your sworn friend, your *beau chevalier*; and in that character I will endeavour to repay the extreme kindness with which you have treated me during our short acquaintance. Be, therefore, no longer under any apprehension of ever saying anything to offend me or make me think less of you. Being sworn friends, we must be blind to each other's faults, even supposing that either of us had any, which I very much doubt. – This paper, I must say, is not very favourable to friendship, for it scarcely affords room to say how truly I am yours Robert Chambers.

March 3 1829

Dear Miss Kirkwood,

In the hush of night – at two o'clock in the morning – after having spent about eight hours in almost incessant study – I seize a piece of paper of a size somewhat more auspicious to friendship than what I last adopted, and begin to answer to your gracious beneficent heart-fraught letter. First, and above all things, how much genuine pleasure do I feel in receiving your acceptance of my friendship! It gives me a pleasure which I cannot describe, but which I am sure is of a pure and most disinterested character. I feel, in receiving your friendship and knowing that you appreciate mine, what I suppose must be the gratification resulting from greatly good actions in the bosoms of those who are enabled by fortune to do them: the pleasure of utter virtue. The only thing that at all distracts from my satisfaction is a fear, a lurking impossible fear that you had formed a hasty and imperfect notion of my character, and may afterwards find reason to think less of me, and to withdraw your friendship. Not that I am conscious of any defects of an extraordinary description, but that I fear no character, however worthy, can be worthy of the very high praise and honour which you are conferring upon me. I fear I am all too rude, too commonplace, too little endowed with external grace, to retain an order of merit which seems to have been thrown over my neck, as Bonaparte threw his collars over the favourite man who performed any sudden deed of heroism, without a proper consideration of my ability to wear it worthily. Somebody says in Latin – pulcrum est laudari a laudato – it is a pleasure to be praised by those who have been themselves esteemed worthy of praise. But, surely, in the case of a mind not possessed of a very firm self appreciation, a cause of distress must sometimes arise from the very merit of the praisegiver. It may be like the poor beggar in the Arabian Nights Entertainments, who, on being seized and dressed and fed sumptuously in a great man's house, could not help fearing that the very menials employed so busily in offices of kindness about his person were to punish him eventually for the strange mistake they seemed to be now committing.

I must, however, beg to pardon for this fearfulness, which I dare say will appear to you very much like the awkwardness of the rustic child who sidles into a corner on finding 'a grand lady' unexpectedly sitting in the room with his mother, and looks with terror at the fair hand held out to fondle him. I assure you, whether it be a silly thing or not, it is a real feeling of the nerves, not an affectation of the understanding.

Now that I think on it – here is a plan for stilling all my fears on this score. Let me accept of your friendship only on this provision, that if you find reason to reduce the high notion you seem to have formed of me, it must be done with a regard to my protest – which is, that I was always afraid from the very beginning that I should be found wanting in the balance, and consequently claim to be held as having lost nothing, and not to be esteemed as degraded, but only as never having risen. With that understanding, and thus prepared to decline gracefully back to the station which I have hitherto occupied, I accept with thankfulness and pleasure of the exalted office to which you have raised me.

To speak of inferior matters, I have to say that I waited at the shop on Saturday night, till twenty minutes past ten, when, thinking that you must have abandoned your scheme, I locked up and went off. What a pity that I did not wait a few minutes longer; and – what a still greater pity that I should have gone away from your aunt's delightful party so soon for nothing! I might have as well spent the hour with you there, and by that means possibly have found some little opportunities of conversing with you on the subject you were so anxious to have discussed. But you must just make up for all the cross purposes of the night, at once, on Saturday next, by coming with me to the Exhibition of the Institution, which you have not yet seen. I will wait the whole day at the shop to receive you. By the way, do not scruple to call any day during the daytime from an idea that you occupy my time, for it is only at night that I shall be doing anything that requires close attention during this and the next week.

I am obliged by your anxiety regarding my health; but it is in the great measure unnecessary. I always stop whenever I find the least distress from exertion. I adopt the plan of working by night from motives of economy – economy of time, I mean. It is necessary, in order to get on clearly with the work I have in hand, that I should have a great deal of time at once, or in one uninterrupted period – say eight hours – to afford a space for the study of authorities, and another space for the committal of results to paper. The period of eight hours thus enables me to do more than I could do in forty or fifty isolated hours with space between. I expect, if nothing occurs to prevent me, to have the volume I am now engaged with, finished in two months; otherwise it would require half a year at least.

I had a call yesterday from the Captain, who gave me such an account of the last hour of your aunt's party as filled me with chagrin and regret. Miller, it seems, sang a great deal more, and most delightfully. You must, you *must* make all this up to me some other time. By the way, the Captain said nothing about the affair of the letter; so I think he must have pardoned it. Indeed, he could scarcely fail to do so; for on Saturday night, I gave him such a flattering account of it – a sincere one, too, mark me – that he must now be rather glad that you showed it to me than anything else.

And now, Miss Anne, I have really no more to say, except that

> I am
> most sincerely yours,
> R Chambers.

PS As you have given me a hint about my paper I may also give you a hint about yours. You should make up your letters in such a way as to leave no part of the writing visible from the outside. A word to the wise etcetera.

March 11 1829

Mr Sharpe, a Roman Catholic clergyman with whom I lately dined at a mutual friend's house, has been so very polite as to send me three tickets of admission to the Chapel tomorrow, when a grand funeral service, with Mozart music, takes place in honour of the late Pope. It has struck me, my dear Miss Kirkwood, that you who are so fond of music and yourself so excellent a musician may take some interest in such an affair, and I accordingly make you offer by these presents, as the lawyers say, of one of the tickets. I propose to take one of my sisters with the remaining ticket, which will afford me an opportunity of introducing two young ladies to each other, who, I think, would make excellent friends. Do endeavour by all means to come. I assure you Mr Sharpe's politeness is not to be sneered at: the tickets are sold to the general public at half a crown each; a circumstance which also assures good company and a perfectly convenient access to the chapel.

I must confess I make this offer with a reservation. I have somehow caught cold in one of the glands of my throat, which has given me some uneasiness during the day, and may possibly – scarcely possibly – make it imprudent for me to go out tomorrow. Now, in the case that all the nine hundred and ninety-nine chances in my favour are passed over by Fate, and the thousandth against me pitched upon: – in plain English, if I should chance to be unable to go with you, you will have no objection to accepting my younger brother James as a substitute. I need scarcely say, after our vows of friendship, that it will only be a regard for life itself which

shall make me forgo, what is almost next to life most agreeable to me, your company.

In case you cannot come, may I beg to have a line of
excuse from you before the hour? If you can come, come at a
quarter to eleven, to the shop, where I shall be.

Ever truly and faithfully
yours,
R Chambers.

10 St Andrew's Street
March 12 1829

My Dear Miss Kirkwood,

I have just received your card, and am sorry you could not
go both for your sake and my own, as I had given William
and Margaret directions to bring you up here to settle about
the ball tonight, in which case I would have been in some
measure consoled for the impossibility of attending you
tonight by seeing you. Fortune, alas, has declared against me.
My throat is not any better today, and my physician advises
me not to go out tonight. It is the most unfortunate thing in
the world, but it might be worse if I were to go out. You
therefore must excuse me. I have made a scheme of compensation for you. If you have no objection, my elder brother
William will come to India Street at the time I was to come,
and ask for you; his mentioning his name will be a sufficient
introduction; and he will squire you to the ball. As it was a
Mr Chambers who sent the card to Miss Greenfield, he will
do quite as well as me, so far as the ladies of the house are
concerned. He will of course wait to conduct you home
again. By the bye, he has one point of superiority over me, as
a companion to a ball: he dances. If you think it necessary
that I should apologise to Miss Greenfield and Miss Montgomery, you and William may perhaps do so for me.

When you call on Saturday – for I do not – cannot question that you will do so – I shall endeavour to complete the
imperfect apology you now receive. Miss Picken has asked
me to accompany her that day to the Pro-Catholic meeting;
but I am told no ladies are admitted, and I therefore shall be
entirely at your service. If you can call early – say about one –
we may perhaps go to the Exhibition. Please to give me some
prefatory notice of your intentions for that day, that I may

know how to proceed in case of having anything else to do or
to attend to.

> Believe me, my dear Miss Kirkwood,
> Most truly yours, R. Chambers.

March 13 1829

My Dear – 'Miss Kirkwood' and 'Madam' are two cold words
to address you with: so, understand or suppose some warmer
phrase unexpressed. I lean from my bed to answer your kind
letter tonight by my brother this morning. But first let me tell
you, I am much better. By an application of leeches yesternight, and a general reduction of the system by starvation, I
have got the swelling in my throat, and consequently the pain,
very much abated. I am now, my doctor tells me, in a fair way
of recovery. Only, and here comes in the damper, I must keep
close in bed all day, and even perhaps all tomorrow, lest I
should give it fresh irritation. So I cannot promise to see you
at the shop. There, however, is a scheme for compensating
that misfortune.

You must come here tomorrow night, and drink tea with
us. To obviate all the awkwardness of your entrée, my
brother will call for you at your aunt's at a little before six,
and bring you up. You must come alone – that is to say, with
no friend of your own, for that would in a great measure spoil
the project. You will spend the evening with us, and at the
hour when you will require to go home, I will perhaps be
permitted to accompany you, or at least my brother will do
so. This scheme might appear awkward at first sight; but it is
not so, when the circumstances are examined. My mother,
indeed, and my sister, both individually suggested the
scheme; (I of course had it all cut and dry in my own head
before); so there can be nothing wrong in it. They are all very
anxious to see you, and prepared to be very proud of you.
More so this morning than before. Formerly, they only heard
me praise you – and that always with a cautious moderation.
They have now heard William talk of you in a much warmer
style. And, as he is a person of far more strict temperament
than I am, they are disposed to pay more deference to his
opinion. You may therefore be quite at your ease in coming
in the way I propose.

The house to which you will be brought is a hotel.[28] My
mother keeps it. She is a widow, and a woman of extremely

active disposition; she is also of a very independent turn of mind; and she has a family of whom only the elder half win their own bread. All these reasons conspire to make her prefer such a mode of life to any other which my elder brother and I can propose to her. The utmost that she will allow us to do for her is to support her with all our power in the business of her adoption. You must therefore, my dearest Miss Anne, be prepared to feel no surprise at the sort of lodgings in which you find me.

A few words, if you please, about my brothers and sisters. William is every way a good fellow, except in one – that, from constant application to mere business and seeing little of society in its more familiar aspects, he has acquired a stern intolerance of the forms of good breeding, which he considers trifling; and thus he sometimes – for it is only sometimes – gives offence when his better nature does not intend it. I do not say this to make you think little of him, but rather to explain away what I consider a very slight defect, and to guard you against taking up a bad opinion of him on account of it. Margaret, my elder sister, is a most worthy sober unpretending character – possessed, I think, of little genius, but estimable in a high degree on account of her high feeling of honour and her good principles. James is a clever boy of 20, with a turn for sly caustic remark. Janet, my younger sister, is the cleverest of the whole family. The wit, the acuteness, the comprehensive sense of this girl are astonishing. She also possesses, what must in all persons be considered a still better quality, good temper – superior temper even to Margaret. She is very much alive to praise; to secure approbation, she will do anything. Her age is sixteen, and she is full of all the delightful qualities proper to that age in woman. I am sure if Janet had been born of another sex, and therefore able to push her way in the world, she would have cut a most distinguished figure.

This matter being settled, it now only remains for me to await the hours till I shall see you, and to form anticipatory visions of the happenings I shall enjoy in your presence. Also, my dear Miss Anne, if you would form the least idea of the state of my feelings yesternight when I should have been with you, I lay prostrate and in pain, unable to think of anything but you, and unable to sleep for thinking of you, the whole night. Busy fancy represented to me every successive scene through which I could suppose you would be passing. At nine, a little after my brother went away, I supposed the scene of his entering the house and speaking to you. From nine to ten, I conceived him engrossed in the splendours of the ball, and in your delightful conversation. I then supposed you and him leaving the house, and walking together towards Clarence Street; and oh how I envied this part of his happiness! All the night after, till he came home, I could only form phantasmagoria-like scenes of the grand ball, and of your appearance there. When he at last came, I traced you to your own house and supposed you composing yourself to that quiet innocent sleep which spirits like yours must always enjoy – disturbed only, perhaps, (pardon the vanity,) by a regretful thought upon me. (No, it is not vanity – it is only one of the natural demands of friendship.) It was only when I had allowed what I conceived a sufficient time for your falling asleep, that I could procure the least repose. I then slept – but it was from sympathy – it was because I thought you would be sleeping too – because I wished to meet you in dreams.

This was my history for the night; and so this morning brought me the transport of a letter from you – a letter calculated by its endearing expressions, by its – oh I cannot tell what – to alleviate all the tedium and distress of my sickbed, though it had been ten times worse. Bless, bless your kind heart for the feelings which caused you to write such a letter!

> I am,
> my dear Miss Anne,
> with the utmost gratitude, affection and respect,
> yours most truly R. Chambers

P.S. Five o'clock. I am now so much better than ever I was when I began this letter that I strongly hope to be at the shop tomorrow. Therefore, my dear Miss A, call there as soon as you can, and take your chance of seeing me. It will just be so much gained.

Second PS. Six o'clock. Another burst of sunlight on the darkness of my soul and its place – another letter! A thousand thanks for your plan of seeing me. It is a good plot, a very good plot as Hotspur says; but it cannot well be carried into execution. My mother and both of the girls will be so much occupied tomorrow in preparing for the reception of a large dinner party, that they cannot see you at the early hour you mention.

March 15 1829

From my chamber – Sunday morning – seven o'clock

Ma chère Amie,

My interview with you yesternight was preceded by so many circumstances calculated to agitate me and was itself so short and so full of unprofitable discussion, that I left you at last in a most dissatisfied and dejected condition. As I walked homewards, I believe I could have fought, as people say, with a fly. If any man had but jostled me, I am sure I would have knocked him down, or attempted to do so. I not only felt my mind disordered, but my very flesh – every nerve – was in a state of tumult which I cannot describe.

When by involuntary instinct my steps had led me to St Andrew's Street, I thought I could have much rather gone to (hide ?) in some lone Arctic sea-cave than enter a dwelling of domestic peace and social happiness. If it were profitable for men to shift up and down the scale of latitude, according to the temperature of their minds, and so as to settle in such a climate as was exactly suitable thereto, I would have yester-night sat beneath the North Pole. I could think of nothing save the dreary period which was to elapse before I would again see you, and in particular of the dreary tomorrow. I could do nothing but make myself miserable. At length midnight came, and I went – no, it was not to *repose*. As a sort of compensation for my distress, I took out all your letters from their bosom place in my clothes, and there I lay for an hour, reading them, kissing them, and bedewing them with my tears. They have lain beneath my head all night, and my first action after awaking was to seize them and press them to my lips. They are dear to me beyond all costly possessions. They assure me that I am an object of solicitude and tender regard to one of the most worthy and amiable of women; and in so assuring me, I can only consider them as a sort of diploma or passport to perfect happiness. Before becoming known to you, and before receiving these letters, I used to consider myself happy in the advance I had made by my own exertions from the humblest possible fortune to a situation in life not contemptible, and from the utmost obscurity to something like literary distinction; I used to live happily in the satisfaction arising from a perfectly inoffensive life, and from finding the endeavours I made to gain the goodwill of my fellow creatures not ineffectual. But you have

opened a new and higher heaven of happiness to my view.
You have possessed my heart with pleasurable feelings which
it never before knew. All that is past seems lame and poor and
incomplete; all that is before, being seen through you, looks
rich and Elysian. Were I successful in an object of ambition
ten times higher than any I ever cherished; were I chosen out
of thousands to be honoured of men above all others; were I
to be the gainer of another Waterloo, or the writer of another
Waverley; nothing – no one of all these matters of triumph
could be so dear, so precious to me as this simple assurance of
your affection.

In explanation of what I have just written, permit me to
say that I have oftener than once, or twice either, admired
individuals of your sex with a sort of poetical admiration, and
been, as the world says in a general way, in love. These
affections, however, though of course the world could not
discriminate the real character, were nothing but fits of
poetical admiration – often, indeed, assumed willingly, for the
very purpose of making the lady serve as the heroine of a few
verses which I wished to write. They were only the heroines
of a night or day – and even that only by fiction. You are
calculated, in my estimation, to be the heroine of a life, and
that in very reality. The reason is, (without the least regard to
your superior merit,) that in your case affection is mutual.
There lies all the charm of my acquaintance with you.

I find I cannot work today. My spirit could not be confined to the desk. It would be perpetually flying away towards you. I may therefore just as well go abroad at once, and
idle away the day with something like pleasure, as stay at
home and only attempt to employ myself. I will watch to see
you go to church, and go there too. Perhaps I may be so
happy as to find a seat within sight of yours. Perhaps I may
catch your eyes. That *would* – that *would* – be happiness!
Possibly, I may even be impelled near you by the crowd in
coming out, and thus be able to touch your hand and exchange a word with you. Oh nay, with the least of these
pieces of good fortune – one but one kind glance of your
eyes, I could live for the rest of the day; and when once the
business-days of the week have commenced, I am safe. Will
you gratify me?

To conclude – if there be anything in this letter which
seems to your delicate perceptions as too violent in expres-

sion, or which can on any other account be interpreted with a
character of offence, may I hope to be forgiven? It is the
sincerest and honestest letter that man could write; it is
written in the vehemence of an incontrovertible passion: its
purpose is disinterested – is honourable – is governed by a
regard for your own good. Need I then bespeak forgiveness?

I am, my dearest dearest Anne, votre cher ami,

R Chambers]

PS I enclose the scroll – another blotted scroll – of a poem
which I wrote yesterday morning under the influence of the
happy feelings arising from the expectation of seeing you here
at night. It is a ridiculous, but a natural idea. What heroine
there is in it, is you. That is to say, in making out the idea of a
woman whom I suppose myself loving, I used some portions
of your person. Some of it is otherwise – for the sake of the
rhyme!

Thou gentle and kind one,
    Who com'st o'er my dreams,
Like the gales of the west,
    Or the music of streams;
Oh, softest and dearest
    Can that time e'er be,
When I could be forgetful
    Or scornful of thee?

No! my soul might be dark,
    Like a landscape in shade,
And for thee not the half
    Of its love be displayed.
But one ray of thy kindness
    Would banish my pain,
And soon kiss every feature
    To brightness again.

And if in contending
    With men and the world,
My eye might be fierce
    Or my brow might be curled,
That brow on thy bosom
    All smoothed would recline,
And that eye melt in kindness
    When turned upon thine.

If faithful in sorrow,
    More faithful in joy –
Thou should'st find that no change
    Could affection destroy;
All profit, all pleasure,
    As nothing would be,
And each triumph despised,
    Unpartaken by thee.

                                    March 17 1829

My dearest Anne,
    I received no injury from being out on Saturday night and
Sunday except what arises from the reflection that I had
approached you with my extravagances. Extravagant I know I
have been though I am now at a loss to recollect how. The
history of my life between Thursday last and yesterday
morning seems to me, as I now stand, to have been a hurried,
wild, tempestuous dream. Weakened in my mind by indispo-
sition, disappointed of an enjoyment on which I had formerly
set my heart, abstracted from the world and its rules of
conduct, given up entirely to one idea which had before only
possessed me partially, I was then more, or less, than myself. I
know that I have acknowledged to you a warmer feeling of
regard than I ever did before. That I remember, and *that I
could now repeat*. But all the other transactions of the period
appear to me like something which I have dreamt or read of
in a romance, and not as a matter in which I was concerned
personally and in my proper character of mortal man. All this
I say that you may find it more easy to forgive anything that
requires to be forgiven in my bearing towards you during my
fever of sentiment. Women would really require to be of
forgiving temper, for, with and without their will, they cause
men to do very strange things.
    I will, my dearest Anne, attend to your requests, which
reason now permits me to see are prudent. I, indeed, find it
must be as necessary in my past as in yours that we should
either know *more* or *less* of each other. The hours I spend in
forming visions of your future visits and recalling recollections of your past ones; the general relaxation of mind which
the thought of you occasions to me; are the most fatal possible to my usual habits of application, and will, if continued,

cause me to think shame of myself as less prudent at nearly seven and twenty than I was at seventeen. I was never before so little master of myself, so unable to command my attention to its proper objects. I begin to feel as if the fabric of good repute which I have been ten or twelve years a-building, were now giving way and tottering beneath my feet. I'm afraid to look the world in the face; for I know myself to be falling beneath the standard of prudence which I had formerly established for myself. This must be checked. My mother used always to prophesy that if ever I were married I would write no more books; but I find the same result almost effected by a mere acquaintance with a young lady, which the said young lady calls friendship. Ah, this friendship! Well might Byron say that, in two young persons of opposite sexes, it was 'love full fledged and ready to fly away.' It is a mere disguise – the most specious deceiver on earth. I think I once told you that I looked upon friendship as a most con-temptible thing. I do so still. I have never found it a thing of the least account. Whatever friendships I have ever had with my fellow men, have only been contracts for mutual conven-ience or amusement. I assure you, my dear Anne, friendship is an inadequate, imperfect thing. It wants object and withers. It requires love to give it sincerity or truth or steadfastness, just as a wall requires mortar to make it hold. But perhaps the real cause of why people never find friendship to be what they expected is that they expect so much from it. They expect from an inferior and temporary sentiment what is only possessed by a superior and more enduring one. They ask for bread at a place where there are only stones.

However, I shall say more of this when I see you on Saturday; and oh for that day!

You will perhaps think the tone of this letter colder than that of the former. It may be so, but it proceeds from the same heart that addressed you on Sunday last, a heart that, I believe, must ever remain equally warm to you. I am now more engaged in the affairs of the world and therefore less extravagant in my expressions. Why should I write warmly to you any more? Does the traveller who has seen Etna and Vesuvius in their fiery (. . . ?) require to carry a paper-full of their ashes always in his pocket as a means of bringing the impressions to his recollection? No. We can understand each other, or will soon be able to do so from a few personal interviews. Writing now so many letters would scarcely make us so well acquainted as one interview.

I am much amused, (among other feelings,) with your request about my name. Do you know I like phrases of ceremony in addressing and being addressed, and can scarcely endure to be called by my bare name by anybody. I will, however, gratify you on your taste. I have pondered over a great number of classical names for you – as 'sister Anne' from Blue Beard, and 'Sweet Mistress Anne' from the *Merry Wives of Windsor*. But none of them are happy. I have also started a fictitious or rather a descriptive epithet for you,[29] which I apply when anxious to avoid the necessity of using your real name. By this name you are known and spoken of at home, also by Captain Gray and Mr Hamilton. I do not know whether I should tell you what it is or not. It is complimentary, or at least intended to be so. But perhaps you have the same prejudice against sobriquets that I have against naked Christian names.

I saw the Captain today, (for he has yet a few dinners to eat in Edinburgh,) and I took the liberty of apologising to him for your non transmission of an apology or card on Sunday last, which apology he has graciously accepted. So you are safe with the Captain. He tells me he is to go away for certain on Thursday. Before then, you may possibly get a card written to him. To conclude this strange letter – believe me, my dearest Anne, I am sensible in the highest degree of the value of what you say in reply to my addresses of Sunday. I am also deeply sensible of the prudence and discretion of your requests, and I shall most scrupulously attend to them. It gives me shame to think that I, a man of the world, and of not the greenest age, should be taught lessons by such a juvenile and so inexperienced a person as you, but with this feeling there goes along a palliative – a willing and most delightful admiration of the good sense which stands as a governing principle over your affections.

Farewell. I am altogether and most affectionately yours
R. Chambers

P.S. Don't let what I say about friendship disturb you. You have not yet got the tinge of the boarding school off your mind, or you would never have talked of such things. Nevertheless I hope I am not and never will be so sagacious and severe a man as to ridicule the amicable though mistaken feelings of youth. Long may you preserve such feelings. The world will do all it can to strip you of them.

By the bye, the Glorious One is to be published on Saturday.

Hanover Street
March 25 1829

My dear Anne,

One violation of your rules, if you please, for the sake of an arrangement about our proceedings on Saturday. It has struck me that, instead of your calling for me at the shop, it would be better that I should somewhere wait upon you, and subsequently walk with you towards Mrs Bell's. We should thus avoid the eyes of my retainers here, which I always fear must be somewhat offensive to you; and, as you, in that case, shall not have called upon me in the forenoon, you might, without giving rise to any suspicions, look in upon me in the evening, as you return from Mrs Bell's, at any time you please *before* nine o'clock. By this arrangement, you may have the advantage, perhaps, of more easily shaking off any officious escort which may be attached to you, than if you were to leave Mrs B's at a later hour.

Be pleased, then, my dear Anne, to let me know if you can accede to this proposal and to appoint an hour and place when and where I may attend. If we must meet on the street, depend that I shall be at the place ten minutes before the hour, to ensure you against the necessity of lingering for me.

I am just on the point of going to call for Miss Jane Robinson at your aunt's, to show her some of the public curiosities of Edinburgh. Oh that *you* could accompany us!

Perhaps, you may answer this in a *verbal way*. May I hope? Most faithfully and affectionately thine, R.C.

March 25 1829 (7 pm)

My dear Anne,

You are a most unaccountable creature. You called upon me today in your own proper person (and a proper person it is) about some fiddle faddle of an album; and lo and behold, six hours after that event, I receive a letter stating in the most emphatic terms that you cannot call – that you *will not be able* to do the thing which you *have done*. There is a confusion of tenses in your conduct that absolutely bewilders me; I don't know whether I am a living man, have been a living man, or am to be so. The world is spinning around me. Am I in the world at all? In answer to your letter, I have to say that I shall most certainly call for you at the Circus. That is an excellent arrangement, because it allows me a little more of your delightful company than I would otherwise have. I only regret that the hour of your emancipation should be so late as two. Could you not make it one, and then we should have a detour – a sweep – before going to Elder Street or to Mr Miller's. One hour for certain, and only a chance of another, is really too little for a Saturday. Oh that Mrs Bell! To have occupied you for such a long time – to have withdrawn you from one who would have enjoyed your society so much. I am sure she makes me poor by doing so, without enriching herself – for what can you be to her more than another female acquaintance? And how much more are you to me than all other acquaintances male or female! My dear, dear Anne, you must quit her house soon; you must let me see you again that night. I should expire with chagrin if you don't. Only think what a dreary Sunday I should have next day (in the event of *surviving* Saturday night) and what a tedious week afterwards – a week, too, which, I fear, will not terminate in a satisfactory interview – since you are to be engaged, as you tell me, at Miss Forrest's. Really, this system of only seeing each other once a week, and that with such uncertainty, is most grievous. We must take some measures to have it amended. The worst consideration connected with it is that we are so soon to part more seriously and effectually. Since that is the case, ought we not to make the most of the time which remains to us?

You fear that I shall forget you after you go to (Hallorig?). Dearest Anne, I never shall. If I can at all calculate upon the faith or the feelings that are in me, I am too much devoted to you to prove inconstant. You have my admiration and affection undivided. Shall an absence which, at the worst, can only be temporary, have the effect upon me you anticipate? Have I lived years without loving any woman to be distracted from one I do love by merely losing sight of her for a few weeks? It cannot be. I grant that I have already felt the impression of your image fade a little after having not seen you for a week or two. Business and ambition come in place

of love. The very pain of absence occasions a little oblivious-
ness; for the mind, fretted to madness by the distressing
sensation of the impossibility of seeing the beloved object at
last naturally takes refuge in some other thoughts, which
occupy and mask it for the time. And thus a species of incon-
stancy arises from the very strength of affection. But

    'I'll have you pictured in my breast,
      The ladye that I love'
and will be strangely deceived if aught on earth can obliterate
the image.

    What would I give, my dear Anne, if you were at this
moment by my side! The shop closed – no possibility of
intrusion or supervision – sitting by the fire in the back-room
– that dear back-room – we, at least, I know *I* should be
perfectly happy. In default of yourself, I have all your letters
spread before me – your beautiful dark ringlet in my bosom;
and, next to yourself, these objects are to me dearer than all
others. I was yesternight supping at the house of a widow
lady of my acquaintance, and, remembering that you had
played the Macbeth Quadrilles, I asked her to give me them
on the piano. She did so, and in a moment my breast was
filled with a gush of – blood shall I call it or tumultuous
feeling, the most delightful I ever experienced, and you rose
before me in everything but reality. I asked her to play them
over and over at various periods of the evening and every
time with the same result. The night was to me one of rapture.
The only drawback from my pleasure was that I was at length
absolutely ashamed of myself for indulging to such extent in
so luxurious a pleasure. It is by these little arts, my dear Anne
– by reading your letters, by gazing on your ringlet, by
humming the tunes I have heard you play – that I contrive at
once to support the pain of your personal absence, and to
keep your image entire in my breast. How much more
delightful, to hear you speak, to see you, to see your whole
person, to hear you play these tunes yourself! But fortune
does not allow that, and I must be content – at least in the
meantime.

    But I fear I am only bestowing my tediousness on you. So
bonsoir.

    Most affectionately – most entirely – yours R.C.
PS In consequence of a request from Miss Picken I have sent
the MS. volume to her, to be revised before you get it.

March 30 1829

My dear Anne

I had an interview last night with my chief publisher and best friend, Mr Tait, of Princes Street – the gentleman who came up behind me, you will recollect, and said something to me, on the day we went together to the Exhibition at Waterloo Place. To him I disclosed the secret of my attachment to you (without mentioning names), and at the same time I asked his advice regarding the proper period for the consummation of our attachment. He advised me not to delay, as I intended, till the end of summer, but rather to bring the affair to a crisis as early in the season as possible. I mentioned, in objection to his counsel, that I had some literary speculations in view which might call me a good deal abroad during summer, but he expressed his willingness to engage me as soon as I pleased on a work which would not require my absence from town, and he had at the same time the infinite kindness to offer to facilitate my measures at any time I pleased by giving me money. This has produced an alteration in the scheme I proposed to you on Saturday night – a blessed alteration, for it will enable me to be *perfectly happy* some months *sooner* than I could have hoped for. You must endeavour to call upon me, at the very latest on Wednesday, when I shall disclose the whole scheme as modified. I will take care to have all my near-rank men out of the way at the hour you mention. In the meantime, may I presume so far on our pledged affection as to request that you will make no engagement with Sir Colin Pringle or any other body before that day?

I can have no objection to your consulting any friend you please on the subject now laid before you, to prepare yourself for giving me a decisive answer on Wednesday. I cannot even object to your having a longer time to consider a matter of such importance. At all events, however, you must at least *see* me on the day in question.

Most affectionately and most faithfully

Yours RC

PS I find I have misstated Mr Tait's kind offer. It referred to a work which I have already nearly completed for him but for which the payment would not be due for some time.

March 31 1829

My dear Anne,

I cannot be angry with your letter, because I know that
you cannot have designed to offend me, but are on the
contrary induced to dictate what I have just read by motives
which abstractly I am much disposed to admire – *motives of
prudence*. It is impossible to answer your letter in another
letter. I must see you yourself. I wish very much that you
would come here tonight after nine o'clock. I will be here at
any rate. So, if you can, come; if not, I shall only be miserable
in so far as the disappointment of an ardent hope can make
me miserable. Perhaps it is not easy for you to get away at
such an hour. But if you can at all, I beg and entreat that you
will come. Possibly, by coming away at eight with a promise
to be home before ten, your conduct or request would not be
considered remarkable. I make this request from a strong
desire to argue with you on the scheme you affect to controvert; and surely, since the object is one of such importance,
you will strain a point to gratify me. By all means come. I will
consider your doing so a test of the affection you profess for
me, and I will not fail to reward it accordingly – that is to say,
if I possibly could love you more than I do.

Most affectionately yours,
R Chambers

Hanover Street
April 5, 1829

My dear Anne,

I am going to write you a very grave and rational letter –
one quite different in style from the extravagant ravings
which I have lately addressed to you. It is to consist altogether of a dispassionate consideration of the relation in
which we stand towards each other since your declaration of
yesternight. What you then said gave me much pain at the
time, and it has since excited some surprise. It seems to me
most strange that love in our case, or rather I should say in
yours, should not lead to matrimony. As the paths of glory,
according to Gray, lead but to the grave, so did I always think
that the paths of love could lead to nothing else than marriage. If, as you say, you cannot find that you regard me with
that endeared feeling which is necessary to matrimony, how,

in the name of all that is wonderful in the heavens above, or in
the earth beneath, or in the waters under the earth, did you
ever give me any reason to think that you entertained any
affection for me at all? How, in that case, do you account for
the warm phraseology employed in so many of your letters?
How do you account for your repeated verbal assurances to
that effect? I love you too much to upbraid you, or rather I
love you too much to think that you *can* have done amiss.
But yet some explanation is here necessary. Is it possible that
the sentiment of esteem and affection with which you regarded me as a mere lover, can have suddenly changed to
aversion on my being presented to you in the light of a
husband?

I do not mean, mark me, to impose myself upon you
against your will, or to exercise the least force over your
affections. I have already told you that my love lives entirely
in the idea that you love me. It would die the very moment
you should tell me that yours had never lived. Its strength has
all along been precisely commensurate with my idea of the
strength of yours; and it would sink by precisely the same
degrees. You need not therefore put the least violence upon
yourself from an idea that your rejection would wound me. It
would not, I assure you, in the very least. Love, in my opinion, has not that bigoted prejudice in favour of individuals
which people generally represent it to have. It seems to me an
independent sentiment which may be removed from one
object and directed to another, in a great measure at will. I
almost fell in love the other day with a lady, merely because
she was somewhat like you. This sentiment must be employed. If deprived of one object it will seek another. Rather
than want a proper object, it will exercise itself upon dogs and
parrots – as we see every day. My power of affection, if not
permitted to rest with you, will, I doubt not, find entertainment either in my ordinary course of studies, or on some
human being like yourself. Therefore, I repeat, do not allow
my wishes, intense and sincere as they are – yes, I may say,
altogether concentrated upon you – to have the least effect
upon your judgement. It is not necessary, either for you or
me, that you should; if you have not the affection I seek, you
are as nothing to me; if you would feign it, you would only
be fabricating our future misery. If you really have not the
affection required, and think you never can have it, it would

be the best action you could do for me to tell me so at once.

I hope you will not think that I say anything here in anger.
You would require to be something very different from what
I now think you, before I could entertain such a feeling
towards you. On the day when you first told me how much
you were alone in the world, and what you would give if you
had had either sister or brother, I formed the idea of becoming to you the friend you wanted; and even although we
should find it impossible to enter into the tender relationship
I have proposed to you, that friend would still continue. I
cannot cherish any feelings towards you but those of kindness. I could never be to you anything less warm than the
warmest friend. I believe therefore, that this letter, though
written in something like sadness, has in it nothing of anger.
It is dictated, if I can believe my own heart in aught, by the
same anxious wish for your happiness which has inspired me
in all the intercourse I have had with you.

My whole object in what I am now doing is to request that
you will patiently scan your thoughts regarding me and say
whether they amount or not to the degree of affection necessary for the relation proposed. Perhaps you should not give
an immediate answer, but take a long time to consider the
case. I would like, however, to hear from you soon, if it were
in never so indecisive a tone. How much should I appreciate a
visit from you during the the week!

I went this afternoon to Mr Hopkins', in the hope of
seeing you; but was disappointed. What added to my chagrin,
was that, if I had not done so, I might have made the four and
twenty pages I have written today thirty.

I am a great economist, you see. By the way, what a poor
preacher Doctor Muir is when you are not in the church. I
could not today take the least interest in his sermon. It was a
lost afternoon.

It is now eleven o'clock, and I have not risen from my seat
since a little after five. So you may judge how wearied I am.
Adieu my dearest love. Bon repos.

Yours with unfailing *admiration*,
R Chambers

PS I send the library journal, which I had in my pocket to
give you on Saturday night but forgot. What will an all
engrossing passion not make a man forget!

                                        April 7, 1829
My dear Anne,

   I receive your letter tonight in the midst of a turmoil of
business and other duties which almost puts it out of my
power to think. But I must say something in answer, however
short, or however ill considered. Pardon, pardon, I pray, the
doubts I have expressed regarding your affection. They
entirely arose from a misapprehension of what you said or
meant to say on Saturday night. My idea was that although
you regarded me with much respect, you did not find that
you loved me; and with my usual diffidence regarding myself
I feared that I was in some way personally disagreeable to
you. I never supposed that you only asked time to love me
better than you now do. I thought you insinuated that you
found an insurmountable difficulty at the beginning. I derived
countenance to this theory from the want of self appreciation
with which, as I once told you before, I am so irredeemably
afflicted. In the misery arising from that dreadful idea, I
penned a letter, which, although inspired with the warmest
and sincerest feelings of love toward you, must, I fear, have
given you great pain. I must say, however, in partial justifica-
tion of myself, that I never formed the idea that you were or
could be a coquette. The utmost of your supposed offence
was that, with an alarm perhaps natural to a person of your
age and character, you shrank from an alliance which in its
earlier stages had nothing in it to offend you. If that had been
the case – as I thank heaven it is not, – I could have easily
forgiven you for it. I would have looked upon it as natural,
and therefore hardly to be blamed.

   To make all odds evens, we must now consider ourselves
again as lovers not to be separated. My love is not ideal,
although it would perish at the idea of yours perishing.
Would you have me to be possessed by a passion which, after
finding no return in you, should turn back upon me and
consume my own vitals? No. Thanks to Nature, there is no
necessity for such a thing. There is a safety-valve for the most
obstreperous and the most unfortunate passions. I only
attempted, my dear Anne, to express what I know to be the
general principle. It was ungracious perhaps, to say so much
to a young lady inspired like you with such notions of the
indestructibility of love, but it was right philosophy after all.
Why, look into any of the works of the great minstrels of the

human heart and you will always see that what man most appreciates in woman or woman in man is love for love. Burns says times without number that the dearest charm of his mistress was her love for him. It is in fact the indispensable requisite. To love without love in return is meanness of spirit – is spanielism. The dignity of man revolts from it. But enough of this.

Our controversies are now all settled. This letter, beseeching your pardon for my last offence, is the last of them. Let us now write one letter more to each other, assuring each other that the collision has not injured our love. Let us write to each other as the next best solace since we are denied the satisfaction of a personal interview. Oh the pain of this cruel separation! To be divided by the space of half a mile, yet unable to see each other. It is truly agonising. How much would I give to see you now return the warm (. . . ?) I am writing! My heart expands in my bosom at the very idea. The tears come into my eye. You come not. I will have to live four weary days before I can see you. Ah, you may doubt that I love you, but it is to myself too fanciful a truth – fanciful since it cannot be gratified by even the pleasure of your company. Write, my dear dear Anne, to make up by your words what I want so earnestly in your personal presence. It will be a kindness just to say that I am still as much to you as before. Your dear subscription alone would be something. My brother, I expect, and both my sisters, if possible, will be with you on Saturday night. On that day you must call upon me at the shop as early as possible, and stay as long you can. In no way could I see you with so much satisfaction. So you must not demur. Believe me, my dear Anne, with increased affection,
    Your devoted R.C.

April 8 1829

I almost regret that I should have written so hurried, so incorrect, and I am afraid every way so contemptible a letter, as that I sent to you yesternight. How unfit was it, my dear Anne, to give you the idea I wished to convey of the great love I bear towards you! How unworthy to serve as an answer to the elegant and eloquent letter which called it forth! If I had not been very much hurried I never would have written such a letter; if I had not been very anxious to reply to yours *speedily*, I never could have despatched it. Permit me to take the earliest opportunity of perfecting the answer, of which you must consider it as no more than the commencement.

The purpose of my letter was twofold – to apologise for the ungracious misunderstanding I had laboured under regarding your declaration of Saturday night, and to assure you that, now being put to rights on that score, my love was the same as ever. I believe I need say no more about my misunderstanding. You must have forgiven it already, as only the result of my own diffidence. You must have seen that, had I not truly loved you, I never could have given such a colour to your meaning, nor ever felt so much chagrin in consequence. So, let this matter rest henceforth for ever buried. As to the reality of my love – if to think more of you than of anything else – if to feel perfectly happy in your presence and miserable and dissatisfied in your absence – if to fall asleep thinking of you and to waken to think of you again – if to calculate the days and the hours which will elapse before I shall see you – and if to gaze upon your letters and that still dearer ornament of you which lately came into my possession, till I sink in a transport of tenderness and almost forget that I live – if habits such as these indicate love, then do I love. Can you really doubt that I love you? Do you think that I would ever have proposed such a step as that I lately proposed, unless I had found myself completely abandoned to you? Ask yourself if there be any external reason that I should. There is none. In asking your hand, I ask yourself alone – yourself and your love. It is evidently impossible that I can have been otherwise than sincere. My use of the word 'idea' should not make you think my love unreal; for what is love but an idea? There is no substantiality about it. It is a thing entirely metaphysical. If I had wanted any proof to myself that I truly and entirely loved you, I should have had it last week, after receiving your short letter of Wednesday's date. I was then so much afraid to receive your next letter, which I feared should prove far more fanciful, that I cogitated a thousand schemes for avoiding the horror of reading it, or for alleviating the (. . . ?) I expected it to produce. Sometimes, I thought of forbearing to read it, in case at a first glance I should find it unkind; and I thought of (. . . ?) it beside me

unread, till I should have made some attempt to explain what
seemed to have given you offence; after which I could have
destroyed it unread. I also endeavoured to prepare myself for
taking refuge from your anger and from the miseries of
disappointed passion in the indifference which I believed I
should be able to assume. But that was very difficult, and
perhaps should eventually have been impossible, notwithstanding all my theories. Indeed, I then found with bitter cer-
tainty, that your favour was indispensable to my happiness –
that I truly and unalterably loved you.

It is, my dear Anne, a thing to be above all things la-
mented, that we should be so completely sequestered from
each other. Is there no way by which we could have an
interview *twice* a week? You can have no idea of the irritation
of mind which I suffer on your account during the week, or
of the derangement which it produces in (what is much
valued by you) the economy of my time. It (. . . ?) my mind,
and actually makes me often idle when, according to all my
previous theories on the subject, I should be working. If I
were certain of seeing you at the distance of three days, or if I
were *un*certain that a *whole week* must be the space to elapse
before seeing you, I would perhaps apply more seriously and
more regularly. At present it is impossible. Even with the idea
ever present in my mind that the more vigorously I labour I
make myself the more worthy of you, and shorten the probable period which must intervene before our union, I cannot
apply in the way I wish. If I have an odd hour at any time,
either in the morning or at night, I cannot spend it in task-
work – I devote it to contemplative reflection upon you – to a
review of our last half-dozen Saturdays, or a perusal of your
letters, or to *raptures* over the elegant fragment of your
person which I am so happy as to possess. Almost every
morning I awake two hours before I require to attend to
business; and these two hours, which might be devoted to the
scribbling of a page, I can spend in no other way than such as
I describe. You have revolutionised my whole system of life,
which was previously one of the most methodical jog-trot
affairs that you could conceive.

Since I saw you on Saturday I have made an arrangement
with the editor of Constable's Miscellany to have my volume
published in June instead of May; which will enable me to
have more time to spend with you before you quit this town,

and also to pay a long-promised visit to Fingask Castle in
Perthshire, the seat of Sir Peter Murray Threipland. This
gentleman is the grandson of a gentleman who was out in the
Rebellion of 1715 and son of another who was in arms in
1745. He possesses, of course, an immense quantity of docu-
ments and anecdotes regarding both these periods. He is now
in town with his family and I was this evening seeing them at
their lodgings. They are most amiable people, and I expect to
spend a delightful week with them hearing their stories and
inspecting their old papers. It will be about the end of this
month that I will pay this visit. Of course I will take care that
it does not involve a *Saturday*. The Misses Threipland, three
fine young ladies, are such enthusiastic Jacobites that when
they first came to see me about a twelve month ago, I thought
they would have fairly overwhelmed me with their kindness.
I have made up a project with them to go this first fine
forenoon to see the Old Town, on which occasion their
mother Lady Threipland, a very old woman, and Miss Gra-
ham of (. . . ?), another devoted Jacobite, are to accompany
us. May not that day be the proudest in the life of the Author
of *Traditions of Edinburgh*? Alas, my dear Anne, how
willingly would I give up a thousand such delightful affairs
for the momentary glimpse of you during the middle of the
week! How stale, flat, etcetera do all the uses of the world
appear without you!

A chaplet when the flowers are fallen –
A shrine from which the god is stolen!

By the way, our next Saturday will be an unusually good one.
We may, I suppose, be together at the shop here for three hours
if we please, before dinner, and as long at your aunt's after. Remember, I depend most completely upon seeing you at the shop.
I will take care to have the boys out of the way at any times you
think you can come, or I will meet you somewhere abroad and
take you to it myself; but the other way will be the better. Is it
not strange that we two who love each other so entirely (for I
love you entirely and you love me at least two thirds) should find
it so difficult to meet? I wonder much how we should feel if we
were left entirely to ourselves, as I think we must eventually be.
We shall run riot, like school-boys at the commencement of a
vacation. We shall really, I am afraid, be a more than usually
foolish pair. In addition to all the (. . . ?) reasons for extravagance,
we shall have one which other people never feel, the delight of

seeing each other *ad libitum*.

I have now made up my mind entirely to the necessity of your going to the country; but I insist that it shall only be for half a year. By taking a long look at you before you go away, and seeing you perhaps two or three times during the summer, I think I shall be able to pass that period of probation without either killing myself or forgetting you. It may also be well that I spend the months of summer, vacant as they are comparatively in regard to business, in intense study. In winter, however, that is at Martinmas, you must be mine for ever. I could not hope to pass that dreary time, during which I should scarcely ever see you, without utterly despairing. It will, besides, be really more convenient for me, more agreeable to my plans of economising time, to have the business of matrimony transacted during winter than summer. During the entire months of winter, I find my time so much broken to pieces by business that I never write any at all or attempt it. (. . . ?), however, there are many vacant hours, and there is a general relaxation as to time, that will be quite enough for the duties of receiving and paying visits and so forth. I will then be less under the necessity of *abstracting* myself than in summer. I dare say you will laugh at me for this arranging the whole business with a view to my own conveniency and without even so much as indicating a doubt as to yourself. But I think it would be a better joke still, a thing more to be wondered at, if you were to refuse accession to my plans. So, I cannot suppose that you will hold out. You ask time to know me better. Do, I pray, endeavour to get acquainted with me as fast as you can and let me then know your resolution.

My sister Janet and brother William will accompany me on Saturday night to your aunt's. Margaret, unfortunately, cannot be spared from home on that night, and she hopes you will excuse her. She expects to have other opportunities immediately of prosecuting your acquaintance.

My dear Anne, I am sincerely and entirely yours R.C.
PS. I expect to hear from you at least once, if not twice, before Saturday.

April 8 1829

My dear Anne,

Since you are not able to come tonight, I will spend half an hour in endeavouring to controvert you on paper. But in the first place let me apologise for an unjust and injurious expression which I used tonight in my letter. I mean my saying that I would consider your obedience to my request for an interview a test of the love you profess for me. The expression was used in a hurry and was nonsense. So pray then forgive it. I need no tests of your affection, and I ask none. It is a precious stone which I have already proved and laid by in the casket of my inmost bosom.

The first grand argument which I wish to employ against you is that, in all human probability, if you quit the town for a year, we shall be separated for ever. As I have often already told you, it is a next thing to impossible to maintain an attachment under such circumstances. The impression of each other's mind and form would wear off from both of our minds before the expiry of that period; and if we still should think it proper to fulfil our former engagements, it would be without that ardour of passion which is so necessary to nuptial happiness. The most likely result is that we shall each alike be distracted towards some other object, the pressure of which upon our senses will wear out the former stamp, exactly as the footstep of a horse obliterates the vestige of a smaller animal. It is almost *felo de se* to my own heart to suppose that I could possibly forget you. It is a thought which agonises me. But I speak from a strong sense of the weakness of human natures. I argue from an established general principle, against which I cannot hope that I will be permitted to bear up when all the rest of mankind fail. The instances which I have known of passion becoming languid from delay are innumerable, and I have always deprecated the idea with a kind of horror. I might grant that the course you propose might be the most prudent if there were any onerous circumstances to render our early union inadvisable. But there are none. I am at present enjoying an income perfectly sufficient to support us in comfort – more than sufficient to gratify any wishes I formed on such a score. It is also such, I am persuaded, as should and would content you. It is rapidly increasing, and indeed *must* increase, if I only continue to retain health and sanity of mind. Such, indeed, I may say is the disposition of the world to befriend me, that I cannot accuse myself of extravagance when I express a belief that I will in a very few years be near the head of my profession in Edinburgh. If I were to argue from the progress I have already made during the eleven years I have been in business, I would say that scarcely as many more years will be necessary to produce this brilliant event. You perhaps have an idea that because I addict myself to literary pursuits I must necessarily want practical energies in business. No notion could be more mistaken. I never spent an hour in such pursuits which I could have spent more profitably otherwise. The only view I ever indulged in literature was to make it subservient to one grand object – the elevation of my fortune and my personal advancement in society. Accordingly, I find it serves me exactly in the way I wish. It has put, altogether, six hundred pounds into my pocket. It has rendered me acceptable to the class of men whom I wish to mix with, but whom otherwise I could never have mixed with. And it sends day by day a flow of friends to my shop whose countenance is of the most solid advantage to me. Literature, indeed, foments business, and business gives dignity and respectability to literature. I never indulged in one vain speculative view on the subject. It is all plain good-citizenship. I think I once said to you that I was sometimes even startled at the extremely worldly turn which my mind had taken. This is really the case. I only console myself with the reflexion that I have ever maintained a good object in all my exertions, the alleviation of the distresses of my friends in the first place, and latterly the enjoyment of matrimonial happiness with the woman whom I should entirely love.

You ask me a very sly question about Mr Tait. I answer it candidly. Tait is by far the most experienced man of the world and of business that I know. He also knows my circumstances. I therefore trust a good deal to what he advises. His advice of Monday night, however, had no other effect upon me than to confirm what I had previously resolved upon myself. The proposal for an earlier alliance than what I spoke of on Saturday night, arose entirely from his offering to engage me upon a work that would not require my absence from town, and his offer to pay me in ready money instead of bills a sum upon which I calculated as necessary to assist in the purchase of furniture. I am in reality

in no want of resources; but in business it is always more or
less difficult to extricate a large solid sum from the current of
one's accounts. The profits of Mr Tait's publications and of
one which I will have ready for Constable and Co before this
day two months, (when it *must* be published,) seemed convenient to me, as saving the trouble and difficulty of extracting
such a sum from the proceeds of the shop; and finding that I
should realise both before Midsummer caused me at once to
propose an earlier day for the completion of our happiness.

I now come to answer your very modest objection to your
qualifications for household duties. This is absolutely nothing. Should you be ignorant of such accomplishments, my
sister will live with us and instruct you till you are mistress of
them. But in no view of the case do you have any pull from
this objection; for how in wonder's name are you to learn
more at Sir Colin Pringle's than you learned at the boarding
school or at Mr Dunstane's? Both of my sisters are expert in
such mysteries, and either of them would be most happy to
exchange what she knows of them for a few lessons from you
on the pianoforte. This is a mere pretext in the way of excuse.
It is quite untenable. As for your increased gravity of character, heaven forfend that you should ever be otherwise than
you are, except as nature shall prompt to you. As for your
prospect of being more attached to me at the end of a twelve-
month's absence, heaven save your wandering wits – heaven
save you from such a trial!

I am glad that your aunt should have stated no other
objections than what she did. You may report all I have said
to you, so as to enable her to revise her judgement, as they
say at the Court of Session.

To conclude, I must say, my dear Anne, that if you, upon a
little further deliberation upon the subject, and a little further
discussion of it with me, shall determine upon taking the
course I advise, I will be most happy, and will look upon our
union as a certain thing. Should you persist in your resolu-
tions, I will consider the case as rendered problematical – will
look upon the treaty as reduced to its elements – as almost
annulled; and I will be truly unhappy. At present we would
form an equal match: a twelve-month hence there will be a
gulf between us that neither can pass. At present we regard
each other with a degree of passion that would make our
union the perfection of human happiness: a twelve-month

hence we shall be estranged and cold: and if our union then takes place at all, it will be rather from a respect for words which formerly passed between us than from love for each other.

In all this reasoning believe me, my dearest Anne, I preserve the utmost reverence for your motives in determining upon a delay. I only question the correctness of your views. In the earnest hope that you will yield to my arguments, I remain most warmly and most entirely yours R Chambers.

P.S. I really wish you would endeavour to see me before Friday.

April 13 1829

My dear Anne,

The wish of presenting myself, even in this metaphorical way, before your eyes, is almost my only reason for troubling you with this. I have one other little reason. Could you possibly get away tomorrow evening, in order to attend Mr Murray's concert and see Miss Inverarity? I would be delighted in the highest degree to accompany you there. It would break the monotonous misery of the week with one note of pleasure. It would people this dreadful desert of 'ilka-days' with the most agreeable images. It would be as a mountain top would have been to the dove sent forth by Noah, when she wandered over the waste of waters and found no resting-place for her foot. Endeavour, my dear Anne, to come *if it be at all possible.*

I wrote a poetical letter for your aunt, and yesterday, after the evening service was concluded at St Stephen's, gave it to Miss Robinson, who conveyed it to Elder Street. I saw them all afterwards and was congratulated in the highest terms. I know, however, it is not so very good as it should or might have been. You will see it in good time. I expect a glorious harvest of jokes from it; for I am sure it will put Iain almost beside himself. It will be the pet topic of 'the back room' for a week. What a pity, my dear Anne, you were not at church yesterday! I really cannot bear the place when you are absent. I will scarcely take the risk again. Poor Miss Wilkie was obliged by illness to leave the church; your aunt and Mr Thorn went with her. She was recovered however about six when I called.

We sat at your aunt's till after twelve on Saturday night, and all were happy but me. How could *I* be happy when *you* were away! It was certainly a charming party – especially the *earlier* part of it. Oh my dearest Anne, when will the time arrive when we shall have no more such fanciful partings as those we are now doomed to endure on Saturday nights – when we shall be under no constraint except in regard to each other – only devoted to each other's happiness?

I send you a present of paper for love letters, to conceal that I am *now* sending you a letter.

I am, with the fondest and most sincere affection, ever and only yours

R Chambers

P.S. Please to let me know if you can come to Mr Murray's concert, as soon as possible. Do endeavour to make me happy by saying you will come.

April 13 1829

How comes it, my dear Anne, that, although I wrote to you this morning, and have not since then got any more to say to you, and, above all things, have abundance of other business to attend to, I cannot help writing to you again? Excuse my weakness. It is that dreadful thing *love* which causes it. And he who acts foolishly from that cause, you know, must be excused, especially I should suppose, by her who occasioned it. N'importe. If you are only by a tenth part so willing to receive a letter from me as I am glad – delighted – enraptured to receive one from you, I can see by the (. . . ?) irrepressible smile upon your face that you will not fall out with me for pestering you in this peculiar manner.

The truth is, my dear Anne, I have such infrequent and miserable opportunities of conversing with you, that I am constrained to take this method of expressing my feelings, as a sort of dernier resort. You will see how few letters we will write to each other, when once we live under the same roof. I have, after all, to do myself justice, one little reason for writing. I have engaged Mr Tait and two or three other friends to come to my mother's on Saturday – female as well as male; I am going to ask Mr Miller, and have hopes he will come. I would also like very much to have your dear – everybody's dear Aunt May; if I thought it would be appreciated by her I would ask her, but I will not do so unless you say you think she would like to come. Now would you let me know your mind on this subject? I am now going to ask a great favour from you. I'm afraid it is too great. But you are *so kind*. My mother and sisters, who are not accustomed to see such company at home from our sequestered mode of life, feel a kind of difficulty – a kind of *fear* of being unable, destitute as they are of music, to entertain so large a party. Mr Tait and I will play like (?furies) on our flutes, and I don't know how many of us can sing. Yet, from the want of that grand resource – a pianoforte, we are a little non-plussed. Now, my dearest Anne, would you play to us a little on the harp? Would your aunt lend her valuable instrument for the purpose? I am so very sensible of the magnitude of the favour – I mean both your favour in playing and your aunt's of lending us the harp – that it is with great reluctance I mention it to you. But if you think it would be improper or dangerous to remove the instrument I beg you will say so and keep the thing a secret from your aunt altogether. Among the reasons I have for wishing you to play is one I'm sure you will sympathise with. My mother has expressed a secret anxious desire to hear you, and as she will not, for a long time probably, have another opportunity for being so gratified, I wish very much she should do so now.

Should this letter not reach you before you despatch an answer to my last, and should you not be able to delight me with your company tomorrow night, may I hope that you will reply to it at your earliest convenience? To make up this letter, I think I will give you – what I have long wished to give you, either in writing or conversation – a little of my history, and that of my family. It is a tale of misfortune and humiliation. But I have heard that you are also a child of misfortune. You will therefore, perhaps, listen to me with sympathy. You will find, possibly, a greater resemblance in our fates, than you would have expected.

My father was the eldest son of a respectable manufacturer on a small scale in Peebles, a man of much prudence and some wealth, the first of which qualifications *only* he left to his children. My father's profession was that of an agent for a great Glasgow manufacturing house; that is to say, he employed about a hundred cotton weavers in the work provided by the Glasgow house, for all which work he had to himself a

good commission. My mother was the orphan and only
daughter of one of the most extensive sheep-farmers in
Tweeddale. She was left with a little fortune. Her beauty was
so very great that she was called the 'flower of Tweeddale'
and was an object of (. . . ?) among all the youth of the town
and country. My father was not her choice. She was attached
to a young gentleman of the name of Bruce who resided at a
boarding school in Peebles, and who was heir to a large
property, I believe in the West Indies. Her mother, under
whose care she was left, was very averse to a match with
Bruce, because it gave her the prospect of losing her favourite
child. The old lady, therefore, while Bruce was absent,
contrived to work so upon my mother's feelings, that she
consented at last to a precipitate marriage with my father,
who had been paying his addresses for some time before. I
have heard my mother say that she did not know on the
morning of the 8th of May 1799, that she was going to be
married before night. She was hurried off in a coach to
Edinburgh, with her ordinary clothes – a girl between seventeen and eighteen – ignorant, I may say, of what marriage
was. The impropriety of my father's conduct on this occasion, and the misery which I am sure it occasioned, are, my
dear Anne, among my chief reasons for expressing last week
so much solicitude regarding the real state of your affections
towards me. My father's character was this. He was perhaps
the most honest man in the whole world. *I* never knew one
more honest. He was also possessed of some powers of mind
– had read a great deal – was fond of scientific enquiries –
was, in fact, a wonderful man for a country town. Here,
however, was the great error – the grand fault of his character.
He was of an indolent, easy, good-natured disposition. He
had no self-denial – no power of saying *no*. The langour,
however, of his life in Peebles, where he never had what may
be called perfect employment, and where, I may add, there
are many temptations, led him into dissipated habits. He
always treated my mother with kindness. He was, I believe,
sincerely attached to her. But yet how many sleepless nights
has he caused her to spend. How often have I sat by her,
conning my lesson, till late at night, and at last left her to wait
in pining solitary wretchedness till he should come home!
The recollection of this, hence, will never leave me. And
never, while the same heart remains within my bosom, will I

give you a similar cause of misery. His habits during my
boyhood were not so bad as to occasion any disorder in his
business. However it could only be said of him *then*, that he
was too often out late at night. So much activity, indeed, did
he then display, that, in 1808, he added to his former business
the profession of a clothier and haberdasher, which he carried
on for some years with much success. Perhaps, but for an
unforseen misfortune, he might have made his way through
life in a very creditable manner, and been a decent shopkeeper
in Peebles to the end of the chapter. But a misfortune did
occur. About a hundred French officers, liberated from
prison upon parole, were stationed at Peebles. They were
genteel men, and gained much upon my father. He was so
foolish as to give them credit for clothes to a great account.
They were suddenly called away from the town. They never
displayed so much principle as to pay him from abroad. Of
course, as his capital was completely ravished from him, he
was in a great measure ruined. To complete his destruction,
two uncles of my mother's, Messrs Phineas and Robert
Grieve, merchants or furniture painters on the North Bridge
of Edinburgh, became his trustees, and sponged him most
grievously. He might have recovered from the French; but he
could not weather the rapacity of these cruel old men. He lost
almost everything he had in the world, and became not only a
fortuneless, but a despairing – a *lost* man. This happened in
the year 1812, when I was only ten years of age; so I do not
remember much about it. I remember however the agony and
the desolation of my mother after the worst of her fate had
been ascertained. Good God! My heart bleeds at the recollection. One of her uncles, who had a dreadful ill-will at my
father, added insult to robbery. He pretended to be her
patron; and one day, while she was sitting with Janet upon
her knee – a child of two or three months, and not expected at
that time to live for two hours – he said to her, 'If you were a
widow, Madam, I might perhaps do something for you': a
laconic at which the blood runs cold.

To fail in business in a large town is ill enough, but to fail
in a country town is truly terrible. My father could not bear
up against it. He resolved to move to Edinburgh. He had not
a very good prospect of employment there; but anything was
better than to remain in Peebles. He removed in 1813. We
lived in Bristo Street, in a flat above one in which the Misses

Picken lived. It was thus we got acquainted with them; their
misery was much greater than ours: that I remember well. My
father endeavoured to carry on his original profession, as an
agent for weavers. But he came no speed. At length after a
year and a half of partial wretchedness, during which my
mother was obliged to work – yes O´God, to *work* for the
villain who had insulted and robbed her, he procured employment as superintendent at the Saltpans at Joppa, near
Musselburgh, to which place – a perfect Pandemonium of
smoke and soot and all kinds of horrors – we removed in
autumn of 1815.

Regarding myself before this period, I have only to say
that, as I was lame on account of my extraordinary toes, and
had always displayed a singular degree of fondness for books
(– even to that degree that I never mingled in the sports of
other boys but stayed at home and read –) I was destined to
be a clergyman. I got, for this purpose, an excellent education,
partly at Peebles and partly at Edinburgh. My teachers were
generally so much pleased to observe my devotion to study,
that they taught me for nothing; sometimes, even before I was
twelve years of age, they employed me as a kind of superior
assistant which made my gratis attendance a fair enough
matter. When we went to reside at Joppa, my mother found it
very difficult, on account of my father's limited income, to
keep me in lodgings at Edinburgh. However, she resolved to
try. My brother was then an apprentice in the shop of Mr
Sutherland, bookseller, Calton Street. He and I lived in
lodgings together. Our room and bed cost three shillings a
week! It was in the West Port, near Burke's place. I cannot
understand how we should have ever lived in it. The woman
who kept the lodgings was a Peebles woman, who knew and
was disposed to be kind to us. She was, however, of a very
narrow disposition – the result of poverty. I used to be in
great distress for want of fire. I could not afford either that or
candle to myself. So I have often sat beside her kitchen fire –
if fire it could be called, which was only a little heap of
embers – reading Horace and conning my dictionary by a
light which required me to hold the books almost close to the
grate. What a miserable winter that was! Yet I cannot help
feeling proud of my trials at that time. My brother and I – he
then between fifteen and sixteen, I between thirteen and
fourteen – had made a resolution together that we would act

through life in a manner entirely different from my father. Instead of seeking sensual indulgences, we determined to try ourselves to the last degree of self-denial. You will scarcely believe me when I tell you what we lived on. Our food was meal, (in two various forms,) milk, and cheese. The whole matter cost us *eighteen pence a week each*. My brother actually saved money off his income. I remember seeing him take five and twenty shillings out of a closed box which he kept to receive his savings; and that was the spare money of only a twelvemonth. I dare say the Potterow itself never sheltered two divinity students of such abstinent habits as ours. In myself, looking back upon it from my present status in society, with all the comforts of life at command, the thing seems a perfect miracle.

My father's prospects blackened towards the end of that winter; and even three shillings a week (my board and lodging!) at length became too much for him. I then for some time spent the night at Joppa, and regularly every morning walked, lame as I was, (you must know I was dreadfully lame when a boy,) to Edinburgh to attend the school. Through all these distresses, I preserved the best of health; though perhaps my long fasts at so critical a period of life repressed my growth and impaired the symmetry of my person. I am sure, at least, I might have been expected from my gigantic proportions in infancy and early boyhood, to rise to greater heights than I have done. A darker period than even this ensued. My father, by a frightful act of imprudence, which I cannot disclose to you,[30] lost about fifty pounds which belonged to his employers, and was soon after discharged. My mother, overwhelmed with shame and horror, was in fearful despair. How much better a fate do the virtues of this excellent woman deserve. She conducted herself on this occasion like a heroine. At once, though with many compunctious (. . . ?), she resolved to abandon the delicate solaces of private domestic life. She determined to open a small tavern – absolutely a wayside tavern. With what feelings did I look upon it lately, in going to mix in much good society at Musselburgh. It is near Joppa, at a decent-looking little village called Willington Place. There, in a house of four little apartments, did this noble-minded woman – for she is no less – this woman born and educated with such different prospects, work, I may almost say, like a menial, for two years. My father, a miserable

disappointed man, was her only embarrassment. I was now
withdrawn in despair from a course of learning which they
saw I should never be able to complete. They hesitated for a
long time what to do with me. I remained idle for a twelve-
month. It was then and there that Mrs Johnston of Newing-
ton knew us: she lived in sea-bathing lodgings next door. (I
did not remember this when you spoke of it, but my mother
has since explained it to me.) At length, my brother, who still
continued with Mr Sutherland at Edinburgh, procured me a
place in a counting house of a merchant who resided in Pilrig
Street; and thither, for four shillings a week, I walked every
morning from Willington Place (five or six miles) walking
back again at night, for six months. I was then discharged on
account of an imprudent intrusion which my father made one
day upon my master. I was afterwards for three weeks with
another merchant at Leith. From that place I was discharged,
for no other reason that I can think of but that Mr McAlpine
thought me too stupid to be likely ever to do him any good. I
was now in the miserable situation of a youth between fifteen
and sixteen, who having passed the proper period without
acquiring the ground-work of a profession, is totally *hors de
combat*, and has the prospect of ever more remaining so. I
was now, however, at the bottom of the wheel. Now came the
very time to rise. You have already some notion of my self-
denial and fortitude of mind. Now came the time to exert all
my faculties. I resolved in my exasperation of mind, to
become a dealer in old books – to begin at the very lowest
step in the profession – become, as the Scripture says, 'as a
little child'. With books to the value of about fifty shillings, I
opened a small shop (the rent I remember was six pounds) on
Leith Walk. My project was quite opposite to my mother's
will. With her delicacy of mind as yet unimpaired, she
thought I should be a sort of disgrace to her by entering on
such a humble course of life. But I persisted in my resolution.
I was completely successful so far as I could be successful
with so small a capital. I made my fifty shillings worth of old
books twenty pounds worth, and supported myself during
the first year. Never was a boyish freak – for I can call it
nothing more – so triumphant in its issue. By and bye, I got
into a better shop. And, as I continued my traffic, my little
stock rapidly increased. I lived then by myself in the back
shop, feeding only upon tea and arranging all my household

matters myself. For three or four years at that time I never got regular dinner, except on Sundays.

During this time my father and mother had also become somewhat promoted in the world. They removed from Willington Place to Portobello and afterwards to Leith, and finally to Edinburgh; still very poor, but yet at every remove getting into a still better and larger house than before. At last in 1821, they took the White Horse Inn in the Canongate, and there at length I began to lodge with them, instead of living by myself in the back shop. In 1822 my circumstances were so much improved by my unremitting industry and extraordinary parsimony, that I was able to take the small shop at Stockbridge where my brother James now is. There I became the author of *The Traditions of Edinburgh*.

During the first years of my shop-keeping, I had had a great deal of leisure time, which I constantly employed in ornamental writing such as what I once showed you. When the King visited Edinburgh, Sir Walter Scott, to whom I had presented a volume written in such a way, recommended me to a number of societies, the presidents of which wished to address his Majesty; and I wrote four of these things, which the King is said to have admired at Dalkeith House on their being shown to him. Authorship, however, has been a more profitable pursuit, as a means of filling my wasted time. I told you before how much I had won by that means in the course of the last five years. Had I been told that I was to do such a thing, when I was sitting by old Jean Marshall's fire in the West-Port, or toiling through frost and snow to school from Musselburgh to Edinburgh, or when I first removed the window-boards of my little shop in Leith Walk, I would have set down the man so telling me as a raving madman.

My dear Anne, I hope I have not tired you with this long narrative. I hope it will be somewhat interesting to you. I intend it principally as a means of assuring you of the security with which you may entrust your fate to my hands. You will naturally agree that the man who like me has undergone every severity and degree of distress, and who has known the express value of every little sum of money, and who has before him for a beacon the fate of such a father, will continue through life to exercise the duties of his status with caution and prudence. This above all things I wish you to think of me. Do not permit your mind to be dazzled with the notoriety which attends my name as a literary man. That is absolutely contemptible. I value it no more than (. . . ?), except as the means of producing substantial profit. Value me, if you value me at all, as a man who will work for you with untiring infallible industry, who will be ever kind to you, who will constantly endeavour to secure your happiness, who will never do anything to bring shame upon you. With you, as with all the world beside, I am far more ambitious of being thought a good citizen and a good man, than of being held up to the world as a second Byron or Sir Walter Scott.

My dearest Anne – my dear dear Anne – let me hear from you soon. Write to me as often as you can. It is so great a pleasure to me, to receive a letter from you!

Believe me ever truly yours,

R Chambers.

P.S. I forgot in my autobiographical sketch to mention that after a long course of the most unfortunate habits, my father died in 1824. His end was finally hastened by an unsuccessful law-suit which preyed much upon his spirits. Since then, my mother, as might have been expected, has done better than ever before. She is now quite reconciled to her situation in life. Indeed, she is rather proud of it, and has often refused to retire with William and me into a private house. She thinks the inactivity of such a life would kill her. You shall be a great deal better acquainted with her before long. Dearest Anne, again adieu. RC.

Hanover Street
April 15 1829

Your letters make me so happy that I do not know in what terms to acknowledge them. You say you cannot write love-letters; but, without perhaps intending it, you write letters more than worthy of that name. I was truly sorry to want you at Murray's Concert yesternight. I went, however, with the moonlight of your gentle spirit beaming on my mind; I went thinking of you, and regretting your absence: and, as I never ceased to have you present before me in idea the whole time, or permitted myself to be for a moment pleased without wishing that you could partake of my pleasure, it was as much as possible the same thing to me. I remembered the kind regret you expressed for my inability to attend Miss

Greenfield's Ball, and endeavoured to repay it by a similar
regret for you on this occasion. Miss Inverarity commenced
her public career with amazing confidence, was most flatter-
ingly received, sung amazingly well for a first effort, and was
encored in two out of her three performances. Partly perhaps
from the embarrassment of a début and partly from her
inexperience in singing in a large crowded room, her voice did
not seem half so powerful as it appeared to me in a private
room. But, since she was well received with only a moiety of
her voice, how will she be received when a little practice
enables her to bring the whole into play? Her manner was remarked by many, as I have often remarked it, to be very
coltish – the curtsey was a perfect duck. How much the better
would she be of a dash of Anne Kirkwood in her manner!
This is the result of evil education – the want of a mother or
of anybody in her place. It will probably wear off. Miss Paton
and she sat, I am told, the whole evening, at different parts of
the dance room without speaking. From some light thoughtless expression of poor Miss I. regarding Miss Paton – which
was carried to that lady – she is possessed by a dislike of her –
which is to be regretted for both their sakes – for they are
both fine girls, and might have otherwise made good friends.
The whole concert was excellent. The room was crowded. Of
your friends, I saw Tom Dallas, Mr Ritchie, Mr Stewart, and
Mr Jos. Macgregor. Your aunt would not go, although I asked
her; she was under the necessity of waiting on Miss Wilkie. I
had a call here from your aunt this morning and asked her to
come on Saturday night, which she, with the utmost frankness, promised to do. The whole company now asked and
who have promised to come are: yourself (*en chef*), the Misses
Picken, your aunt, a Miss Miller from Eddleston (probably),
Mr Miller, Mr Tait, Mr John Aitchison, stationer in Register
Street, an old school fellow of mine, and Mr (. . . ?), the
clever, and most droll, author of a book which has lately
made a great impression in England, the *Life and Times of
Archbishop Laud* – he is to be the buffo of the party, and an
excellent one you will find he makes. He wrote the review of
Mr Mackray's book in the same number of the lit. jour. which
contains the (. . . ?) one. He writes a great deal in the periodical. What is very strange, he writes about nothing but the
gravest subjects, chiefly religious or at least ecclesiastical; and
he talks about nothing but young ladies, or other such

nonsense (forgive me). Perhaps we shall have Mr Lithgow, the painter, who lives in the same stair with your aunt. We are sure of Mr Fairly, the young gentleman who knows you a little from Leith. *He* is to bring his fiddle. By the bye, or rather *especially*, you must really try to get leave to stay a little later than usual on Saturday night. Could you not make it out by proposing to leave the house at a somewhat later period of the afternoon than usual, by way of compensating as to time? I am almost sure my little party will be a felicitous one, for they are all clever, lively people – not an ounce of dead weight in the whole parcel. It would be particularly grievous to lose you so soon as nine. I really cannot think of it. It would be taking the head off us, as Cuddie Headrigg said of the losing party at the B. of Bothwell-bridge, as clean as ye wad bite it aff a sybow[31]. My dearest Anne, exert yourself to do what you can in this matter. I make it a particular request. And there is one other thing I must beg of you. Call upon me, as you pass to make your necessary calls – though it were but for a moment. Give me only one sun-blink of the brightness of your presence; throw but one ray of your kindness on me, and I am content – for the forenoon. Also, apropos, that I may have as much of you as possible, come home with me at five to take your dinner. You must dine somewhere, and as well with me as with any other body. But I will leave this in abeyance till you call in the forenoon of Saturday. You do not surely need to dine with your aunt on that day, for you will see her at six in St Andrew's Street. Moreover you can dress with my sisters. I requested the favour of Miss Wilkie's company, but from her continued insecurity of health she is to go out of town before that day. You delight me beyond measure by your frankness about the harp. It really *will* be a great accession to the strength of my entertainment; and it will give myself the utmost pleasure personally; for I absolutely dote on that instrument – as played by *you*. I have already possessed Mr Tait, who is a devoted musician, with some idea of the treat he will have in hearing you play, and he is accordingly prepared to be very much interested in you. I will introduce you to him, and endeavour to make you converse together: for he is so remarkably fine a fellow – so hearty, so frank, so agreeable, so sensible – that I am sure you will like him on acquaintance. He is really the dearest male friend I have; and he is a friend who can be of service to me as

you already know. I think the great cause of our liking each
other so much is that we are alike in our perpetual efforts to
unite worldly prudence and commercial accuracy with good
fellowship and a taste for the pleasures of life. I am *really*
gratified, my dear Anne, to find that I have not sunk in your
esteem by the free expression of my early history. I was just a
little afraid that your being made fully aware of the degradation of my youth would alarm and shock you. We may
admire the struggles of an unfortunate man, and think more
of him in his rise than of a man who has been born high and
never needed to rise. But we might hesitate before making
such a man our bosom friend and equal. I thought it but
justice to you, however, to make this disclosure in time. It
was even *better*, as a means of anticipating and obviating any
garbled or malicious accounts of me which might have
reached you through other channels. Candour is with me, as I
am glad to find it with you, a favourite virtue. I practise it
simply as a matter of advantage and convenience. With my
many and various duties, I never could afford time or thought
to act with duplicity. With *you* I think aloud and ever will do
so. I have one thing, above all others, to congratulate myself
upon, in looking back upon my misfortunes and hardships
and degradations. Through them all, I never lost the mind I
had in the better days of my early boyhood. I never lost heart,
or became one of the herd around me. I might condescend a
great deal, for the sake of expediency. But I always preserved
within that pure and lofty spirit appropriate to a better
condition in society; confident all along that in time I should
regain my original place. I believe there are many, and *friends*
too, who look upon me as a wonderful instance of a rise from
the lower ranks to the better. They are completely mistaken.
My mind was pitched *in alt* at the very commencement, and
has never experienced the least *rise* all along. It has only
become *externally developed*, as I found circumstances made
it prudent to do so. I firmly believe, my heart was as ambitious and my soul as full of generous thoughts, at the time I
sat scanning the gracious lyrics of Horace by the old woman's
fire in the West-Port, or when I was carrying on my humble
traffic in Leith Walk, as it is now or ever can be. How much
mistaken is the world sometimes in judging of men and their
motives! From its levity in regard to the interests of others it
generally judges cruelly. It is very apt to suppose something

bad; but dreadfully reluctant to imagine anything good. I
have no hope of ever making my fellows believe that I am
better than a lucky plebeian. They have seen the humility of
my circumstances in youth, but they know nothing of my
better condition and prospects in boyhood. They do not even
know that my *education* was that of a gentleman. They
suppose me, therefore, a man far elevated above my proper
rank. I am anxious that *you* should know the truth of the
matter, my dear Anne, for as you are to be adopted, as it
were, into myself, it is but proper that you should know everything about me. Perhaps you will scarcely be able to
suppress a smile at my anxiety on such a score; and I must
acknowledge that it really might be interpreted into vanity.
But you will judge more generously. You will ascribe it to its
proper motive – love for yourself, and a wish to recommend
myself to you. Enough of this, however.

Please to copy the enclosed scroll into your letter to the
Captain. It strikes me that this would be the most convenient
way of expressing my thanks to him for his kind attention to
the poem. I hope you will excuse the trouble.

I am obliged to conclude – and without having said half so
much as I would like to say of the true and most fervent love
I feel for you. It is my idol thought. It occupies me night and
day. I waken now every morning about five and lie awake for
three hours thinking over all your various noble and elegant
qualities, and enjoying the delicious idea that *I* am chosen to
be the companion of so much excellence. Do you know I
have become quite of a lacrimose turn lately? I frequently
find tears in my eyes when I think of you. They are tears of
(. . . ?) pleasure. My dearest, believe me most truly, most
entirely yours

R Chambers.

P.S. I must hear from you as soon as you can spare time.

St Andrew's Street
Sunday morning, April 19 1829

My dear Anne,

I write this early, to give you agreeable information on a
point about which you expressed some anxiety yesternight.
You wish to know how my mother felt disposed towards
you, and what she thought of our proposed alliance. I can

now answer that she has formed the most favourable opinion
of you. She would have done the same thing at her first
becoming acquainted with you three weeks ago, but the
opportunity was not so favourable; neither can one speak
with so much confidence after a first interview as after a
second. *Now*, the whole of my friends, from my mother to
little David, are perfectly in love with you. I am afraid, if I
had not got the start of them so completely, I should have
found rivals in my brothers. For an hour after the departure
of the company yesternight, and at breakfast this morning,
the conversation was upon you alone, or at least upon the
party which your good nature and accomplishments did so
much to render charming. But you were the observed of all
observers yesternight, and I was given to understand by my
sisters that you produced an equally favourable impression on
all the rest of the company. As for themselves, they are
already your sisters – they love you with an affection which is
only dashed by their feeling of humiliation in your presence.
They could only love you more if they admired you less. I
have taken my mother to task on the subject of our proposed
union; and you shall have the candid result. As I told you
yesternight we are more intimately fond of each other than
any of the rest of the family. I was her companion and fellow
sufferer for her misfortunes – her servant, her friend. I have
also been brought by circumstances into such a situation and
course of life, that she has received more homage and flattery
on my account than on account of any of the rest of her
children. Thus she loves me so much that, as you may easily
conceive, the idea of resigning me to any other woman is not
agreeable to her. Like all mothers, she thinks it scarcely
possible that her children can find matches worthy of them.
The very idea of the separation which must take place when I
am married, is death to her. Yet, as she is also acceptable to
reason as well as affection, she tells me that she will make up
her mind to what she cannot help acknowledging to be a
necessary and even an advantageous thing – however much it
may pain her. She acknowledges the prudence of both my
brother and myself in remaining single till such time as she
was re-established in the world, until we had secured the
comfort of the junior members of the family left in our hands
by my father. She also allows that in my case especially,
matrimony cannot now be considered imprudent in any

respect. Therefore, she cannot abstractly have the least objection to it.

She felt at first great solicitude about the individual I had selected. When I informed her of your situation in life, she was alarmed by the fear lest your education and habits should have unfitted you, as she says they very often do, for undertaking the management of a domestic establishment of moderate splendour. In learning, however, something regarding your early history, and being assured that you had as yet lived so short a time in an aristocratic house, she was inclined to join me in thinking that there was no danger on that score. Now, since she has seen you, and heard a *great deal more* about you, she has not the least fear. She still says, with a laugh, that if you were the *Queen of Britain* instead of the Queen of Barbary, you would not be *too* good for me. But such is her opinion of you seriously, that she says you come nearer to the standard of perfection she has assigned for her sons' wives than anybody she ever saw; and therefore she elects you to the *high office* in question without a single expression of either disappointment or regret.

I hope all this will be agreeable to you. It is delightful to me in a very high degree. Perhaps you may think that the approbation you have procured among my friends has scarcely been bestowed with sufficient readiness, or, when it did come, with abundant enough flow of expression. But I think you should rather congratulate yourself, as I congratulate *my*self, on the reverse. I could scarcely have expected that any young lady coming before a family under such peculiar circumstances, (for of course they all knew what was going on,) coming as it were to be *judged*, should have so completely triumphed after only two appearances in court. That you have been favourably received at all is a great deal; for you must remember, the question was not, are you worthy to be our friend or acquaintance, but, are you entitled by your merit of mind and person to deprive us of the society of a son and brother. You did not start as a candidate for our friendship, you came in the character of something like an enemy, and had all that enmity (of the kind it was of) to overcome, before you advanced a single step in friendship. What reason have I to be pleased, since you have been able, my dear Anne, to achieve so much both negatively and positively in so short a time!

Since this grand step has been accomplished, since you have secured, in addition to my warmest love, the affection and esteem of all I hold dear, I feel increased confidence in the probability of our connubial happiness. The concurrence of collateral relations is not absolutely indispensable to such an event; but I am sure it must further it greatly. How much pain do we feel in ordinary life, when two friends, each of whom is alike endeared to us, fall out, or commence to do! How much more must we feel when the two relations whom of all others we hold most dear, whose happiness respectively is almost equally an object of our wishes, find it impossible to continue in terms of friendship! I am sure nothing would be more painful to me – nothing would contribute, on the other hand, more to the accomplishment of my happiness than to see two such relations friendly.

I have, I believe, little more to say. I could fill a letter, as I could spend six hours in simply repeating the expression, *I love you*. But it is needless. You are already assured of my affection. I may only say that, although I often think it incapable of increase, I find to my own surprise that at every successive interview I *do* love you more than before. My love is not of that sort which disposes men to prostrate themselves before woman, as before a divinity, to worship her. I do not *worship* you. That is not my feeling at all. I rather feel disposed to protect and befriend you; which must be quite a contrary sensation. I love you because you are so gentle and so kind, because you throw yourself upon my protection. If I thought of you as a superior being, or with anything of worship or reverence, I should not *love* you. I don't see how these feelings can be compatible. *My* affection disposes me to press you to my bosom, to my very heart, my heart of hearts, to make you part of myself – to guard you from all harm – to strain and struggle for your happiness. I never yet was more anxious for my own interest than I am for yours. You fairly divide the principle of self-love and self-preservation with me. You have a full half. Every triumph – every good – every pleasure I can secure in this world, I am disposed to share with you. It will even have an additional relish in being participated in by you. Life itself is now more valuable to me than before, since it is enriched with the hope of being spent in your presence and in your behalf.

My whole soul is now turned, my dear Anne, upon a

means of securing your comfort after you shall have become
mine. I have examined my resources with the most careful
inspection. They even surpass my expectations. I believe that,
what with the proceeds of my little establishment in Hanover
Street, and what with writing a book every summer during
the recess of business, I must clear a good deal above three
hundred a year. I was lately offered, or next thing to offered,
the Editorship of the *Caledonian Mercury*: the salary attached to which is above two hundred a year; but I have
declined accepting it because my present mode of life is both
more agreeable to me and more profitable. If I now clear what
I mention, I must clear a good deal more every successive
year; my business is increasing at a very rapid ratio of pro-
gression, and I must also, I believe, be able to make more of
my pen than hitherto, as my literary reputation becomes
more consistent and certain. At the very worst, you see, I can
fall back upon an excellent reserve – an editorship; the stock
necessary for which can never be impaired by either (. . . ?).
Everything considered, I cannot see that there is the least
danger. My resolution, which has been so dreadfully tried in
boyhood, and when I had comparatively few connections, can
never, I should think, desert me in manhood, when I have
you, my dear Anne to depend upon me, and the eyes of the
world fixed at me. – No, never. Let only health be granted,
then, (and from my robust frame and the circumstances of my
never having had a week's illness from childhood, I am
entitled to hope for that greatest of blessings) – let health be
granted, and *you* are safe. You are worthy, my dear 'lassie', to
use Miss Dallas's phrase, of a man of higher fortune than me;
but you never could have found one who was supplied by a
more ardent affection for you or who was more inclined to
seek your happiness. And, after all, there is little additional
happiness, I am afraid, to be hoped for above the medium
station in which I can place you. We will be able to live at
first with perfect comfort upon two thirds, or little more, of
my estimated income; and that, I think, with love, should be
enough to content two such adventurers as we are. Dearest
Anne – my own chosen Anne, adieu. I hope to get a glimpse
of you at church this afternoon; in which case I will put this
letter into your hands. Let me hear from you soon – if possible by tomorrow evening's post. I am really anxious to hear
what you have to say on the various topics embraced by this

letter. *Ever – only* yours,

R. Chambers.

April 20 1829

My dear Anne,

I have not been able to communicate my letter of yesterday the way I expected: it is therefore enclosed in this sheet
for today's post. Since I wrote it, I have had another private
and familiar conversation with my mother on the *subject of
subjects*; and I think it worth while to state to you that I have
had the pleasure of hearing her express still more warmly than
before her approbation of my choice. I have heard her, my
dear Anne, speak of you in terms almost as warm as she could
have used in regard to her own daughter. She anticipates,
from your gentle and flexible disposition, (for such she
rightly judges it to be,) that you shall be to her exactly as a
child of her own. She will love you, she says, with the warmest affection: she will be your counsellor and guide in everything you chuse to consult her upon; she will congratulate
you on every good that befalls you, and be your stay and
refuge in every distress. My dear Anne, she will be *your
mother*; and that (how well can I assure you!) will be enough.
You shall, indeed, be happy.

I have also learnt, from this endeared relation of mine,
something further regarding the opinion that my brothers and
sisters have formed of you. They have been expressing their
sentiments more freely by many degrees to her than to me.
Their opinion is a very high one indeed – much higher than I
ever knew of them expressing in regard to any other individual whatever. I will not offend your modesty by repeating the
terms of it. Enough be it for you to know that you reign in
every heart. Ever since Saturday night, the chief conversation
has been about you; and I have been feasted with the music of
your name till I am perfectly intoxicated. I have had almost
everything that you said or did that night recounted to me.
Even David seems to have been affected with the admiration
which possesses his seniors to such a degree. He said yesterday to my mother, in the childish innocence of his heart,
(they were talking of female beauty at the time,) 'I never saw
ony bonny women but our Margaret and the Queen[32].'

I called yesternight for your aunt, for no other purpose, I

believe, but just to have the pleasure of speaking to her and
hearing you spoke of; a miserable (?substitute) for the pleasure of seeing and speaking to yourself, but the best possible
under the circumstances. I talked for the first time of our
intentions, being anxious to hear what your nearest relation
and most immediate protector thought of them. I rather think
she herself fears about the propriety of the step – some fears,
perhaps, about myself. I am probably mistaken; but it is best
to give my candid impressions. She perhaps thinks me too
young and as yet not firmly enough anchored down upon
society; my principles, and my means of subsistence, not yet
sufficiently ascertained. If she does, she surely does me great
injustice. But it is only a vague suspicion with which I tor-
ment myself. And I beg you will not let her know that I have
had any such suspicions; for she is the last person in the
world, besides my own family and yourself, that I would like
to give pain to or to offend. Perhaps, you might attempt to
assure her on the subject in question. I would not condescend
to such an attempt myself for the world, or for *you*. But yet I
wish her to be assured. Do you know I have received a deal of
reaction on this score in the world at large? People seem to
have invariably the idea that a literary man should be a
vagabond. I have sometimes observed them stare when I
refuse to take a second tumbler of punch! This annoyance has
caused me, I dare say, to be more puritanical in my manners
than I would otherwise be. Very often, I don't taste either
spiritous or malt liquors for weeks. I have an alarm – a horror
at such things, lest I should become, as people seem to think I
should become, a drunkard. For the same reason, I am often
much sterner and keener in matters of business than I would
otherwise be. The least slip I made in such matters – the least
weakness I should betray – the least negligence of 'the main
chance' – would subject me to imputations which I know I do
not deserve and which I abhor. I believe, if I be not softened
by you, I shall at last become a miser and a puritan from mere
habit.

My dear delightful Anne,
Adieu, R Chambers

For heaven's sake write to me soon. I really will be anxious to
hear your thoughts on what I've said.

Hanover Street
April 21 1829

My dear Anne,

It is delightful at all times to receive a letter from you; but it is peculiarly delightful to have one in which you express yourself pleased with anything I may have proposed to you. Your grateful expressions tonight in regard to the opinion my friends have formed of you, and your approbation of a certain other matter propounded in my last letter, are pleasing to me in the highest degree. Now, everything is right, and there can be no misunderstanding between us. Even my suspicions about your aunt are banished, and I now wish to say no more to either her or myself on that matter. If you are content to entrust yourself to me, and she have never expressed any reluctance to permit you to do so, I can have no more to say. Perhaps I should never have expressed any fear on such a score: it might be interpreted into either consciousness of guilt or want of pride. But really circumstances have made me peculiarly tender on these matters; and with you, my dear Anne, I wish to have no secrets – no point of reserve. The Captain is a great bore with his poems. I obey your request by sending two which you left with me on the 21st of March last – I remember the chronology and the circumstances of all your visits. They have lain on my writing table, to be restored to you. I hope you will be able to make out your criticisms. It would be a sad thing if he were to find you so oblivious of his verses as to ascribe the wrong criticisms to them. You say I *silenced* you yesterday when you began to talk of the Captain. I am afraid I have been thought rude. If I changed the conversation, it was only that I might have more time to speak about more important matters. I could not *afford* to spend any of the brief space you would allow me on the Captain. It was all too little for – what shall I say? – for love. On Friday night, if you can allow me an hour, I will give the Captain about one and a half percent – I will give him one minute. Although he were twenty Captains, and on double instead of *whole* pay, I could give him no more. With that he must be content. I will be glad to hear your request on Friday night. *Whatever it be*, I promise to grant it. I could deny you nothing. Friday night will be a happy night. It will be *something* into the bargain. I only wish it could be made Sunday instead of Friday night; for it is then, I feel, above all other

times, that I could most enjoy your presence. Sunday, indeed,
is now to me a most tormenting day. The pleasure of Saturday is reflected in gloom upon *it*. It is the dark side of Saturday. But the good time *will* come. My dear Anne, you say
you would be alarmed if I were displeased with you. I cannot
now suppose it is possible that I can ever be displeased with
you. Our life, I anticipate, will be one long cloudless summer
afternoon, like one of those in June and July, during which
the sun burns on and on through dinner time, and tea time,
and seems as if it never would have done. I allow, at least, for
every contingency, every misfortune, but never can allow for
a cessation of our love or our good temper. Upon *these* our
happiness will chiefly depend. By the bye, I must tell you I
have not yet called upon your aunt for the work basket,
because I have not had time. I will probably call tomorrow.
But now I recollect, my mother had some intention of calling
at Elder Street tonight. If she have, she will have got the
basket. My mother says she will be very glad to see you on
Saturday; but I rather think I will not be able to spare you
from myself. I will *not* have had enough of you at three.
However, we shall see. Mr Tait is projecting a party at his
house, to take place during your interval of liberty and to
have you and me at it. You will, I am sure, be glad to go. You
must also attend another at our own house; for all the people
who were there on Saturday night are so much pleased with
what they saw and heard that they insist with one voice for an
encore. Next (. . . ?) will be one long Saturday, and the
succeeding half year will be one large Sunday. How happy
the one – how miserable the other! I do not know how I shall
part with you. I am afraid to think of it. – I am going tomorrow to escort Lady Threipland and her troop of tall daughters
through the Old Town. They will be there in body; but you
will be there in spirit. I never cease to think of you *all together*, I believe, except in sleep; and it is perhaps only
because I never remember what I dream about that I cannot
say I think of you then too. I wonder if you ever think of me
in the same way. William Kuon says in one of his poems,

> 'Tis sweet to think that thou shalt share
> When thou in distant lands art wandering,
> The spotless spirits' fervent prayer,
> That ever on thy fate is pondering.

But I cannot hope that you should permit your mind to be
so much affected as all that. For my own part, the thought of
you, I can say, is a perfect part. It would be nothing if you
only came in my mind when I was idle; but you intrude at all
times. I read a book for information about my new rebellion;
suddenly I find that for three pages back I have not picked up
a single idea. The eye was reading, but the mind was engrossed by Anne Kirkwood. And in many other cases, you
harass me in a similar manner. I suspect that I will save
nothing by your absence this next half year. – But I *must* have
done.

Dear puzzling tormenting creature, adieu. I am ever yours
                         R.C.
May I hope to hear from you before Friday.

                    St Andrew's Street
                    April 28 1829
You most mischievous person,
    I waited upon you till about ten o'clock on Saturday night;
and all I made by my exposure for such a length of time to the
cold night air was a return of rheumatism, which has confined
me ever since to the house. What have you to say for yourself? What can you say to prevent me from passing judgement
upon you as the most faithless and tormenting of your sex? I
am afraid you can bring no exculpatory evidence. You must
plead guilty and implore forgiveness. You may implore it, but
I will not grant it. So long, at least, as this agony remains in
my jaw, such a thing is not to be expected. I must have
thoroughly recovered from my present dolorous condition –
I must have completely forgot that I was ever was ill, and you
must have spent a week at the least in abject penitence for
your fault, ere I shall be able even to listen to your apology.
    You would laugh, I believe, – yes, you would be wicked
enough to laugh, if you saw me just now, wrapped up as I am
cap-à-pie in flannels and handkerchiefs, and sitting close by
an enormous fire, endeavouring to coax my rheumatism into
peace. I have tried all kinds of cures. Yesternight, it was
proposed to blister my cheek, and the whole womankind of
the house resolved themselves into a sort of jury of matrons
to consider whether I would require to shave my whisker
before such a thing could be applied. At last, my grandmother

expressed herself clearly of opinion that it would be absolutely necessary to do so; and I was so horror struck by the
proposal that I rejected that mode of cure. To lose a tooth
would be nothing to such a dire expedient. *Le petit diable*, as
I am inclined to call it, has been a little pacified today; but I
trouble for the approach of night, when he is sure to resume
his empire over my head in its fullest extent. I sometimes
attempt to think of you, as a sort of lenitive; but you have
quite the contrary effect; I might as well take *sweetmeats*! I
have all my books about me, and study hard for the Rebellion
of 1715; so that my time is not altogether lost; but I writhe
dreadfully under the demeaning circumstances of a sick-
chamber. I think if I could get one glimpse of you, or could
hear you touch but one tune on the harp, I would be quite a
different creature. Alas, the usual gulf is betwixt us. It would
be some consolation, tomorrow night, (should my pains
continue so long,) if I were to receive a letter from you.
Perhaps, as you will get this by the evening post today, you
might manage to gratify me so far. It would really be a piece
of Christian charity in you. I will forgive you a great deal
sooner if you can do so. Tell me at the same time all your
plans for next Saturday – and if there be a possibility of seeing
you before the end of this week.

  This letter is very short, and it is all about myself. But
really I am scarcely to blame. I see nobody but myself just
now. To make up for it, let all your letter be about your own
delightful self; then we shall be even.

  Adieu, my dearest Anne.

R Chambers

P.S. Could you possibly leave the school tomorrow for a
quarter of an hour to call for me? It would be worth while to
endure all this irksome illness and confinement for the sake of
such a pleasure. But I fear, I fear –

St Andrew's Street
April 29 1829

My dear Anne,

  You take my nonsense about Saturday night and the
rheumatism a little more seriously than I expected. Indeed, I
do not accuse you in the least. I would have had the complaint at any rate. I only said what I said because I had

nothing else to say and yet wished to write to you. One must
say something, you know. Perhaps you will ask why I wrote.
Do not ask such a thing. Or ask as well why I love you. Ask
why I am a different thing to you from all the rest of your
sex. Ask anything that is reasonable. – I am sorry you should
request permission to call me by my first name. Your wishes
oblige me to impose what is perhaps a weakness in me.
Somehow or other, I do not like to be so titled. I acknowledge, mark me, that you can only wish to do so from a kindly
feeling towards me. I even acknowledge that I *should* have no
objection to your doing so. I thank you for proposing it. Yet,
yet, I really would not like it. Perhaps it is as well you should
not do it; for you might forget and call me so in company,
and – *what then?* We might as well proclaim the banns at
once. Mr Tait does not usually call me by my first name. I
never heard him do so; and I believe he only did so on Saturday night, to distinguish me from a set of brothers in whose
company he is not accustomed to see me. Pray, forgive my rejection of your request. It really does not matter. I could not
think more of you, nor trust more implicitly in your affections than I now do, though you were to call me by an angel's
name. – I am glad you like Mr Tait so much. I love and
admire him so much myself, and he is so very much my
friend, that I would have been vexed had you not liked him.
You shall yet have much pleasure in his company. – My rheumatism is very easy today, but I still keep the house. I shall
probably do so till Saturday. As Janet remarks, I will make
strong effort to be well before *that day*. My time is by no
means misspent. I am writing my book with prodigious
speed. One day of complete abstraction here is worth three at
the shop. But I am sorry to neglect the shop too. N'importe.
It is only for a few days. – Excuse this wretched scrawl. It is
written on my knee. – I will be well again, I believe, the
moment the east wind goes away. You need not fear about me
for the interval of your freedom for a fortnight hence. But it
is really kind of you to express a fear about that. I am delighted to think that you study these things. Many, many
thanks for your kindness. – I should not have asked you to
come today. It was foolish and you would have been right to
stay away, even though you could have come. It would have
been too marked an expression of care even for me. Besides,
my illness is not such as to justify much amity in any way of

my friends. It is the most trifling thing imaginable, but for the
pain. I will now take more care of myself, according to your
request. Mr Hamilton tells me that all the night of the
Musselburgh ball on Friday last, he never spoke to Miss Inglis
once! He only gave her a distant bow. Isn't it odd – he who
was formerly so distracted about her! Miss Robinson was not
there. All the young ladies at M. are alike hostile to Miss I.
Not one has a word to say in her favour. The Captain is still –
not the man. Farewell, my own dear Anne. Let me know
your plans for Saturday by your earliest convenience. Do, do
let me have a great deal of you that day. I would need it after
so many inconclusive interviews as I have lately had. Console
me in the meantime.

Most affectionately, most devotedly yours
R.C.
P.S. Eleven o'clock. I have continued the whole of this
evening free of pain, instead of being, as for the last three
nights, afflicted with an unusual portion of it. This gives me
reason to hope that I am already recovered. But I will go on
till I am surer of the fact. Again, yours most truly R C.

St Andrew's Street
May 5 1829

I am again ill, and confined at home. After being a great
deal abroad both on Friday and yesterday, without any
symptom of a return of my malady, it rose upon me during
this last night while I was sleeping, like a giant refreshed with
strong drink. It prevented me from enjoying any rest during
the whole morning, but is now (three o'clock) somewhat less
painful. I attribute its recurrence to excess of fatigue yesterday and to the bad weather which had come back during the
night. I am now resolved to be very sparing of myself, to
attend the shop only for a few hours in the afternoon, and by
no means to go abroad in the evening. For really I must get
better before the end of next week – I must arise before then,
as Milton says, or be forever fallen.

I waited for you on Sunday, as I promised, but you had
not succeeded in getting away. When the church bell had
rung in, I went to St Stephen's Church, hoping to see you
there, and perhaps get you away after the congregation
should be dismissed. Alas, you were not there neither. Think-

ing I had thus fairly broken the day, and being too much
excited by desire of seeing you to settle to any work at home,
I wandered about till the time when the evening service is
generally concluded. I then lay in wait at the door of St
George's, hoping to catch at least one glimpse of you as you
passed out. But woe is me you were not there neither. What
could possibly have become of you on Sunday? I really was
very unfortunate. You will say I was very foolish to waste so
much time, even although I had been certain of seeing you at
last. How differently you think on that subject from me!

I long very much to hear what Miss Forrest has said in
reply to your letter. If you have yet received an answer, pray
by all means let me know the gist of it by the earliest post, or
by your earliest convenience. She has done a mischief she
little thinks of. She caused me for one moment – it was but
for *one* moment – to think less of you than I wished to think;
and I could not help execrating her afterwards for the bitterness of that moment. Though, but an instant after, I had
resolved not to blame you, even mentally, till I should hear
your account of the matter, yet I regretted that moment very
much: it seemed a kind of treason in love; I had sinned
against myself and against you, and could not hide the offence
from my own conscience. I hope no such thing will ever
occur again, or that the time will soon come when we shall be
so confident in each other as never to entertain a disloyal
thought, even for a moment, whatever may occur.

I had a call from the Captain yesterday. He was to go away
today at two o'clock. He had called again at Elder Street on
Sunday night, but without seeing your aunt. He desired me to
convey his kindest respects to you, and to say how much he
regretted not seeing you. He is not to be again in Edinburgh
till the end of the year.

I have no news to tell you but this. Mr Hamilton has
learned through some good-natured friend that Miss Inglis
talks despitefully. He had offended her by making rather too
free with her, and by talking as if he hesitated greatly about
paying her his addresses. In consequence of this, she is
understood to have said that 'she wondered Mr Hamilton
should think her come so low as to marry a schoolmaster!'
which, you must confess, is a dreadful stab. How much I pity
him! And *how much reason* I have to do so!

Will you be so good, my dear Anne, as to bring me a

ringlet on Saturday? I promise to take a great deal better care
of it than of the last. By the way, I have *one* hair of the last
preserved. It is a white one! For the curiosity of the thing, and
that I might rally you upon it, I laid it aside in the case of my
watch, where I found it today. So I am not so poor as I
thought myself. However, I would like one full ringlet – and
that not of *white* hair. Pray let me know by letter tomorrow
night what you do on Thursday. Will it be like an ordinary
Sunday? Or will you perhaps steal a moment of it for me? Let
me at least hear all your plans for Saturday. Believe me, my
dear Anne, ever with the utmost affection and esteem, your
own

R.C.

Undated fragment
. . . So you must just hold by the proposals in my above
letter. In the shop for me at your hour of emancipation –
about one, I believe – and if that fails, you (and I) must just
wait till the evening. By the bye, if I be much better tomorrow night, and say (mark me) that I hope to be abroad on
Sunday, will you understand that as a hint that I will lie in
wait for you near the Circus at the time the church goes in, so
as to accompany you, first to church, and afterwards on a
walk. You said last Saturday that you would be able to get
away on this evening Sunday. The day, however, must be
fine; otherwise I shall stay at home and write my book. You
must permit me to be so selfish and unmannered as to say so.

Miss Kirkwood, Mrs Duniston's, 14 Royal Circus

Here this series of letters ends; we must suppose that Robert and
Anne announced their engagement, and Edinburgh society allowed
them to see each other frequently enough to make letters unnecessary.
At any rate they were married in December 1829 at the church of St
Stephen's, Edinburgh, and began raising a large family.

Part 4

EPILOGUE

Chapter XXI

Robert had won his bride, but the last letter of the previous chapter indicates that he had no intention of letting marriage slow down his literary activities. Books on Scottish history, ballads and songs, his own poetry, topography and biography emerged from the back of his bookshop every few months, and all of them advanced his reputation and fortune to some degree. It was a time of burgeoning awareness in Scotland, and with the struggle for political reform went a great appetite for knowledge at all levels. Ideas of self-instruction, self-improvement, acquiring useful facts which would help individuals to exercise some control over their lives – these driving ideas fitted in with the spirit of the times, and were a product of the great surge forward in Scottish endeavour which has come to be called the Enlightenment. Robert and William were by inclination and from their own tough experiences completely in sympathy with this movement, and well poised to contribute to it. They had already in the past attempted periodicals; now they considered the possibility again.

The crucial aspect of publishing a periodical at this time was observance of the stamp laws, which imposed a tax of four pence on any sheet that printed 'news and occurrences, or commented on matters of church and state.' Anything like a newspaper therefore paid the tax and was sold at sevenpence or more (*The Scotsman*, for example, cost tenpence), but a literary periodical could avoid the tax if it was scrupulously careful.

William and Robert had tried to exploit this gap in the stamp laws with their short-lived *Kaleidoscope*, which sold for threepence, and there had been other attempts, notably George Mudie's *Cornucopia*, also priced at threepence. The brothers at their separate bookshops by now had twelve years' experience of dealing in publications of this kind. They knew that the Scottish reading public sought to educate itself, and that people appreciated good writing but had few pennies to spare. Furthermore they had noticed that periodicals were often conducted somewhat haphazardly and were irregular in their appearance, thus losing a great part of their appeal and failing to build up the momentum which comes from people and libraries who like collecting a whole series and binding them into a book. Was there not a market for a cheap, well-run, literary magazine that would instruct and educate as well as amuse?

William thought so. Robert was not so sure, but offered all possible literary assistance – which at first amounted to writing almost the whole of the journal himself. On Saturday 4 February 1832 the first number of *Chambers' Edinburgh Journal*[33] appeared, outlining its aims in a rather sententious leader by William, announcing that it would appear regularly every Saturday, and priced at *threehalfpence*. Within a few days the unprecedented number of 30,000 copies of the first issue had been sold. The circulation climbed to 50,000 a week by the end of the year, exceeding all expectations, and pirated copies began to be produced in America.

It was a brave enterprise, and paid off handsomely. The Chamberses were now in the centre of the publishing world. Robert developed, and some would say perfected, a style that contrived to be both elegant and homely, and he addressed all topics that interested him: history, philosophy, modern life and manners, geology. In doing so he established himself among the literati of the day as an essayist of distinction, or as he himself described it 'the essayist of the middle class'. His range is so extensive that it is difficult to choose an example that seems typical, but the following opening for an article entitled 'Led by Ideas' indicates the amiable perceptiveness which endeared him to a wide audience:

A man is properly and ordinarily the king of his ideas; but it sometimes happens, as in other empires, that one of the subjects, rising into too much favour at court, becomes practically the real monarch. We have then presented to us the singular phenomenon of a Man led by an Idea. Let any one dip for a month into the more intellectual circles of London, and he will be astonished at the number of such revolutionised monarchies which meet his observation. Talk of spoiled children ruling their weak parents; of easy-natured people governed by their servants; of kings in the hands of too powerful ministers; all these are nothing to the spectacle of a man – probably a clever and well-informed one – led by an idea.

Men led by ideas are usually of benevolent character, and their master-thoughts are generally of the nature of plans for putting the whole faults of the social machine at once to rights. It is a curious feature in the condition of the greatest country the world has yet known, that it ever believes itself in the most dreadful state imaginable, and expects nothing but ruin in a very short time. Tenderly concerned for themselves and their countrymen, a few worthy persons are continually going about with nostrums for averting the calamity. One holds that over-population is the cause of the whole mischief, and proposes to bleed off the disease by a system of emigration: which, it becomes quite clear, would carry away units for the tens added in the ordinary course of things each year. Another has a faith in pauper colonies, or allotments of inferior lands. With a third, more schools is the cry. Some, again, are ostentatiously material in their views. What, they say, can be done with the minds of men until they have got plenty of four-pound loaves? They hold it to be necessary to give the people a more ample store of good things in their larders and cupboards. Unfortunately, no one pretends to show how this is to be accomplished otherwise than by the usual means of a prosperous industry. Some have dilettanti ideas. They are all for honey-suckled cotttages and schools of industry. A few think a more universal diffusion of cricket, with gentlefolks bowling to labourers, and spiced ale sent down from the manor-house, the true plan for setting Britain on its legs. Mr Owen stands smiling by, fully assured that no good is to be expected till the plan of competition has been exchanged for that of co-operation. But, meanwhile, somehow the commerce of the country takes a start; new fields of capital are found, and hardly an idle person is to be seen: all the difficulties which we lately contemplated then vanish, and John Bull is found to be a safe enough person after all, so that only he has work to do, and money and grub to get by it.

Such a denouement is rather awkward for the leading-idea men; but the fact is, the ideas are good enough ideas nevertheless, taken simply by themselves, and not as panaceas. Scarcely any doubt exists that colonisation, and cottage-gardens, and cricket, and schools, are all capital things: the error lies in thinking any one of them sufficient to patch up a diseased commonwealth, and going about seeking to pin down mankind to that narrow conclusion. It seems, however, to be essential to enthusiasts of this class to have but one idea – at least at a time ...

By 1844 when the circulation of the *Journal* reached 84,000 it made the firm of W. & R. Chambers one of the biggest publishing concerns in the world. It is not difficult to identify, in the context of that information-thirsty age, the ingredients of their great success: entertaining and wholesome articles that no one could object to, cheapness, absolute regularity. Behind these obvious qualities were the rigorous efficiency of William's management, Robert's flair for hitting the right note, and the prodigious industry of them both.

William knew all about printing from the days when he had worked day and night on a creaking hand-press in Leith Walk, but even with his expertise the early difficulties were formidable. To produce the 25,000 copies required weekly in Scotland, two large presses now had to be operated all round the clock. Twelve men sweated away up to midnight on Saturdays when everything stopped for a bare twenty-four hours. The pressmen were not averse to bringing drink along to sustain them, much to William's disapproval. Austere and uncompromising, he would visit the presses and, on one occasion, 'found much of the work damaged, and the pressmen lying asleep on the floor, the consequence of a night's carousal.' The London edition was achieved by sending the London agent a copy which was then reset. The fact that this was done weekly from April 1832 in time for the London edition to come out on the right day is a tribute to William's remarkable powers of organisation, but it was an expensive process and made the London edition barely profitable.

The printing problems were solved by installing a steam-press. It cost William £500 to buy and install, but it easily doubled the previous hand-press capacity while requiring only two pressmen and a stoker to work it. Stereotyping was another innovation quickly adopted; extra plates could then be made in Edinburgh and sent to London, which avoided the expense of having to reset each issue. In 1833 William made arrangements for a separate edition to be printed in Dublin, making the *Journal* the first periodical to be printed simultaneously in all three capitals of the United Kingdom.

Circulation rose to a peak of 90,000, and each copy was probably read by several people. The poet Allan Cunningham described the *Journal* circulating among the shepherds of Galloway:

> The shepherds, who are scattered there at the rate of one to every four miles square, read it constantly, and they circulate it in this way: the first shepherd who gets it reads it, and at an understood hour places it under a stone on a certain hill-top; then shepherd the second in his own time finds it, reads it, and carries it to another hill, where it is found like Ossian's chief under its own gray stone by shepherd the third, and so it passes on its way, scattering information over the land.

With this kind of hand-to-hand circulation it has been estimated that the actual readership of the *Journal* was something in the neighbourhood of a quarter of a million.

Robert managed the literary aspects with skill and great attention to commercial possibilities, but he was never too busy for a friendly word to would-be authors. Hugh Miller wrote of him in *My Schools and Schoolmasters*:

> There is perhaps no other writer of the present day who has done so much to encourage struggling talent as this gentleman. I have for many years observed that publications, however obscure, in which he finds aught really praiseworthy, are secure always of getting, in his widely-circulated periodical, a kind approving word – that his criticisms invariably bear the stamp of a benevolent nature, which experiences more of pleasure in the recognition of merit than in the detection of defect – that his kindness does not stop with these cheering notices, for he finds time, in the course of a very busy life, to write many a note of encouragement and advice to obscure men in whom he recognises a spirit superior to their condition – and that the compositions of writers of this meritorious class, when submitted to him editorially, rarely fail, if really suitable for his journal, to find a place in it, or to be remunerated on a scale that invariably bears reference to the value of the communications – not to the circumstances of their authors.

Even his reject-notes were encouraging. What could be more courteous than this one to an unidentified contributor?

> I very much regret that my brother has not joined me in thinking the enclosed contributions suitable. I return them very unwillingly, and would hope that you will not be discouraged from allowing us a sight of any other little effusions which you may produce in the intervals of your laborious profession.

Charlotte Brontë, after much discouragement from other publishers, had this to say about W. & R. Chambers:

> From them I received a brief and business-like, but civil and sensible reply, on which we acted, and at last made way.

Chapter XXII

The success of *Chambers's Edinburgh Journal* inspired the brothers to other ambitious projects: *Chambers's Information for the People* (1833), *Chambers's Educational Course* in 64 volumes (1835-1849), *Chambers's Miscellany of Useful and Entertaining Tracts* (1846), *Chambers's Papers for the People* (1848) and later *Chambers's Encyclopaedia* (1859). These titles, which speak for themselves, are monumental compilations by Robert and other authors, and were all commercial successes under William's guiding hand. The firm expanded hugely, and by 1845 there were ten steam presses working.

Robert's literary output was astounding. In three years he contributed in the *Journal*:

117 essays, and part of 44 others
76 articles
15 biographies
4 tales
3 poems

All the while his other works poured out in full flood. He had always understood the need to strike while the literary iron was hot. In 1824 his *Remarkable Fires of Edinburgh*, including an account of the great fire of 15-17 November, had reached the public within six days of the event, during which period his father had died. On the death of Sir Walter Scott on 21 September 1832 Robert wrote his 110-page *Life of Sir Walter Scott* which was published just two weeks after the funeral. The reward for such industry on that occasion was a vast sale of 180,000.

His *Scottish Jests and Anecdotes* and the two-volume *History of Scotland* came out the same year. A simple calculation reveals that his total published writings during that single year amount to about 1600 printed pages.

Many other books followed from Robert's pen. *The Cyclopaedia of English Literature* (1840-1843) is a vast survey of the whole field which endeavours to put all notable British authors into their historical and critical contexts, together with biographies and generous extracts from their works. Nothing so comprehensive had been attempted before. Like all Robert's major undertakings, it was very successful, and revised editions were still being issued in the nineteen-thirties.

But his interests were becoming more scientific, as can be seen from some of his articles in the *Journal* and elsewhere. In 1840 he was elected to the Royal Society of Edinburgh. He began to go on geological investigations and correspond with the experts of the day. Robert had always tended towards the broad perspectives of a subject, and his survey of the science of geology, and in particular its impact on the question of the evolution of species, was leading him to some strange and far-reaching suppositions which appeared to challenge the orthodox view of creation. He needed time and privacy to examine these matters further, but in the hidebound religious atmosphere of Edinburgh this seemed to him to be fraught with danger to his reputation.

For this reason in 1841 he moved to St Andrews, and for three years worked away at a book in great secrecy. It was to be published anonymously, so Anne copied out the manuscript herself and Robert's handwriting was destroyed. The sheets were then sent to a friend in Manchester, who had agreed to act as a go-between, and by him transmitted to the London publisher. The proofs went back by the same route for checking. There were therefore no direct links with Robert or with Scotland.

When the book was published in the summer of 1844 under the title *Vestiges of the Natural History of Creation* it caused a sensation, perhaps more than any book since *Waverley*. It went through four editions in the first seven months; by 1860 there had been twenty editions in Britain and America. It was translated twice into German, once into Dutch and once into Swedish. It caused a particular furore among churchmen, who referred to it as 'that book', and preached against it in countless sermons, many of which Robert himself endured. Scientists were split; a few saw it as a major advance, but most were hostile to its lack of technical expertise, and the book provoked vigorous criticism, some directed at small mistakes, of which the book had its fair share. Contemporary novelists, poets and playwrights referred to it, usually sarcastically. It probably helped to drive poor Hugh Miller to suicide.

Vestiges was the first thorough exposition of evolutionary theory in Britain. It was based on a thesis which Robert summarised as follows:

> The proposition determined on after much consideration is, that the several series of animated beings, from the simplest and oldest up to the highest and most recent, are, under the providence of God, the results, *first*, of an impulse which has been imparted to the forms of life, advancing them, in definite times, by generation, through grades of organisation terminating in the

highest dicotyledons and vertebrata, these grades being marked by intervals of organic character, which we find to be a practical difficulty in ascertaining affinities; *second*, of another impulse connected with the vital forces, tending, in the course of generations, to modify organic structures in accordance with external circumstances, as food, the nature of the habitat, and the meteoric agencies, these being the 'adaptations' of the natural theologian.

Today such views seem old-fashioned, but in religious terms surely unobjectionable. To understand their effect on the contemporary world they must be read alongside the then unreconciled version of events in the first chapter of Genesis, which in 1844 was beginning to look threatened in circles familiar with Lamarck and Lyell, but was still required dogma everywhere else. Here was an anonymous work that appeared to discredit the bible and elbow the Creator out of his own creation, or at the very least diminish his creative powers. To the early Victorians, scientists and non-scientists alike, this was playing with fire.

There was much speculation as to who was capable of having written it. Among candidates were Lyell, Prince Albert, Thackeray, Darwin – and Robert Chambers. This rumour did him some harm. In 1848 he was put forward as a candidate for Lord Provost of Edinburgh. He appeared to be a particularly happy choice, being generally respected, well-liked in a way his brother never could be, devoted to Edinburgh, and successful. It seems certain that he would have enjoyed being Lord Provost, and done more credit to that ancient office than many. But his candidacy was opposed by a man who challenged Robert to deny he was the author of *Vestiges*, the godless book that threatened public morals and indeed all Christianity. Robert could only admit it or withdraw, and withdraw he did. Not for the first time in the annals of Edinburgh, religious bigotry carried the day.

Yet 'that book' is not irreligious and certainly not atheistic. There seems something almost mediaeval in the way it was viciously attacked by ordinary God-fearing people as if the whole structure of their faith were tottering. Robert was reluctantly driven to further explanations:

> The purpose (of *Vestiges*) is to show that the whole revelation of the works of God, presented to our senses and reason, is a system based on what we are compelled, for want of a better term, to call *Law*; by which, however, is not meant a system independent or exclusive of Deity, but one that only proposes a certain mode of His working.

The attacks continued, but all the while the book was being bought, read, and debated; and little by little prejudice began to be exposed and eroded.

Darwin was at this time working on his own theories, and annotated his copy of *Vestiges* extensively. During the next fifteen years it was at the centre of the evolutionary controversy until overtaken in 1859 by *Origin of Species*, which established evolution in scientific terms. Thereafter, among experts, the substantial personality of Darwin soon eclipsed the shadowy author of *Vestiges*. But in the mind of the reading public of 1859, *Origin of Species* was seen not so much as a philosophical watershed, but more as technical reinforcements for the campaign of bible-demolition started in 1844 by *Vestiges*.

Darwin disagreed with some aspects of *Vestiges*, and was at first uncharacteristically reluctant to acknowledge the contribution it had made. In February 1845 he wrote to a friend:

> Have you read that strange, unphilosophical, but capitally written book, the *Vestiges*? It has made more talk than any work of late, and has been by some attributed to me – at which I ought to be much flattered and unflattered.

In *Origin of Species* he added this:

> The work, from its powerful and brilliant style, though displaying in the earlier editions little accurate knowledge, and a great want of scientific caution, immediately had a very wide circulation. In my opinion it has done excellent service in this country in calling attention to the subject, in removing prejudice, and thus preparing the ground for the reception of analogous views.

But he still felt uncomfortable as to whether he had given the author of *Vestiges* his due, and if one compares *Origin of Species* with *Vestiges* it is easy to see why. Very large chunks of Darwin are merely more carefully elaborated lines of evidence already presented in detail by Chambers. It is true that Darwin did more to explain the mechanisms of evolution, and he removed several of Chambers' minor technical errors and one major piece of naivety concerning the creation of life in a test-tube, which had attracted much adverse – even derisory – criticism. But some similarities between the two works are striking.

When Robert died Darwin tried to make amends. Writing to Robert's daughter in 1871 he said:

> I beg leave to thank you very sincerely for your extremely kind communication through Sir J. Lubbock. It has been highly gratifying to me to hear that so distinguished a man as Dr Chambers felt an interest about my book during the last hours of his valuable life. I have always felt a most sincere respect for your father, and his society, the few times I enjoyed it, was most

pleasant to me. Several years ago I perceived that I had not done full justice to a scientific work which I believed and still believe he was intimately connected with, and few things have struck me with more admiration than the perfect temper and liberality with which he treated my conduct.

In his lifetime Robert received no credit for *Vestiges*, although he must have made a lot of money. He took the hostility of the scientists with good humour, and with his usual perception had this to say – still anonymously:

It is no discredit to them, that they are, almost without exception, engaged each in his own little department of science, and able to give little or no attention to other parts of that vast field. From year to year, and from age to age, we see them at work, adding no doubt much to the known, and advancing many important interests, but, at the same time, doing little for the establishment of comprehensive views of nature. Experiments in however narrow a walk, facts of whatever minuteness, make reputations in scientific societies; all beyond is regarded with suspicion.

Robert did not by this stage seek fame, and it was his choice to remain anonymous, a decision taken presumably to safeguard family and firm. Anonymity may be a slightly troublesome thing to the scientific community; certainly it obliged him not to take too prominent a part in the controversy he had largely contributed to. But he kept up with the level of events, travelling the country on its new railway system to attend discussions and hear lectures. Indeed it was he who in June 1860 persuaded Huxley to confront Wilberforce at the famous Oxford meeting of the British Association, when the new thinking and the church clashed head on, and after which things were never quite the same again.

The author of *Vestiges* has been mostly forgotten, while Darwin is rightly commemorated throughout the world. But Chambers deserves his place in the record of evolutionary thinking. His book had persuaded the scientific and general public that there was massive evidence for the fact of evolution. Yet today in the extensive Evolution Section of the Royal Museum of Scotland in Chambers Street, Edinburgh, the permanent display covering the development of evolution theory omits Robert Chambers entirely. Perhaps history could have been a little more generous to the man who, in Darwin's words, 'prepared the ground'.

After *Vestiges* was published Robert returned to Edinburgh. He acquired a new and expensive town house at No 1 Doune Terrace, which immediately began to be the centre for a circle of friends interested in music, literature, and science. Robert and Anne were both competent musicians, and the eldest daughter Nina was a brilliant pianist. All the other eight children performed in some way, and the Chambers' house was frequently the scene of lively musical evenings. Robert had a gift for friendship and good-humour, in spite of his protestations to the contrary eighteen years before, and many people who knew the family at this time have commented on this. Writers, scientists, and politicans were frequent visitors to No 1 Doune Terrace, which was a well-known part of Edinburgh life in the 1840s and 1850s.

It all seemed a long way from a dreary room in the West Port and a young lad who had flogged his schoolbooks from a Leith Walk stall.

Robert continued his literary output which included the seven-volume *Select Writings of Robert Chambers* (1847), and a massive *Life and Works of Robert Burns* (1851) which interleaves poems with biography and criticism – an unusual and, most people thought, particularly effective technique here. His geological and physical investigations continued, resulting in more field work and more books, this time less controversial than *Vestiges* and published under his own name. From a tour to trace raised beaches in England he wrote to his children describing the journey:

>   ... Then he came
>   To see if Liver-
>   Pool and Birken
>   Head had ever
>   Been in Neptune's
>   Deep Dominion;
>   That they were
>   Is his opinion;
>   And he means
>   In time to show it;
>   Meanwhile you
>   Are first to know it.
>   Now he has
>   Invaded Chesshire
>   Where he means
>   To take his pleasure;
>   All tomorrow
>   With his level,
>   Dee's old beaches
>   To unravel.

Then he's off
      Like crack of pistol,
Stopping not
      Till he reach Bristol . . .

He became enthusiastic for life assurance, and wrote a small tract on the subject. According to William it had a circulation of 'several hundred thousand copies', which seems astonishing in Scotland with a population of just over two million. He took out no less than five policies himself, and became a director of the Scottish Equitable. Like all his enthusiasms, he pursued this one whole-heartedly.

Meanwhile his children were growing up and setting out in promising directions. Nina married Frederick Lehmann, a prosperous businessman who made a fortune during the American civil war. Nina was an outstandingly lively and attractive personality. Some of her exuberant letters have been published, and all of them deserve to be. Her grandchildren include the famous Lehmann siblings, Rosamond the novelist, John the publisher and poet, and Beatrix the actress.

Nina's younger sister, Amelia, married Frederick's elder brother Rudolf, who was a fashionable portrait artist and author of 'An Artist's Reminiscences.' One of their three daughters was the composer Liza Lehmann.

Robert's fourth daughter, Elizabeth, married the Queen's physician, Sir William Priestley, and published her memoirs. And the eldest son, Robert secundus, went into the firm of W. & R. Chambers and carried it along on its unstoppable course.

With his large family requiring him less at home Robert the elder began to do more travelling at home and abroad. His visits to Iceland, Norway, France and America were all the subject of books or articles in the *Journal*, and his letters home are fascinating. His last major work, *The Book of Days*, was published in 1864. Then Anne died and his own health began to fail. After a long period of increasing weakness Robert died in 1871 at St Andrews, and was accorded the singular honour of being buried inside the old tower of St Regulus.

Robert Chambers is remembered for *Traditions of Edinburgh*, almost continuously in print for 166 years and still going strong, for some contributions to Scottish history and to *Chambers's Edinburgh Journal*, and for the publishing firm which pioneered cheap literature for the people and still bears his name. But he was 'a man for a' that,' which his early life and letters handsomely show.

Principal Sources

Short titles are shown in brackets.

Chambers, Robert: Untitled fragment in National Library of Scotland probably dated 1868 (*Auto 68*). Unpublished except for about 14 pages which were included in *Memoir*.
- Untitled fragment in collection of Mr A S Chambers dated 1833 (*Auto 33*). Unpublished.
- Letters in collection of Sir Mark Norman (*Norman*). Unpublished, except for part of the letter dated 13th April which was included in *Memoir*.
- *Vestiges of the Natural History of Creation*, 1844 et sqq (*Vestiges*).
- Select Writings, 1847.
  Chambers, William: *Memoir of William and Robert Chambers*, 1st edition, 1872.
- ditto, 13th edition, 1884 (*Memoir*).
- A History of Peeblesshire, 1864 (*Peeblesshire*).
Chambers's Edinburgh Journal, various dates (*Journal*).
Cooney, Sandra Miley: *Publishers for the People*, 1970 (*Cooney*). Unpublished.
Lehmann, John: *Ancestors & Friends*, 1962 (*Lehmann*).
Milhauser, Milton: *Just Before Darwin*, 1959 (*Milhauser*).
Priestley, Lady: *The Story of a Lifetime*, 1904 (*Priestley*).
Scott, Sheila: *Peebles During the Napoleonic Wars*, 1980 (*Scott*).

Chapter I is based on *Auto 68* and *Peeblesshire*. Chapters II-XI are all *Auto 68*. Chapters XII and XIII are mostly *Auto 68*, except for the hexadactylism which is *Auto 33*. Chapters XIV and XV are largely *Memoir*. The letters from French prisoners in Chapter XVI come from the private collection of Mr A S Chambers, the girls left behind are described in *Scott* and *The Prisoners at Penicuik* by Ian MacDougall (1989), and the rest of the chapter is *Auto 33*, except for the description of the lodging in the West Port, which is *Memoir*. Chapters XVII to XIX are all *Auto 33* except parts of the electrical experiments and Leith Walk, which are *Memoir*. Chapter XX is all *Norman* except Gray's poems which were eventually published in his *Lays & Lyrics* (1841). The Walter Scott quotation is from his Journal of 1829.

Chapter XXI. Information on the stamp laws comes chiefly from an article in the *Journal* No 35, October 1832. *Memoir* covers some of this ground also, and deals with the start of the *Journal*. Circulation figures come from Robert's private letters in *Norman* and from *Cooney*, which also deals with printing. Cunningham's letter is in the National Library of Scotland and has been quoted by several people. The estimate for total readership is in *Lehmann*, but he seems to be quoting some other source. *Cooney* has the three quotes concerning Robert as editor; Hugh Miller wrote his in *My Schools and Schoolmasters* (1858); the Brontë quote comes from Mrs Gaskell's *Life of Charlotte Brontë* (1857).

Chapter XXII. *Cooney* has supplied the data on Robert's contribution to the *Journal*, *Milhauser* the details of the reception of *Vestiges*. Robert's summary comes from *Vestiges* itself, 10th edition. Darwin's first quote comes from a letter to William Darwin Fox in February 1845, the second from *Origin of Species* 4th edition, and the third is quoted in *Priestley*. Robert's reply to scientific compartmentalism is in the later editions of *Vestiges*, quoted in *Lehmann*. The Lord Provost incident comes from *Memoir* (1st edition only, and bowdlerised) and *Milhauser*. Robert's defence of the religious basis of *Vestiges* comes from *Explanations, by the Author of Vestiges of the Natural History of Creation*, which was first published separately in 1845 and subsequently became an annex to later editions of *Vestiges* itself. *Lehmann* and *Priestley* describe the family and social circle at No 1 Doune Terrace. Robert's poem comes from *Norman* in a letter dated 16 February 1847.

The list of works of Robert Chambers comes chiefly from *Milhauser*, but I have made considerable amendments by checking it against the 'Catalogue of the Principal Writings of Robert Chambers' deposited in the National Library of Scotland by C.E.S. Chambers in 1898.

Notes

1. Wooden bowls
2. Coal dust
3. Close and fasten
4. *Rejected addresses*, a popular work of verse parodies by London wits James and Horace Smith (1813).
5. A species of ganoid fish akin to the lizard. Dr Hibbert's discovery was, with others, a fact of some importance to palaeontology and evolution theory, and is discussed in *Vestiges of the Natural History of Creation*.
6. John Wilson, 1785–1854, professor of moral philosophy at the University of Edinburgh, poet and critic. He collaborated with Robert Chambers in producing *The Land of Burns* (1840).
7. I.e. the Eighteenth
8. Andrew Fletcher of Salton or Saltoun, 1653–1716, patriot, republican, and social polemicist.
9. Meal-bags
10. Strolling beggars.
11. See Pitcairn's Criminal Trials (R.C.)
12. Cupboard
13. A fact. The provost and the commander of the regiment stationed in the town, were seen in a loft of that U.P. church next Sunday, but their expectations of a similar escape of sentiment were disappointed (R.C.)
14. Home-made fireworks
15. What is proper
16. Exact meaning not traced, but the sense requires 'dung'
17. Auction
18. Soft mud
19. Pinafore
20. Fledglings
21. A natural arrangement of the hair, not of very common occurrence, making it start up off the forehead on one side (R.C.)
22. Scratch
23. Dressed
24. Eel
25. Sermons
26. Meaning untraced
27. Published afterwards in *Chambers' Edinburgh Journal* No 27
28. The White Horse Inn in the Canongate
29. 'The Queen of Barbary'? - see letter dated 19 April below
30. He was in fact mugged, and severely injured. The presumption is that it happened coming home after a drinking session.
31. Onion
32. The Queen of Barbary
33. Later *Chambers's Edinburgh Journal*

Works of Robert Chambers

The Kaleidoscope, or Edinburgh Literary Amusement	1821-2
Illustrations of the Author of Waverley	1822
Ocean Rhymes	1824
Traditions of Edinburgh, 2 vols.	1824
Notices of the Most Remarkable Fires in Edinburgh	1824
Walks in Edinburgh	1825
Popular Rhymes of Scotland	1826
Picture of Scotland, 2 vols.	1827
History of the Rebellions in Scotland, 5 vols (Part of Constable's Miscellany)	1828-9
The Scottish Ballads	1829
The Scottish Songs, 2 vols.	1829
The Picture of Stirling	1830
Life of King James I, 2 vols.	1830
Gazetteer of Scotland (with William Chambers)	1832
Scottish Jests and Anecdotes	1832
Chambers's Edinburgh Journal (editor and contributor)	1832 ff
Home Pictures and Familiar Counsels (from Chambers's Edinburgh Journal)	1832
Life of Sir Walter Scott	1832
History of Scotland	1832
Reekiana, or Minor Antiquities of Edinburgh	1833
Chambers's Information for the People, 2 vols. (editor and contributor)	1833-5
Biographical Dictionary of Eminent Scotsmen, 4 vols.	1833-5
Life and Works of Burns (based on Currie's edition)	1834
The Spirit of Chambers's Journal (with William Chambers), 5 vols.	1834-8
Jacobite Memoirs of the Rebellion	1834
History of the English Language and Literature (Chambers's Educational Course)	1835
Poems	1835
The Land of Burns (with Professor John Wilson), 2 vols.	1840
Cyclopaedia of English Literature (with Robert Carruthers), 2 vols.	1840
Chambers's People's Editions: Essays, Fiction, Travel, History, 4 vols. (editor and contributor)	1840-1
History of the Rebellion of 1745	1840
Vestiges of the Natural History of Creation, 2 vols.	1844
Twelve Romantic Scottish Ballads	1844
Explanations	1845

Chambers's Miscellany of Useful and Entertaining   1846
    Tracts, 9 vols. (editor and contributor)
Select Writings of Robert Chambers, 7 vols.   1847
Ancient Sea Margins   1848
Chambers's Papers for the People, 6 vols. (editor and   1848
    contributor)
Tracings of the North of Europe   1851
Life and Works of Robert Burns, 4 vols.   1851
Tracings of Iceland and the Faroe Islands   1856
Domestic Annals of Scotland, 3 vols.   1859-61
Sketch of the History of the Edinburgh Theatre Royal   1859
Memoirs of a Banking House, by Sir William Forbes (editor) 1859
Edinburgh Papers   1861
    i. Ice and Water.
    ii. Testimony – its Posture in the Scientific World.
    iii. The Romantic Scottish Ballads, their Epoch and Authorship.
    iv. Ancient and Domestic Architecture in Edinburgh.
    v. Edinburgh Merchants and Merchandise in the Olden Times.
Songs of Scotland Prior to Burns   1862
Preface to 'Incidents in My Life', by Daniel Dunglas Home 1863
The Book of Days, 4 vols.   1864
Life of Smollett   1867
The Threiplands of Fingask   1880

Scientific Papers

'On the Existence of Raised Beaches in the Neighbourhood   1843
    of St. Andrews.' *Edinburgh New Philosophical
    Journal*, Vol. XXXIV
'Sur la variation du niveau relatif de la terre et   1846-7
    de la mer.' Paris Société Géologique, *Bulletin*, IV
'Geological Notes on the Valleys of the Rhine and Rhone.' 1849
    Edinburgh New Philosophical Journal, Vol. XLVI
'On Glacial Phenomena of the Neighbourhood of   1850
    Edinburgh.' *British Association Reports*, part II
'Personal Observations on Terraces . . . in Scandinavia.' 1850
    Edinburgh New Philosophical Journal, Vol. XLVIII
'Memoranda Regarding an Ancient Boat Hook Found in the   1850
    Carse of Gowrie,' *Edinburgh New Philosophical Journal*,
    Vol. XLIX
'On the Eyeless Animals of the Mammoth Cave of Kentucky.' 1853
    Edinburgh New Philosophical Journal, Vol. LV
'On the Glacial Phenomena in Scotland and some Parts   1853
    of England.' *Edinburgh New Philosophical Journal*, Vol. LIV
'Further Observations on Glacial Phenomena in Scotland   1854
    and the North of England.' *British Association Reports*, part II
'On the Great Terrace of Erosion in Scotland.'   1855
    Edinburgh New Philosophical Journal, n.s. Vol. I
'On Glacial Phenomena in Peebles and Selkirkshire.'   1855
    Edinburgh New Philosophical Journal, n.s. Vol. II

'On Denudation and Other Effects Usually Attributed to 1855
    Water.' Paper read before the British Association, Glasgow
'On the Recently Discovered Glacial Phenomena of 1857
    Arthur's Seat and Salisbury Crags.' Royal Society,
    Proceedings, Vol. III
'Notice of an "Eskar" at St. Fort, Fifeshire.' 1864
    Geological Magazine, Vol. IV

Acknowledgements

I am particularly indebted to Mr Tony Chambers for much assistance with the papers of his great-great-grandfather, and for letting me use the unpublished material. Sir Mark Norman also gave me full access to his large collection of letters. Without these two generous men this book could not have been put together.

The late Mr John Lehmann provided encouragement and advice. Professor Jon Dorling of the University of Amsterdam was kind enough to comment on my attempt to summarise Robert's contribution to evolutionary theory. Mr Neal Ascherson aided and abetted. Miss Sheila Scott assisted with Peebles research. Mrs Christine Pike helped me puzzle out the letters with magnifying glass and dictaphone, and typed them faultlessly. Mrs Maxwell-Scott kindly let me see Robert's handwritten book in the Abbotsford library.Mr Eric Carter, Mr Hugh Pinney, Miss Sylvia Cave and Mr Gordon Nichol took the photographs. My daughter, Alexandra, made a number of improvements to the text. Mrs Ellen Middelhuis and Ms Jeanne van der Velde put the MS in order.

To all these, and to many others, I am most grateful.

Index